IMAGES
*of America*

# SCOTT

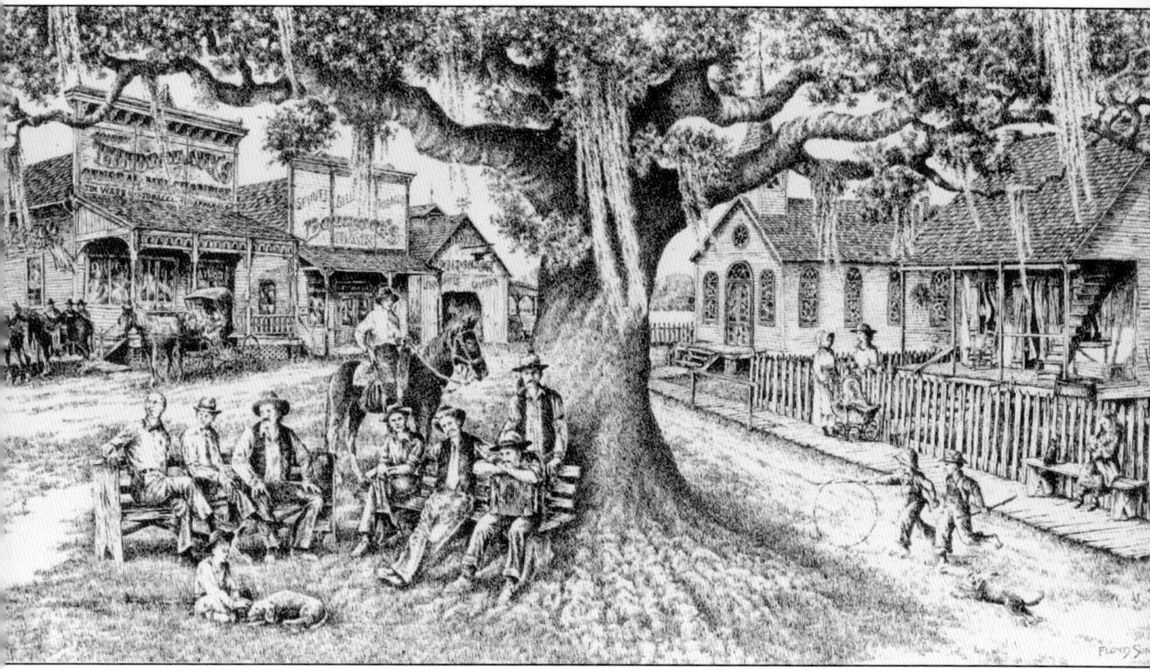

*La Ville Ste Marie*, a fictitious Cajun village created by artist Floyd Sonnier, captures the spirit of Acadiana. This charcoal drawing, inspired by memories and old photographs of the area, depicts Bourque's Bar, along with the artist, his wife, his children, and local residents. (Courtesy of the estate of Floyd Sonnier.)

**On the Cover:** Childhood friends known as "The Gang" spent their summer days on their bikes. From left to right, this 1946 photograph shows (first row) Fred Domingue and David "Boo" Prejean; (second row) Rodney "Petoo" Lormand, James Lee Martin, Elmo Broussard Jr., James Leewood Breaux, Charles Oran "Poochie" Abdella, and Carl Hebert; (third row) Barbara Broussard Magnon. (Courtesy of Claudette Prejean LeBlanc.)

IMAGES
*of America*

# SCOTT

The Scott Historical and Genealogical Society

ARCADIA
PUBLISHING

ISBN 978-0-7385-9066-0

Published by Arcadia Publishing
Charleston, South Carolina

Printed in the United States of America

Library of Congress Control Number: 2012943202

For all general information, please contact Arcadia Publishing:
Telephone 843-853-2070
Fax 843-853-0044
E-mail sales@arcadiapublishing.com
For customer service and orders:
Toll-Free 1-888-313-2665

Visit us on the Internet at www.arcadiapublishing.com

*The community still turned to Noelie Martin Provost, into her 90s, for answers. Always the teacher, this installment of Scott's history is dedicated to her.*

# Contents

# ACKNOWLEDGMENTS

This project began with the creation of the Scott Historical and Genealogical Society, which wants to express its appreciation to the individuals, families, and groups who allowed their photographs to be included in this work. We owe thanks to the past and present mayors of the city of Scott and city hall staff, along with many community members who assisted us: Annette Sonnier, Pat Ferguson, Leana Miller, Mona Caldwell, Cassie Richard Blair, Becca Begnaud, Lynn Hargrave, Murphy Boudreaux, Fran Bihm, Angela Jean-Batiste, Cherri Foytlin, and Paul Begnaud. Louise Sonnier, who was always ready with a story for any photograph, deserves our special thanks. Her wealth of knowledge about the history of Scott was priceless. She is dearly missed. The book would not have been completed without the tremendous support of June Broussard and Annadine Credeur. June knocked on doors to collect photographs, bought supplies, ran errands, conducted fact-finding missions, and supported us when we needed it most. Annadine Credeur loaned us books and articles that her mother, Noelie Provost, had collected through the years. The information was invaluable when writing the captions and introduction. She also shared her own recollections and made numerous phone calls to collect photographs, ensuring that as many people as possible were aware of this project. We would be remiss if we did not extend our sincere appreciation to the Lafayette Parish Clerk of Court staff for their support in loaning photographs. We want, above all, to extend our gratitude to Dennis and Pam Carr. Not only did they offer technical and organizational support, their love of Scott inspired the project; the use of their home and the gift of their time made it possible. Our sincere thanks go to Claire Manes for her editing assistance and Theresa Rohloff for her final editing and layout expertise. We hope that this book will inspire everyone to help preserve our history. To that end, this society will continue to collect photographs, documents, artifacts, and stories with the hope of establishing a museum to allow others to learn about "Great Scott." The Scott Historical and Genealogical Society can be reached at www.scotthistorysociety@yahoo.com.

# INTRODUCTION

The city of Scott is located very near the geographic center of the 22 parishes (counties) officially designated as Acadiana by the State of Louisiana for showcasing the music, dance, food, heritage, and living culture of the Cajun and Creole people.

This part of Louisiana was under Spanish control when the British in Canada, about 1755, began Le Grand Dérangement, the exile of Acadians from the former French colony in Acadie, Nova Scotia. After deportation, the British scattered the French-speaking Acadians into the 13 British colonies in America, as well as to England and France. A few of the exiled Acadians then traveled back across the Atlantic from France to New Orleans and spread the word about a friendly Spanish area with available new land. Eventually, 1,600 Acadians migrated to Louisiana, arriving in New Orleans in 1785 on seven ships from Nantes and St. Malo, France. Surnames on the passenger list included Dugas, LeBlanc, Hebert, Trahan, Richard, Guidry, Bourque, and Boudreaux, which continue to be common family names in Scott today. The Acadians scattered along the East Coast of America, while the French immigrants and others gradually moved westward from New Orleans to the prairie lands of Louisiana. As farmers, ranchers, landowners, and businessmen, they set the stage for the growth that followed in what became the Scott community.

It is believed that early settlers Jean and Andre Martin purchased land from the Attakapas Indians during the period from 1815 to 1830; others, including Aurelien Breaux and his son Louis, applied for and received land grants from the federal government in 1836. The large land grants and the influx of these industrious peoples meant that land was cleared, settled, and cultivated. During the late 1870s, farmers grew corn and potatoes and raised poultry and cattle for their personal consumption. Cotton, too, was grown and became a cash crop but needed transportation to become a commercial venture.

The need to transport crops was handled with the founding of Scott. This endeavor was due in large measure to two farmers: Dominic Cayret, a French immigrant, and Alcide Judice, an Acadian who masterminded efforts to bring the railroad to the area. Judice traveled frequently to New Orleans on business, which provided him with early information pertinent to the future development of the railroad. Cayret negotiated land deals in the area for the building of a railroad depot and station in 1880 by the Louisiana Western Railroad. When the railroad requested a name for its new location, the area residents chose Scott Station honoring Scott, variously identified as JB, GP, or SP Scott, the superintendent in charge of building the tracks. From the rail industry, the area got not only its name but also its motto: "Where the West Begins." Travelers to and from Scott Station were required to pay "western rates" for travel going west from the station. The railroad thus became the backbone of the village and its economy.

The arrival of the railroad in 1880 meant that cotton, sweet potatoes, and other crops could be grown for distribution as well as private use. Farmers had a wider venue for their produce, thus impacting the economic and cultural development of Scott Station. The proximity of rail transportation enabled Scott businessmen to operate three cotton gins during these times and to plant sweet potatoes, shipping them across the United States and Canada. In the case of the sweet potatoes, shipments to Canada were made under the Regal Yam label. Controversy hovers around any suggestion that this was to honor the king of England, the titular ruler of Canada, part of the British Empire.

With commerce coming in and out of the area, Scott began to grow. In 1880, Alcide Judice opened a general merchandise store. By the mid- to late 1880s, Scott Station had a hotel, a boardinghouse, blacksmith shop, two taverns, rural schoolhouses for both black and white children, steam-powered cotton gins, a molasses mill, and a large mercantile store. Progress came to the area but so did unforeseen tragedy. Martin Begnaud, the owner and operator of Begnaud's General Store, was brutally murdered in 1896 by two individuals known as the Blanc brothers, who purportedly emigrated from France. They worked in Scott and were befriended by Begnaud, but their obsessions of acquiring wealth and fame like the James brothers led them to kill the kindhearted businessman. The murder and subsequent conviction and hanging of the two men brought further interest and notoriety to the area.

From the earliest years, education was a priority, and generous landowners and businessmen donated land for schools. The first public schoolhouse bearing Scott's name was built on land donated by Louis Gustave Breaux. Others, over the years, ensured that a semblance of "bus service" (a wagon pulled by livestock) and meals were made available to the children since cafeterias were not yet available.

The booming rail business shifted before the turn of the century, changing the name but not the spirit of Scott Station. By 1896, the Southern Pacific Railroad Company, which had purchased the Louisiana Western Railroad in 1883, was consolidating its operations in Lafayette, the parish seat. With the decrease in railroad operations in Scott Station, people began to refer to the village simply as Scott. Scott was officially incorporated in 1907 as the Village of Scott and later changed its name to the town of Scott in 1960. As the community grew, new schools and businesses continued to develop. In 1920, Scott's first all-black school was completed, followed by the new high school in 1928. In 1951, a new elementary school, L. Leo Judice Elementary, was built. A bank was incorporated in 1911, a silent movie theater was opened in 1915, and a pharmacy began operating in 1919. Gulf States Utilities wired Scott into its electrical grid in 1927. All the activities were indicative of the prosperity and growth of the community.

Even more important than the buildings and businesses were the people themselves, who were loyal to their community, rich in faith, appreciative of everyday life, respectful of education, and generous in their sacrifice for their country. Images of America: *Scott* wishes to celebrate the spirit of its people. Chapter one, "It All Started Here," chronicles the beginnings of Scott, especially with the railroad. Chapter two, "Businesses, Buildings, and Landmarks," recalls the unique structures that were and are Scott. Chapter three, "School Days," reinforces the central role of schools to the community. Chapter four, "Our Faith Defines Us," recognizes the primacy of religion and the churches to Scott believers. Chapter five, "Everyday Life," celebrates the daily life of Scott's citizens. Chapter six, "People along the Way," remembers the leaders of the community. And chapter seven, "Honoring Those Who Served," pays tribute to some of the military men and women from Scott. Thus, Scott from unnamed prairie lands to a rich cultural community appears in the following images for readers to view and cherish.

# *One*

# It All Started Here

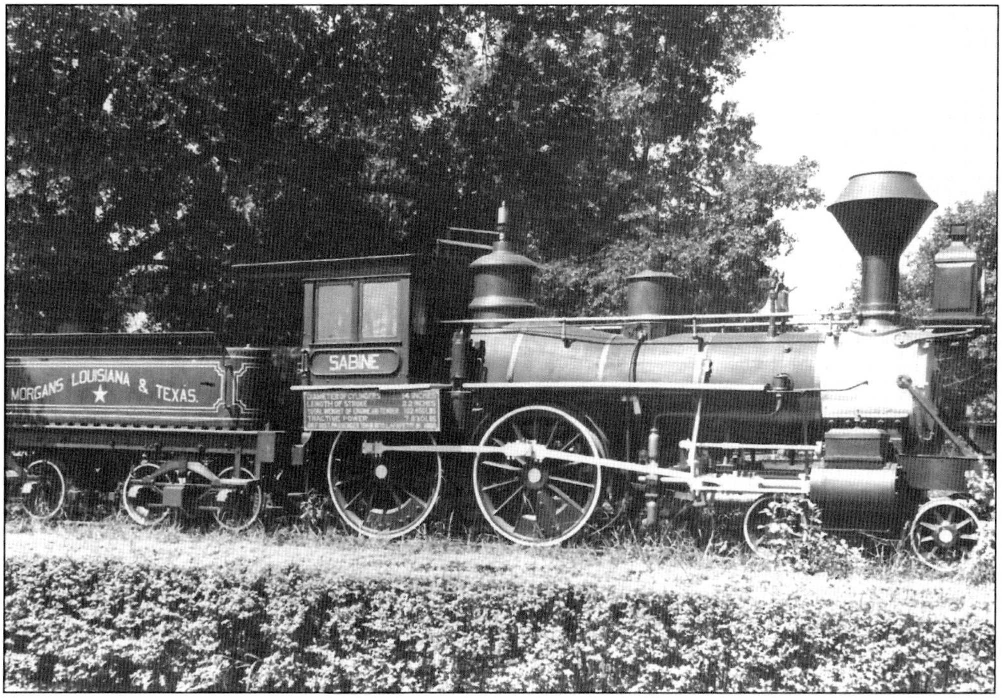


The arrival of the Sabine engine inaugurated rail service in Scott. The Louisiana Western Railroad acquired property from Dominic Cayret in 1879 for the rail line right-of-way and subsequently acquired additional property from Cayret for a depot and station house. (Courtesy of Lafayette Parish Clerk of Court.)

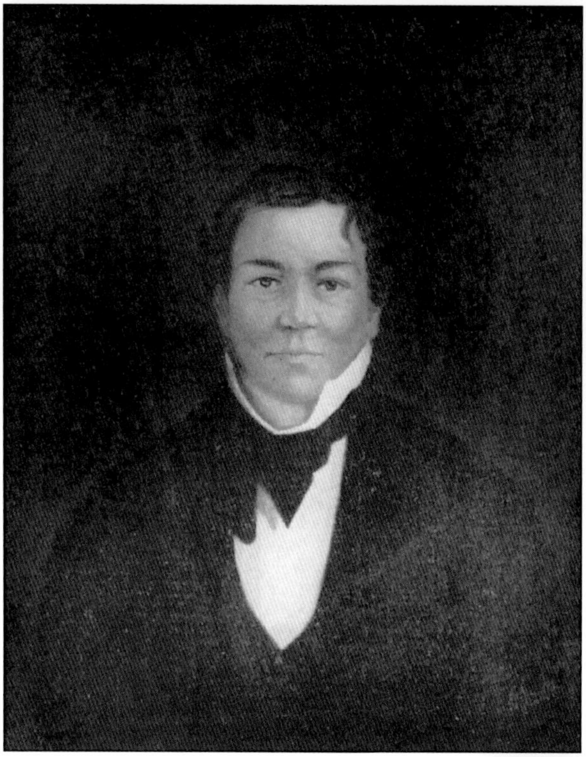

Land grants acquired by Aurelien Breaux (pictured) and his son Louis A. Breaux from 1836 to 1855 made the family among the most prominent landowners in Scott. Aurelien's son Gustave and grandson Louis inherited property, as did his daughters M. Arthemir, M. Olivia, and Anatile, who wed Joseph L. Bernard, Alexander Delhomme, and Dr. George Scranton, respectively. Through purchases and marriages, much of Aurelien's property comprises the current city. (Courtesy of Dupre Library, University of Louisiana Lafayette, and the Breaux family.)

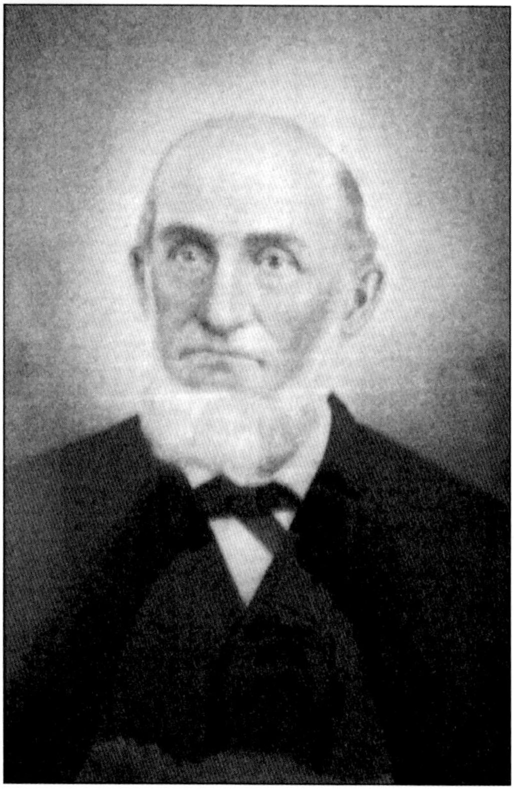

Early settler Alexander Delhomme moved to Scott after his marriage to Olivia Breaux, the daughter of one of the first landowners, Aurelien Breaux. Alexander and Olivia moved into the Breaux family home, located on present-day Oak Street. They had nine children; the two youngest lived in the home until the 1960s. Delhomme, a successful farmer, owned and operated the first cotton gin in the area, as well as a hay-mowing machine. (Courtesy of David Delhomme.)

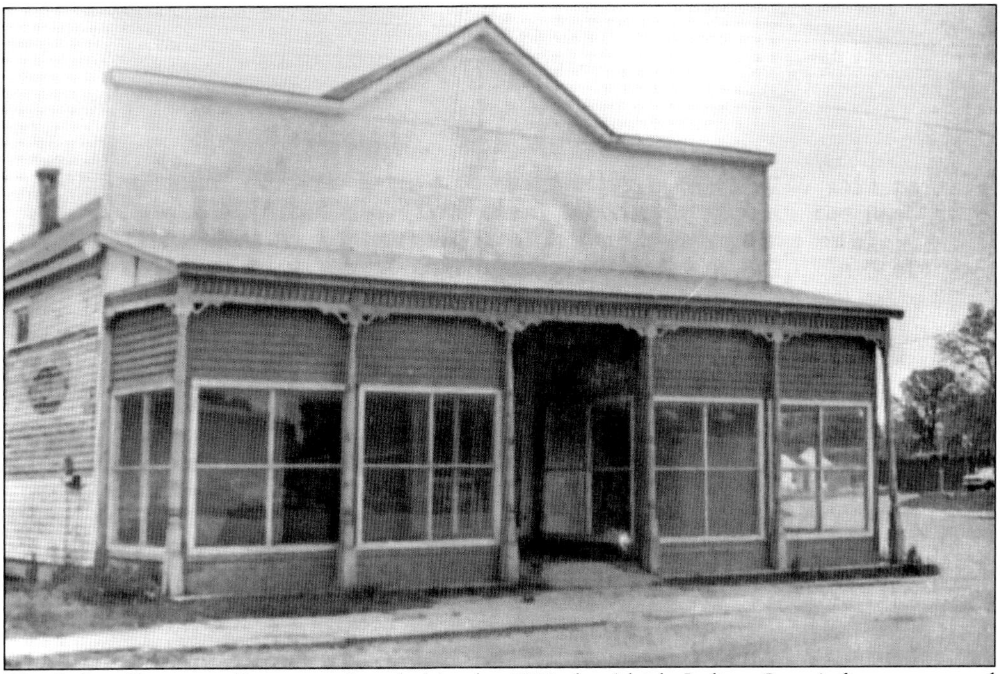

The Judice Company Store was founded in the 1880s by Alcide Judice, Scott's first mayor and businessman. His store coincided with the advent of the railroad at Scott Station. From his store, Judice loaned money to area farmers for their future crops. His son Louis Leo eventually joined him in the business, selling general merchandise to the people in Scott and the surrounding area. The store remained vibrant until the mid-20th century. (Courtesy of Lafayette Parish Clerk of Court.)

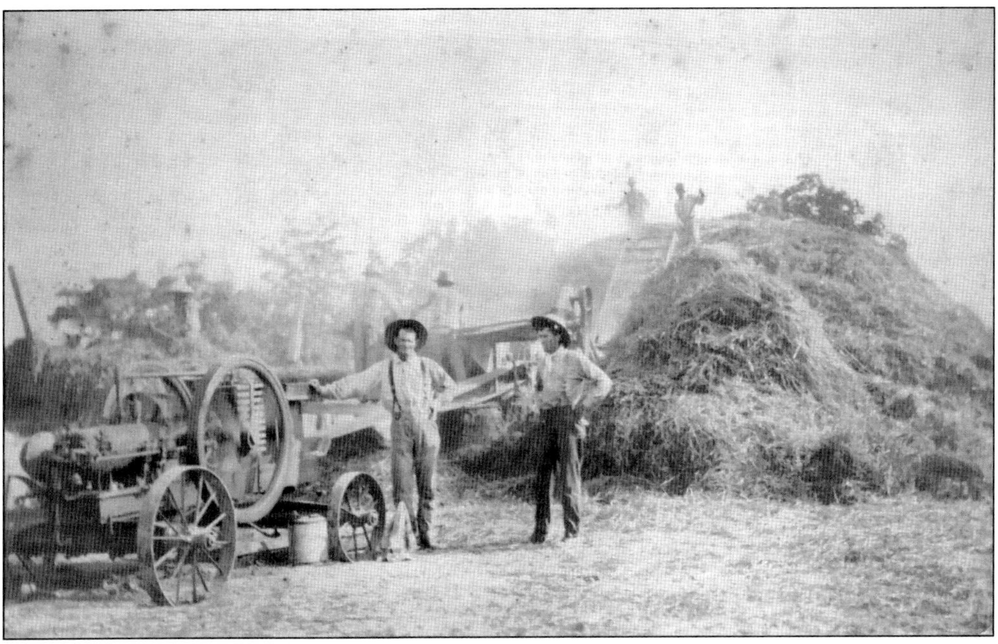

People traveled from miles around to see the area's first-known hay-baling machine in operation. Without the machine, hay was left in loose stacks. (Courtesy of Cheri Norton Broussard.)

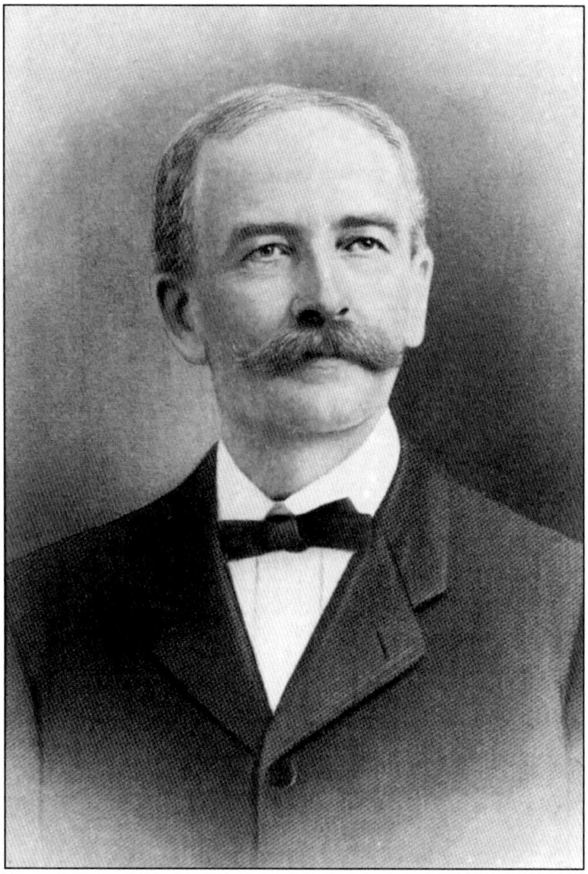

Alcide Judice settled in Scott in the 1870s. In the 1880s, he married the daughter of Dominic Cayret and opened the first general merchandise store. As Lafayette Parish's father of public education, he helped build area schools and arranged "bus" transportation for students. He was also a benefactor to Sts. Peter and Paul Catholic Church. (Courtesy of Louise Sonnier.)

The home of Louis Leo Judice and his wife, Hunter Ferguson Judice, was considered one of the most elaborate houses in Scott. Hunter was known for establishing a soup kitchen for area schoolchildren and maintaining garden flowers used for graduations and all church functions. (Courtesy of Lafayette Parish Clerk of Court.)

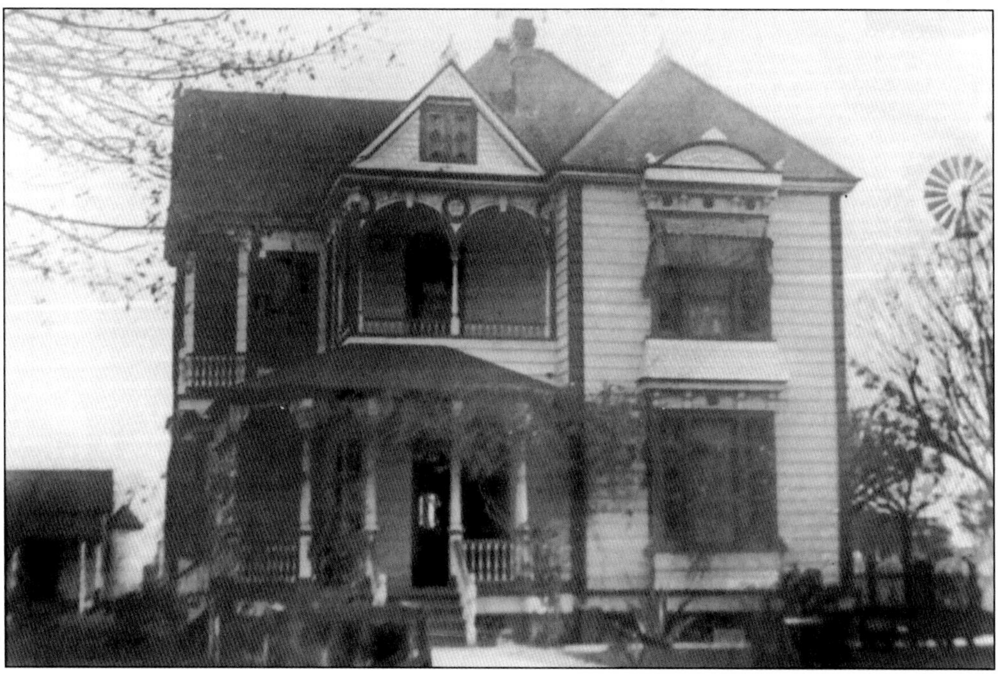

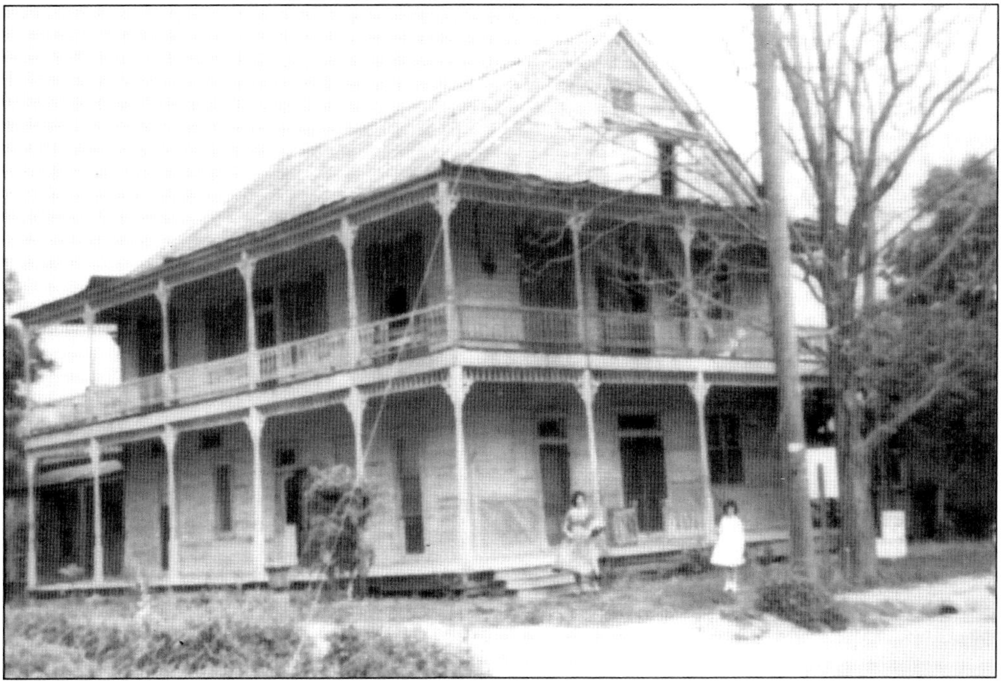

Sharon (left) and Paulette Delana stand in front of the home of their grandfather Leon Bernard. The house, surrounded by a large veranda, served as the St. Paul Hotel in its early years and then as apartments. In World War II, a tower built on the roof served as a lookout for unfamiliar airplanes. (Courtesy of Donald Arceneaux.)

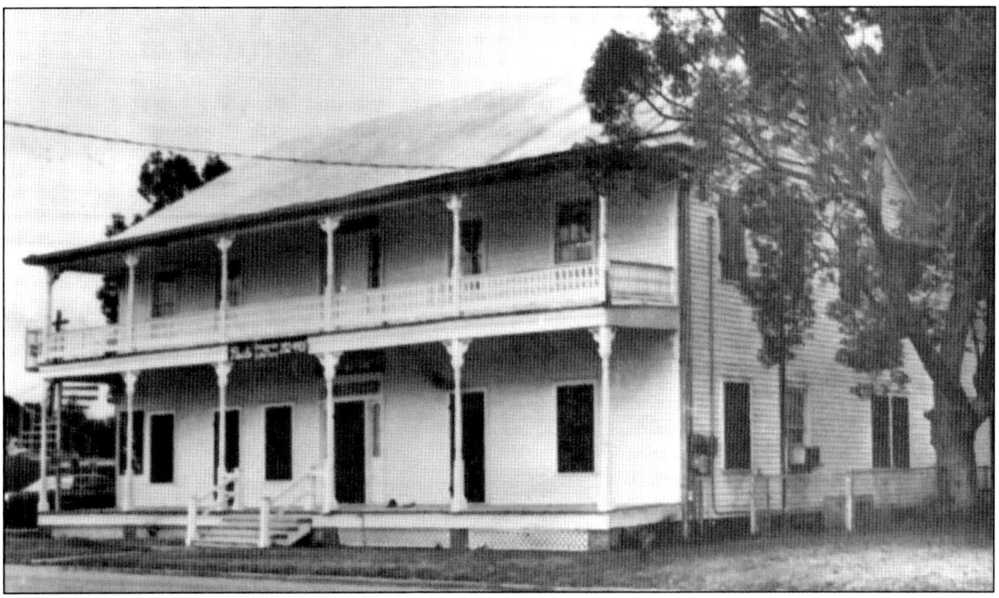

Felix Foreman's house was built by Duperon Morvant in 1895 and was located on Cayret Street in Scott. The house served as a rest stop for traveling salesmen, also known as "drummers." Foreman bought the house and used the upstairs as a dance hall from 1910 to 1940. Paul H. Begnaud used the building for commercial purposes starting in 1971. In February 1993, it burned to the ground. (Courtesy of Lafayette Parish Clerk of Court.)

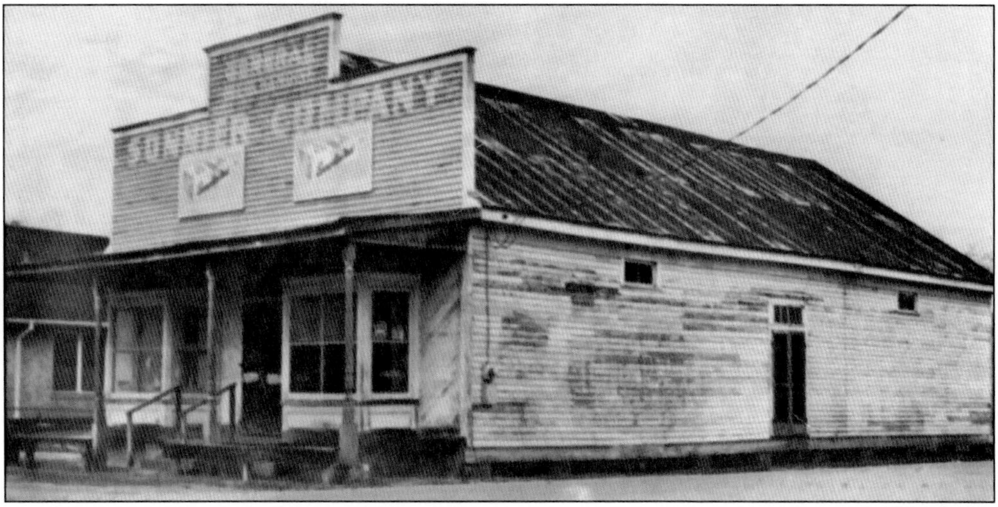

The Sonnier Company business, which later became a fabric store, still stands today. It supplied residents with a variety of food staples, clothing, and notions. Bins of beans and potatoes sat beneath the counter, and coffee was ground from whole beans while customers waited. The owners accepted fresh produce in exchange for food staples and offered "lagniappe," meaning "a little extra," to children buying candy. (Courtesy of Lafayette Parish Clerk of Court.)

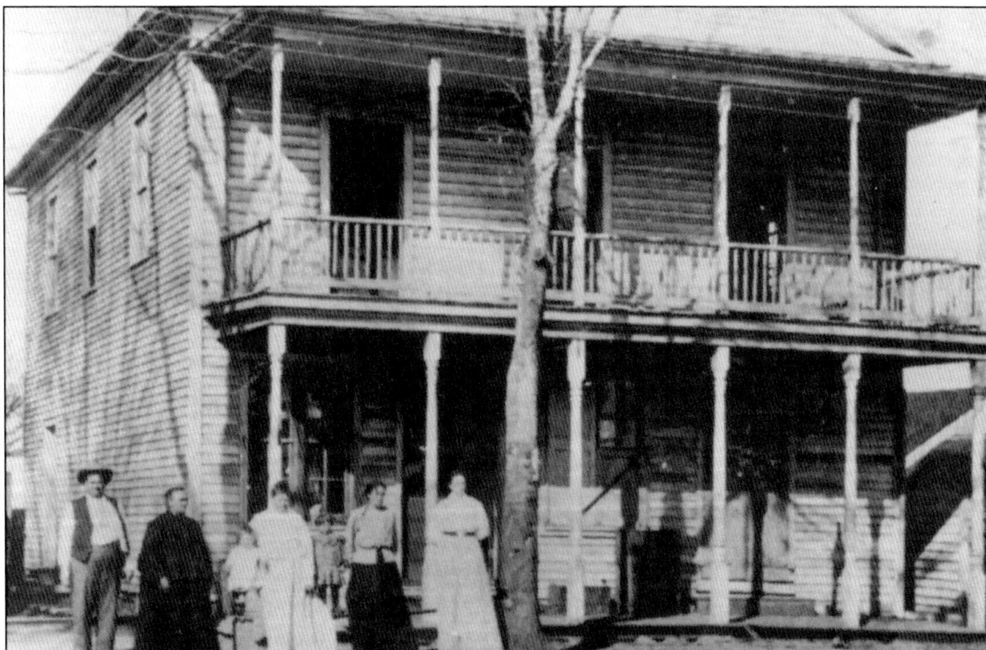

The 1904, the Sonnier Company building and home was located across the street from the Sonnier store. The home burned in the 1900s, possibly during a dynamite explosion at a warehouse/workshop in town. Pictured here from left to right are Joseph Sonnier, Celima Sonnier Prejean, Lee Sonnier, Mrs. Joseph Sonnier, Mary Sonnier Mouton, Mrs. Basile Sonnier, and Bernadette "Taunte Badette" S. Chiasson. Lee became a prominent doctor in Lafayette. Taunte Badette always dressed in very long skirts. In later years, a Shell service station was built on this location. (Courtesy of Lafayette Parish Clerk of Court.)

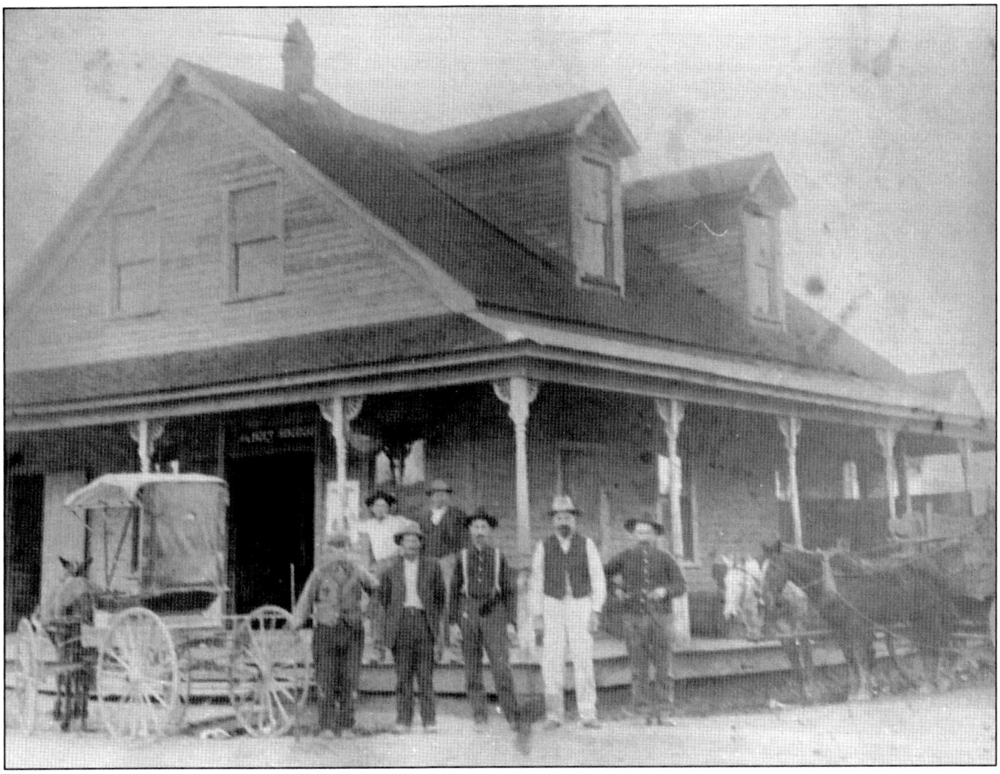

Opened in 1902 by Albert Bourque, this famous landmark on the corner of St. Mary and Delhomme Streets was known as an "exclusive" all-men's bar, a meeting place for many local citizens. Pictured from left to right in front are Delmar Broussard, Alcide Martin, Albert Bourque, Burchman Deshotels, and Antoine Hernandez. The "wanted" poster near the door featured escapees from Angola Penitentiary. The bar later became the studio and gallery of artist Floyd Sonnier. (Courtesy of Macqueline Thibeaux.)

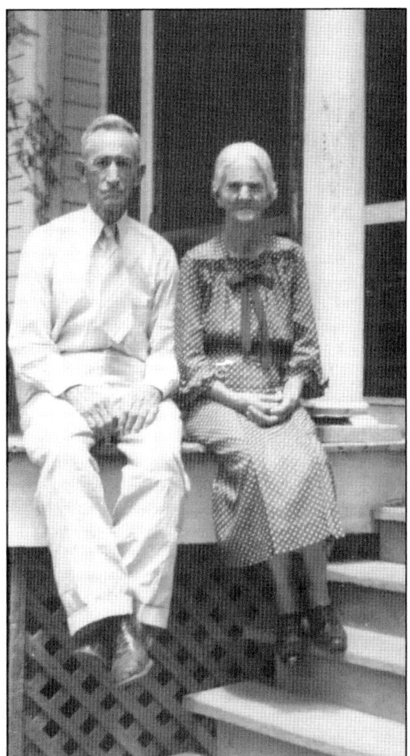

Albert Bourque and his wife, Zeoline, rest on their front porch on St. Mary Street across from Bourque's bar. The bar was owned by Bourque and run by his sons Clovis "Pete" and Wilson "Toot." The Bourques were the parents of Editha, Lester "Lep," Clovis "Pete," Wilson "Toot," George, and twins Milton "Tan" and Milta. (Courtesy of Macqueline Thibeaux.)

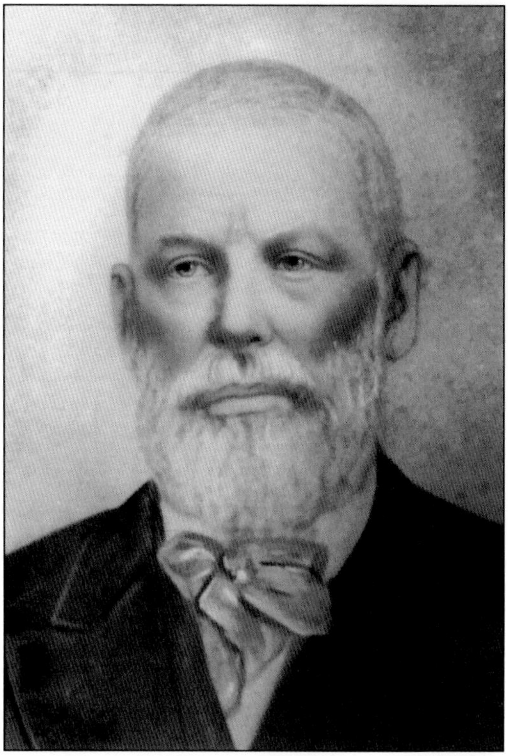

Col. Aurelin Drouzin Boudreaux was the patriarch of a large family. He owned an extensive plantation and was a leader in the Louisiana Confederate Army. A generous man, Colonel Boudreaux befriended the Blanc brothers, young French immigrants who eventually admitted guilt for the 1896 murder of Boudreaux's good friend Martin Begnaud. (Courtesy of Mona Stutes Caldwell.)

Built around 1835, Colonel Boudreaux's family home was located east of Scott city limits. The extensive plantation included orchards of fruit and pecan trees, over 20 buildings, and the Chinaball Racetrack. (Courtesy of Mona Stutes Caldwell.)

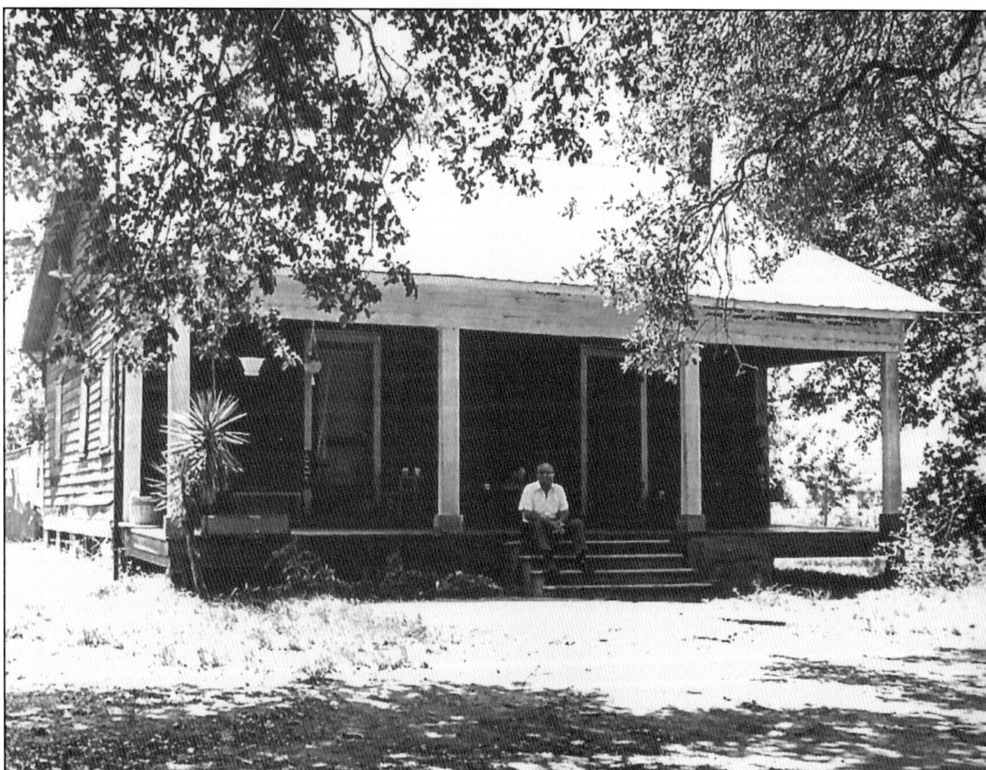

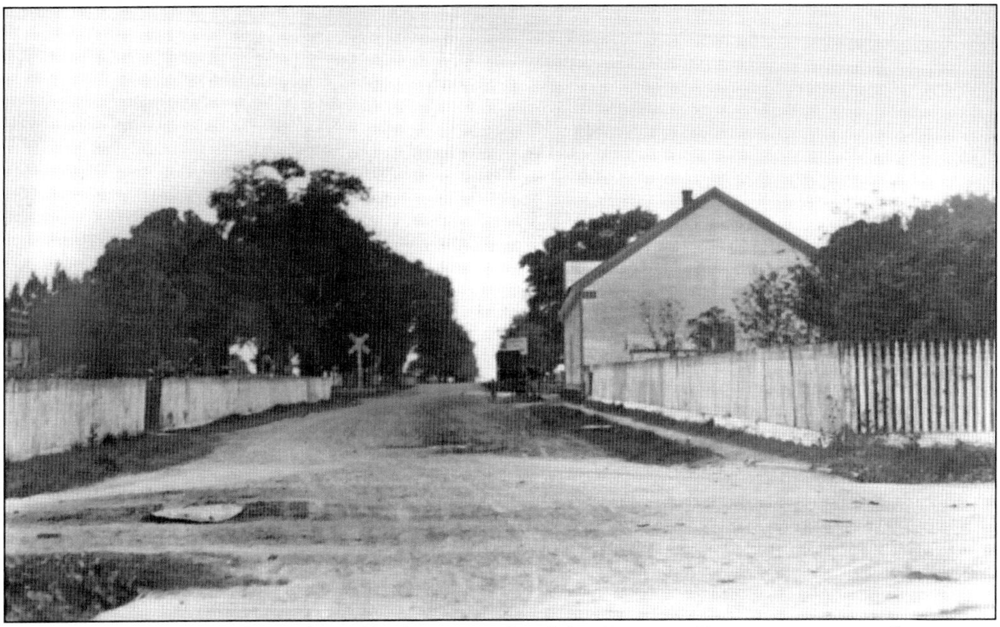

A horse-and-buggy park on the Alfred Street side of the Sonnier Company store in downtown Scott is pictured in 1926. The railroad was still important to this community of dirt roads. (Courtesy of Lafayette Parish Clerk of Court.)

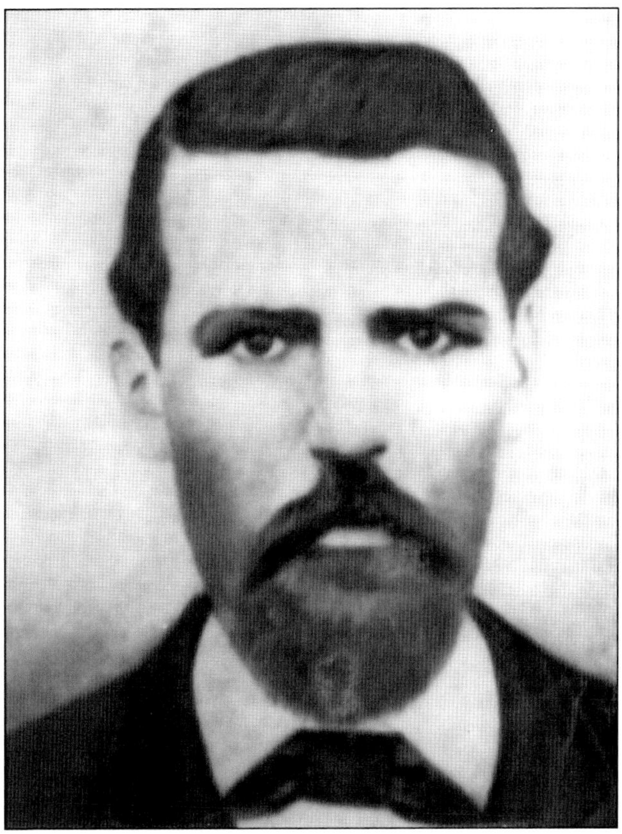

General store owner Martin Begnaud was known for his business skills and generosity to his customers. (Courtesy of Lafayette Parish Clerk of Court.)

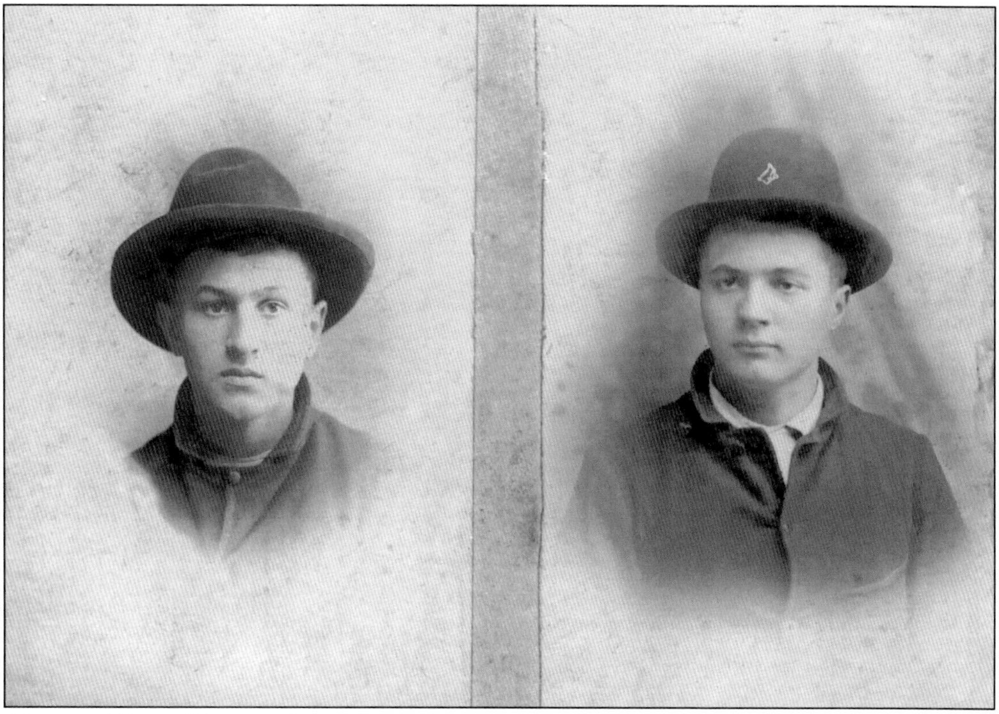

Alexis and Ernest Blanc settled in Scott after coming to the United States from France. Col. A.D. Boudreaux hired them as farmhands, but they dreamed of greater wealth after reading western stories about the James brothers. Subsequently, they robbed and brutally murdered Martin Begnaud. (Louise Sonnier and Lafayette Parish Clerk of Court.)

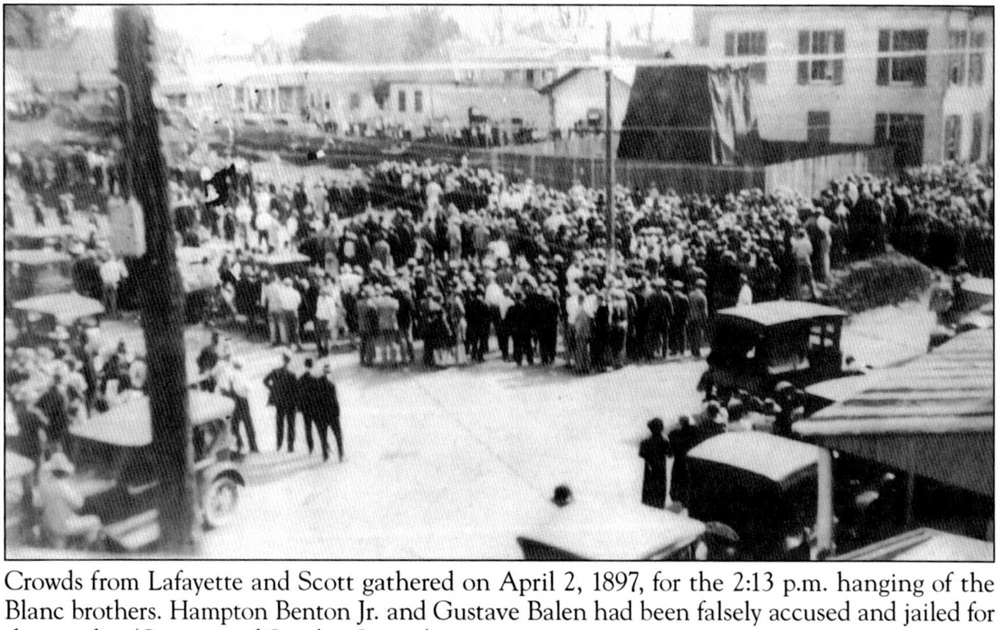

Crowds from Lafayette and Scott gathered on April 2, 1897, for the 2:13 p.m. hanging of the Blanc brothers. Hampton Benton Jr. and Gustave Balen had been falsely accused and jailed for the murder. (Courtesy of Carolyn Stutes.)

# *Two*

# Businesses, Buildings, and Landmarks

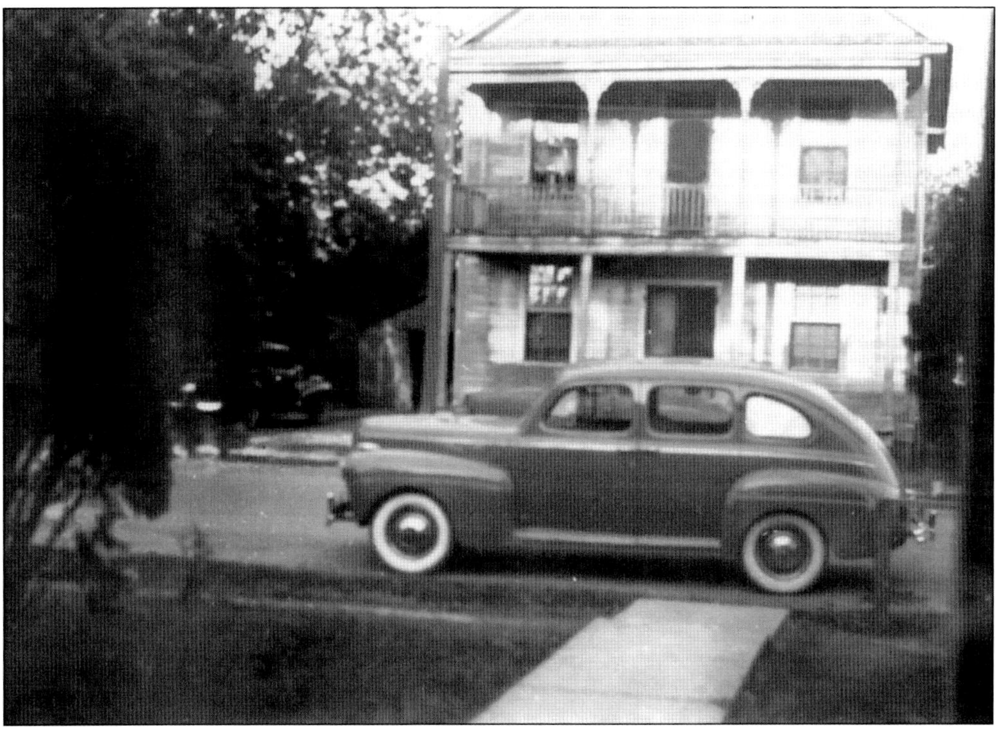

The Victor Dugas Store served as a business and home for the family. The store was located on the first floor, and the family lived upstairs. The back area had two rooms and a small porch. Leon "Doc" Sonnier later purchased the house and property. In the middle of the property was a garden, and in the back was a hen yard. This house was dismantled between 1948 and 1949, and the lumber was used to build a new house a couple of blocks away. (Courtesy of Georgie Bourque Duhon.)

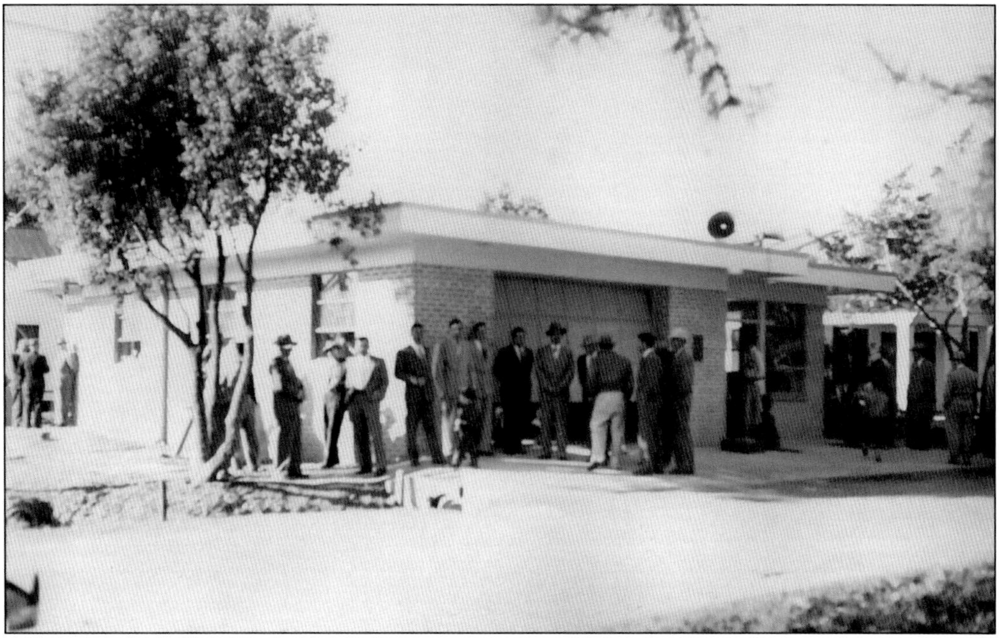

Scott's first multipurpose municipal building consolidated the fire station, two jail cells, and the municipal offices. Built in the 1950s, the structure served Scott until 1984. A siren would sound from the building, alerting villagers of a fire; the fire location was then written on a chalkboard so the volunteers who missed the truck could drive to the fire. (Courtesy of Scott City Hall.)

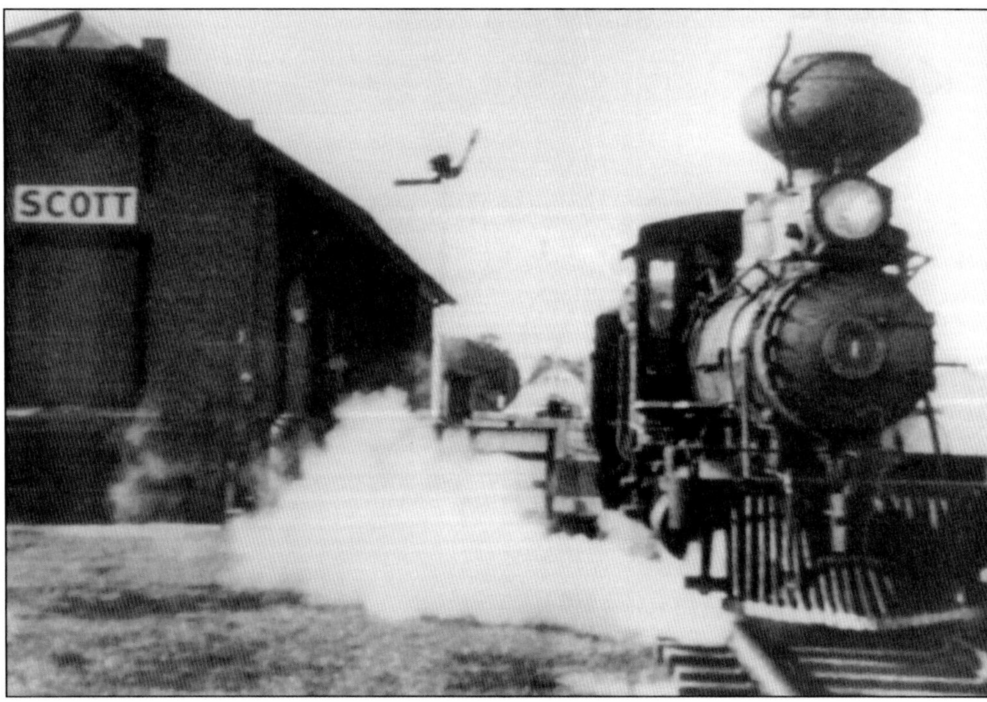


An engine steams into Scott near the railroad depot. The railroad was a source of commerce, a means of transportation, and the stimulus for growth and business in the area. (Courtesy of Lafayette Parish Clerk of Court.)

Families that did not own property worked as sharecroppers. They were paid in produce and cash for their work. In this 1940s photograph, Ulinor Pitt Jr. (a sharecropper) and a group of people helping him stop for the camera in a cotton field. Pictured from left to right are Natalie Carriere, Velior Carriere, Pitt, Kermit Boss, and Sarah Leger. (Courtesy of Earlene Carriere.)

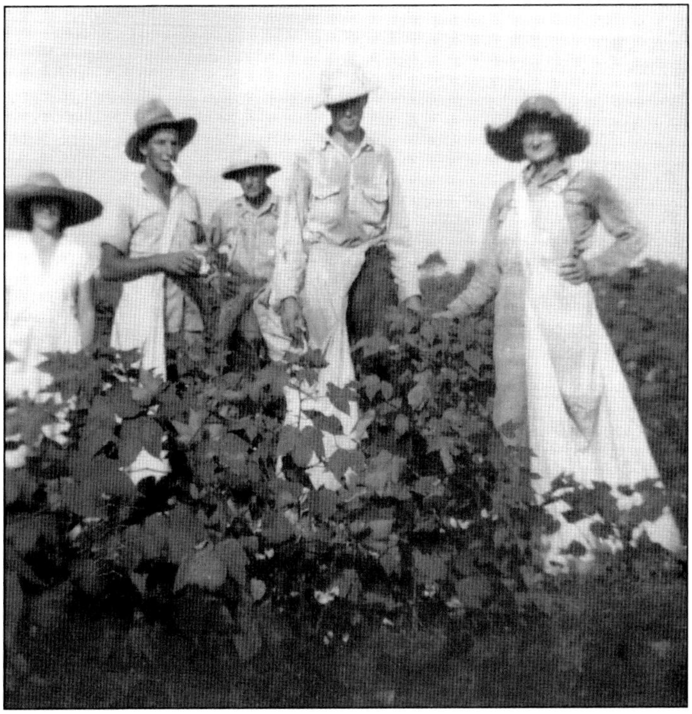

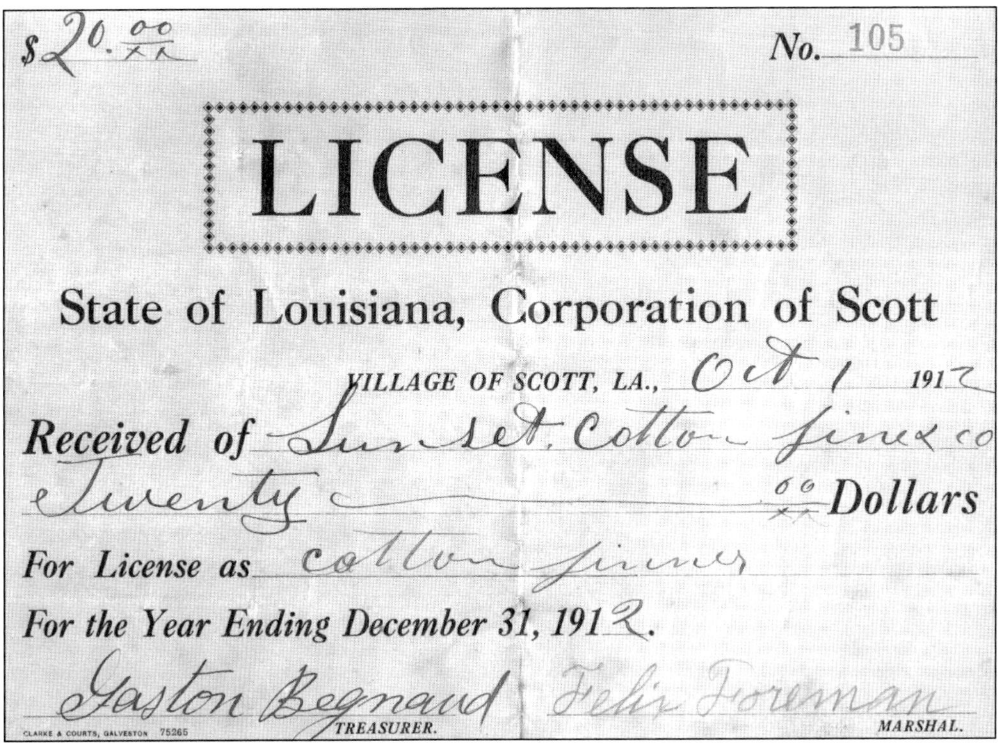

$20.00/xx No. 105

LICENSE

State of Louisiana, Corporation of Scott

VILLAGE OF SCOTT, LA., Oct 1 1912

Received of Sunset Cotton Ginner co

Twenty 00/xx Dollars

For License as cotton ginner

For the Year Ending December 31, 1912.

Gaston Begnaud TREASURER. Felix Foreman MARSHAL.

CLARKE & COURTS, GALVESTON 75265

Companies needed a state license to operate a cotton gin in the village. The license seen here was issued to the Sunset Cotton Ginner by the Scott village for $20 in 1917. (Courtesy of Tina and Johnny Thibodeaux.)

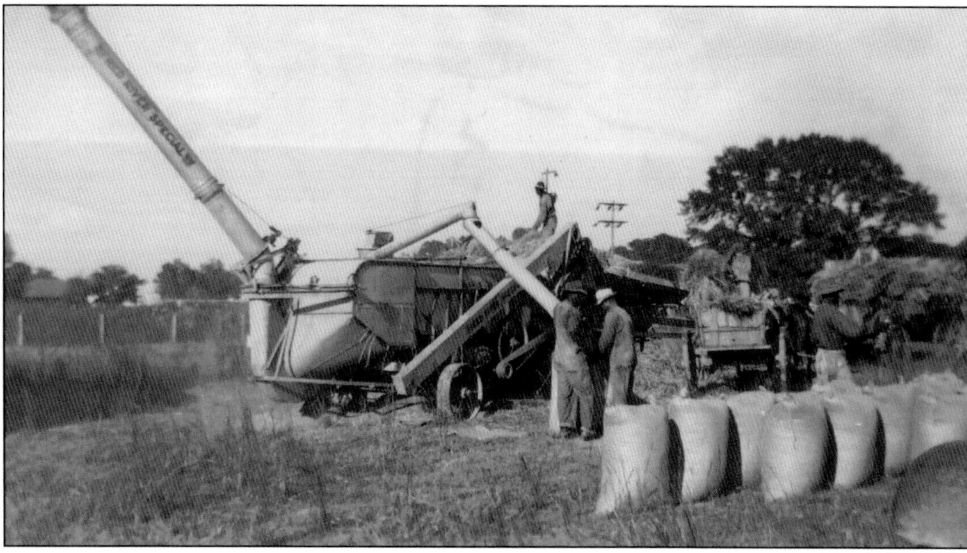

Rice was one of Scott's dominant crops in the 1940s. It was planted in the spring and harvested in the fall. Here, tenant farmers bag the rice to be stored until it could be sent to the mills by rail. (Courtesy of Annadine Credeur.)

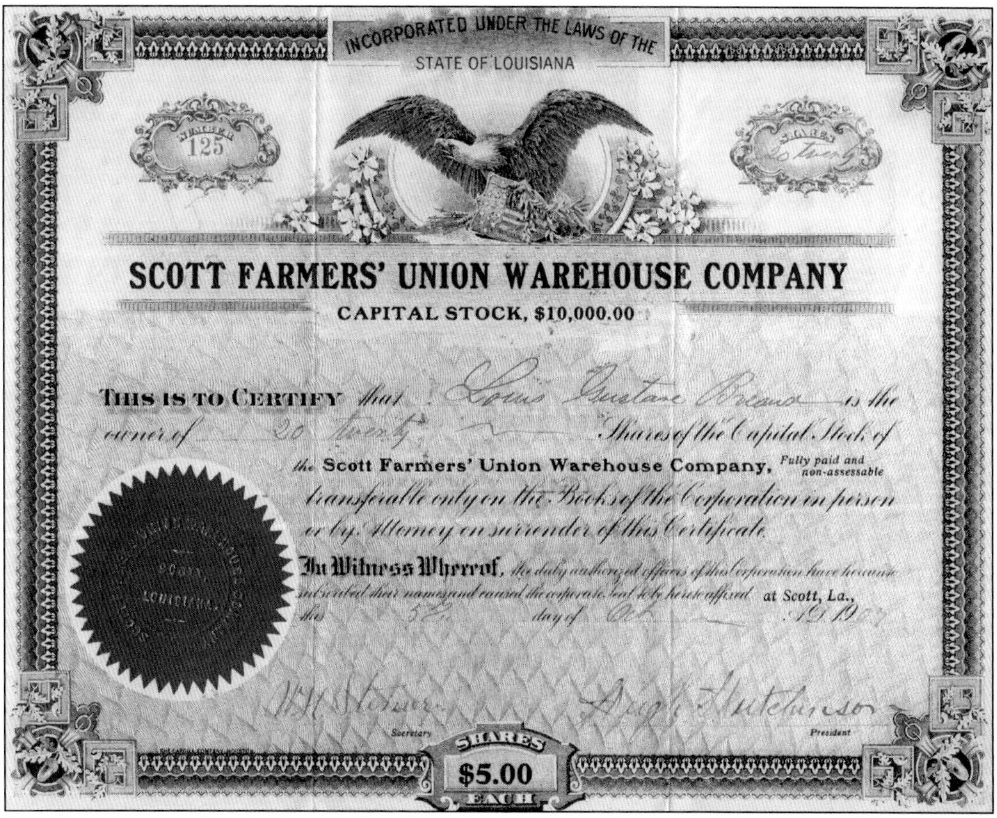



Local businessmen bought shares of stock in the Scott Farmers' Union Warehouse Company, and investors were issued stock certificates like the one pictured. Farmers would store their harvest in the warehouse until it was ready to be shipped by railroad. (Courtesy of Annadine Credeur.)

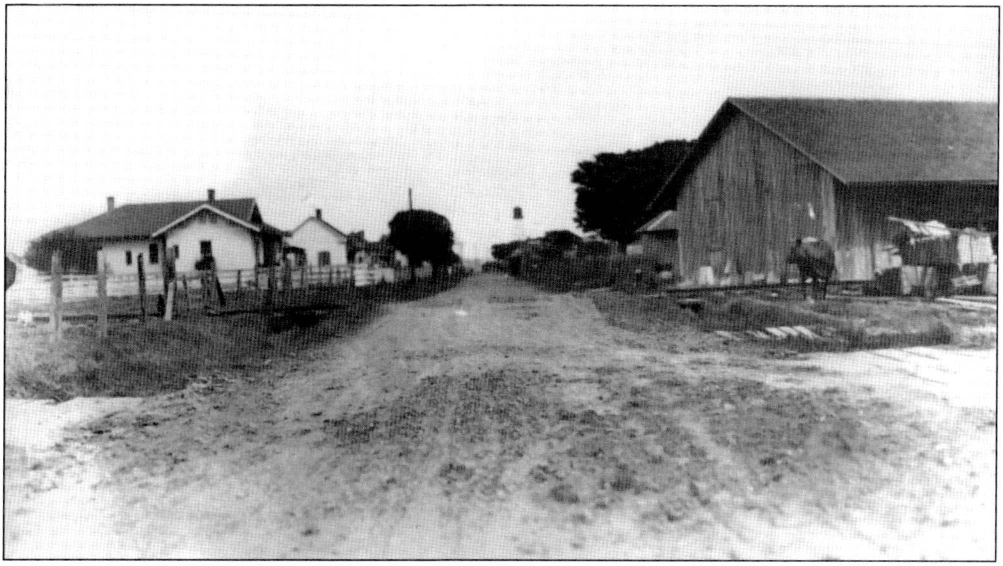

In 1926, Delhomme Avenue was the main road through Scott. The Guidroz and Madame Neville Prejean houses are situated on the left, and on the right is the Brandt Lumber Company storage warehouse. The railroad spur crosses Delhomme Avenue and goes to the cotton gin. The Guidroz house burned in 1973. (Courtesy of Lafayette Parish Clerk of Court.)

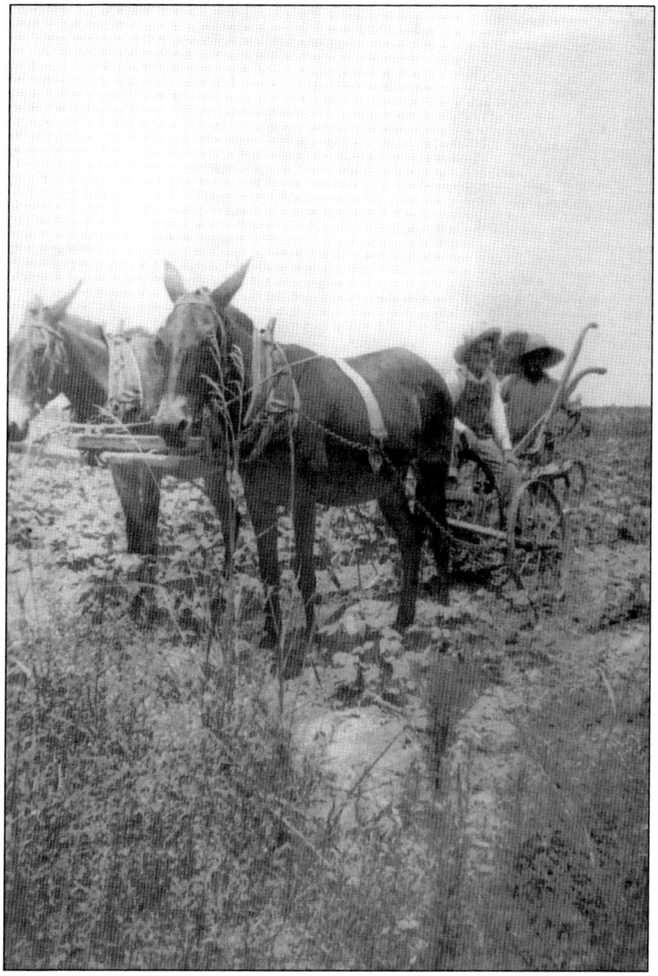

In the early years of farming, mules and sometimes horses were used for plowing the fields. A person walked behind the plow to guide the animal pulling it. The work was laborious for both animals and men. (Courtesy of Annadine Credeur.)

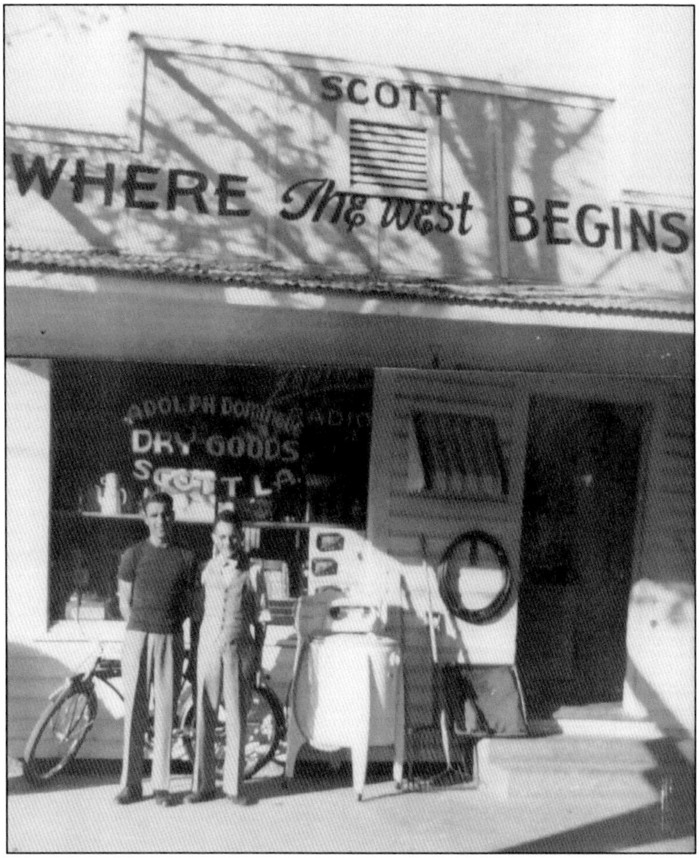


This general store, located on the corner of Cayret Street and Highway 90, sold a variety of goods, household items, and odds and ends. It was owned by Adolph Domingue, who proudly displayed a sign that read, "Where the West Begins." (Courtesy of Wayne Burton.)

Elmo Broussard Sr. owned Broussard Welding and the Western Auto Store on St. Mary Street. He served individuals while he was on 24-hour call for the oil industry. From left to right, Elmo Broussard Jr., Elmo Broussard Sr., and Eric Domingue stand in front of the welding shop. (Courtesy of Judy Broussard Leger.)

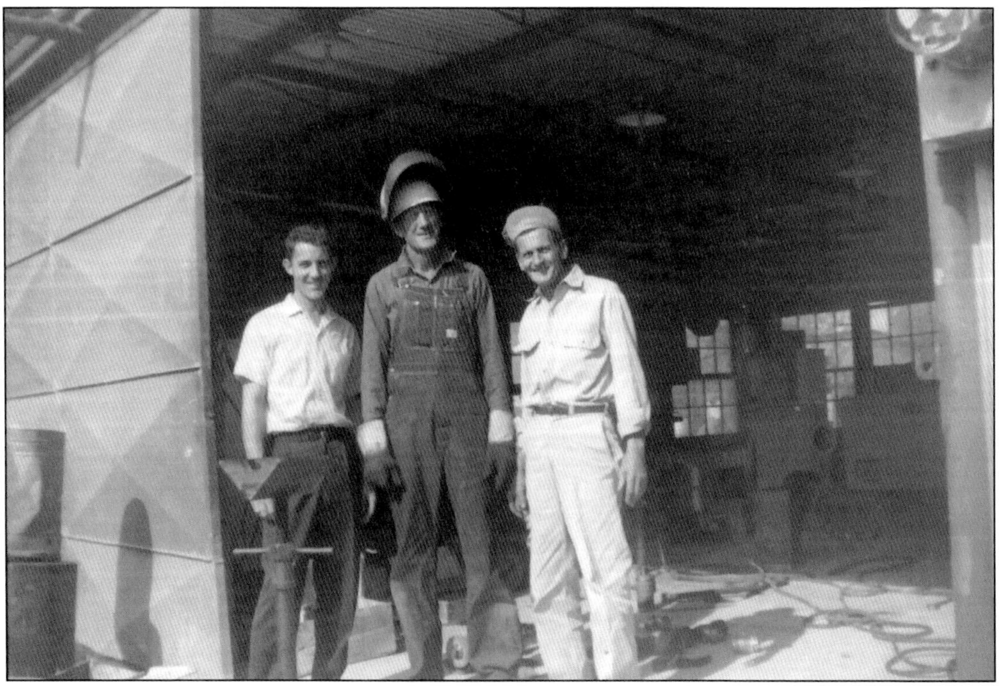

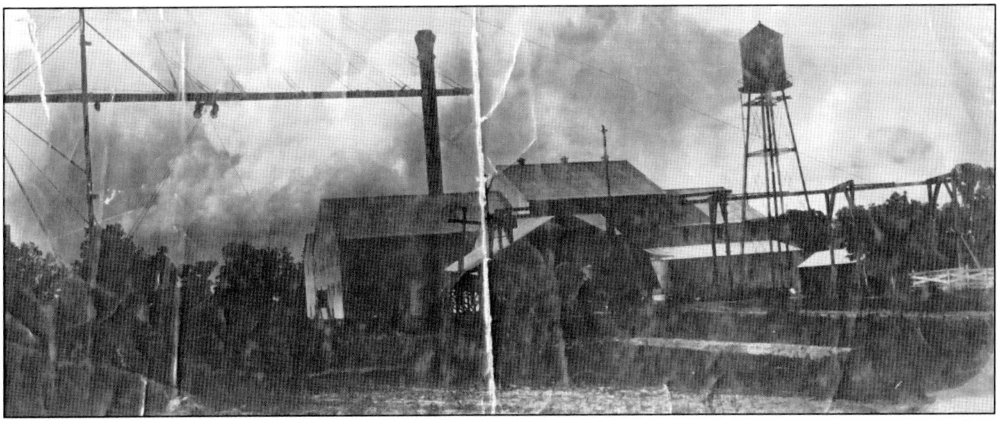

This is a photograph of one of the cotton gins in Scott in the early 1900s. Cotton was transported to the gins by mules and wagons and later by trucks. The gins cleaned and baled the cotton to be shipped by the Scott railroad. Each bale weighed about 500 pounds. (Courtesy Annadine Credeur.)

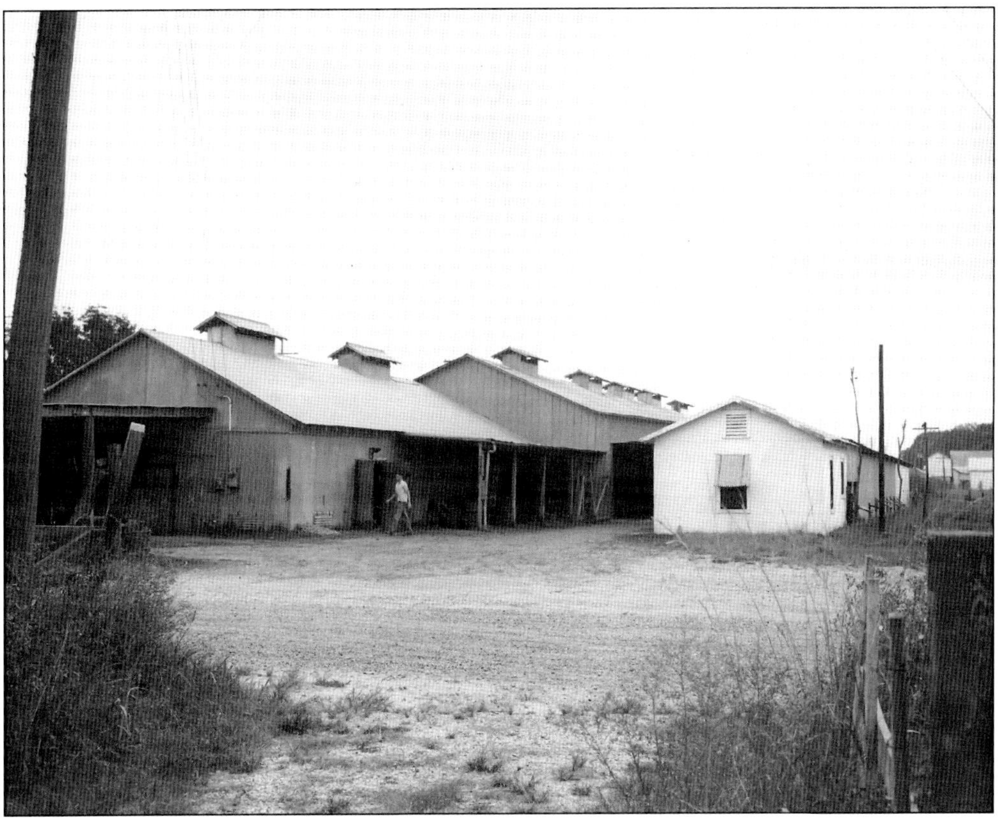

Hubert Sonnier walks from his office towards the potato kiln. The kilns were used for drying and storing yams to be shipped by railroad across the United States and Canada. (Courtesy of Mila Handler.)

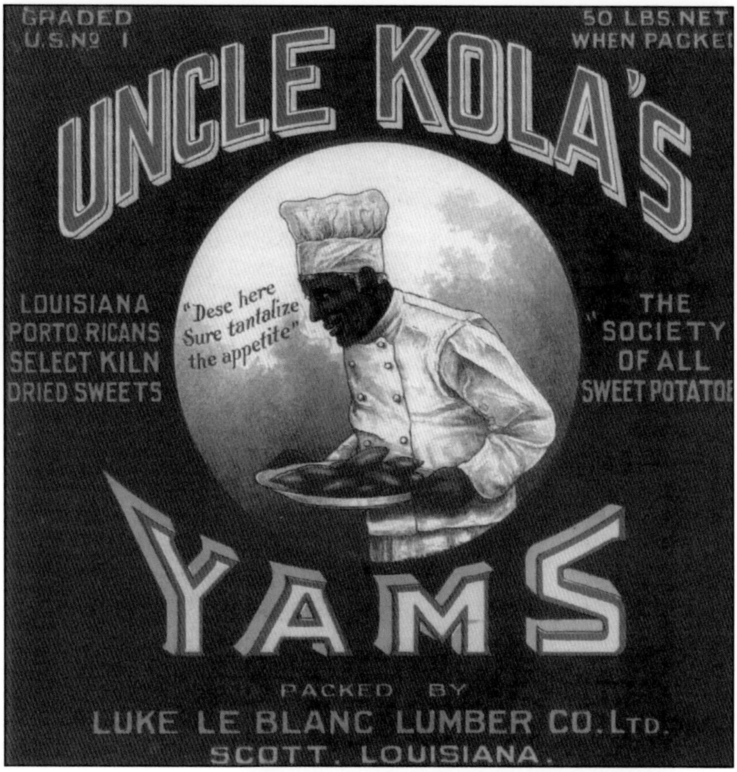


Yams became a successful commodity during the Depression era. Luke Leblanc's sons-in-law Arthur O'Conner and Clay Leblanc were involved at the inception of this industry. Uncle Kola's Yams label was one of those used for shipping yams in the United States. (Courtesy of Cheri Norton Broussard.)

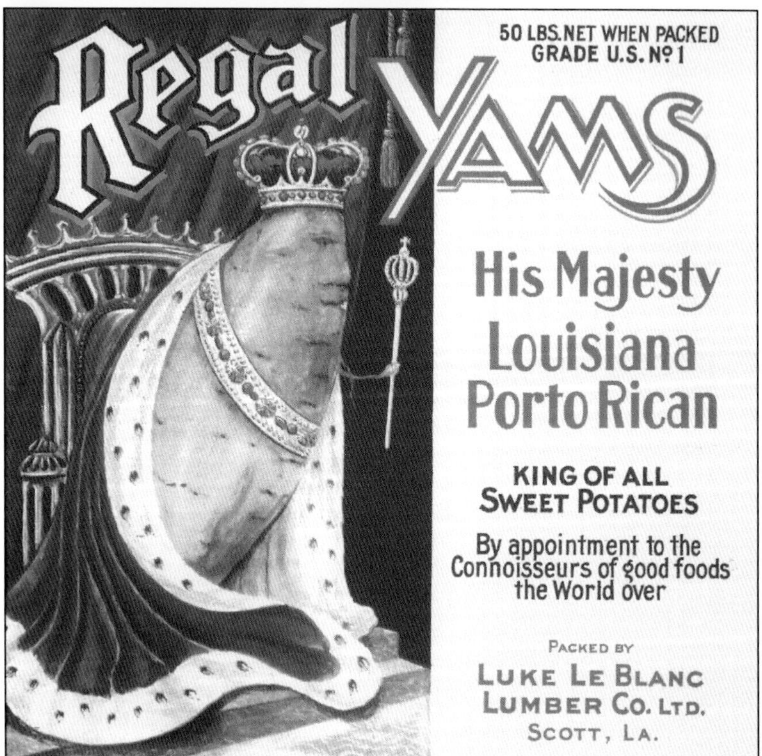


The Regal Yam label was used specifically for yams shipped to Canada; yams shipped in the United States used other labels. All of the yams were harvested from the same fields. (Courtesy of Wayne Domingue.)

The Sonnier brothers—Alcee, Freddie, and Saul—were involved in the sweet potato business during the 1930s, shipping Puerto Rican yams under several labels, including this one. (Courtesy of Cheri Norton Broussard.)

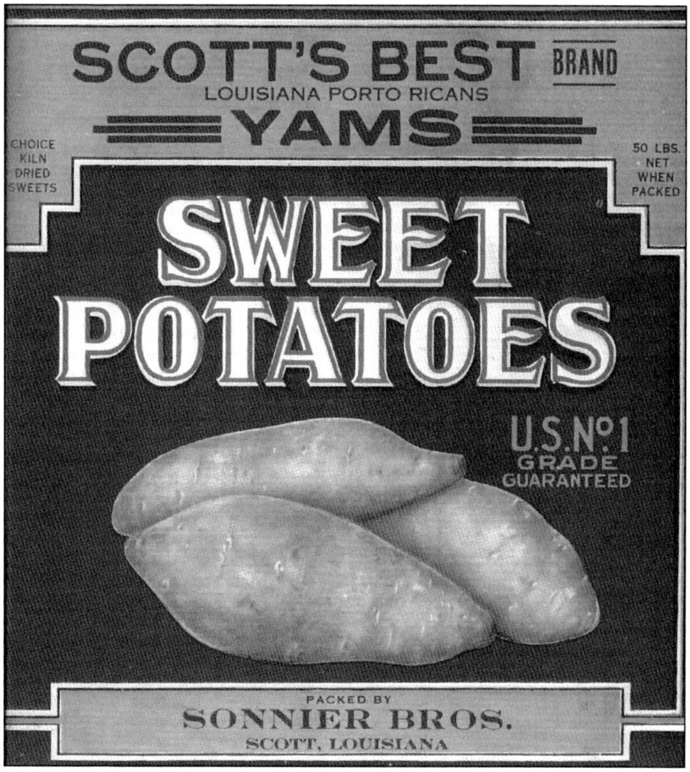


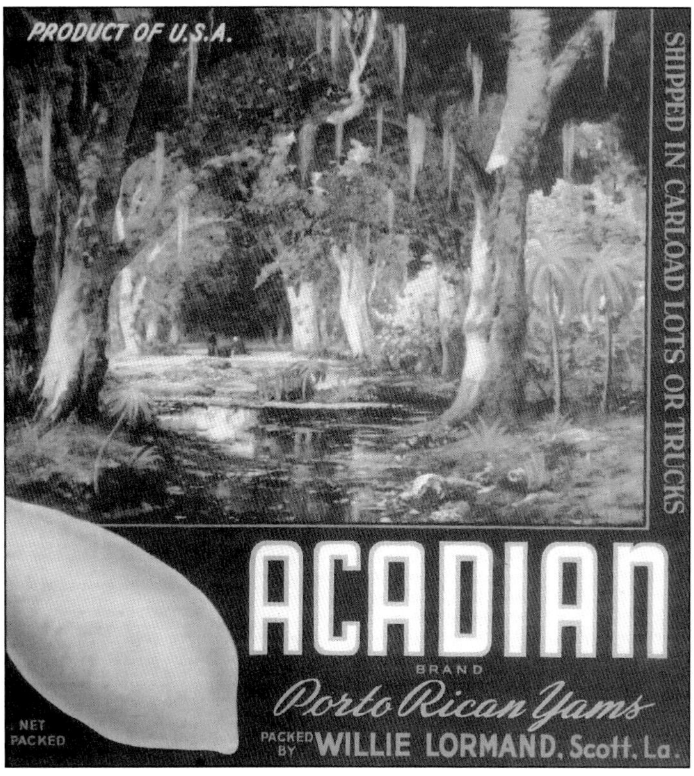


Willie Lormand packed and shipped sweet potatoes under the Willie Lormand label. This label shows that the yams could be shipped by carload lots or trucks. (Courtesy of Cheri Norton Broussard.)

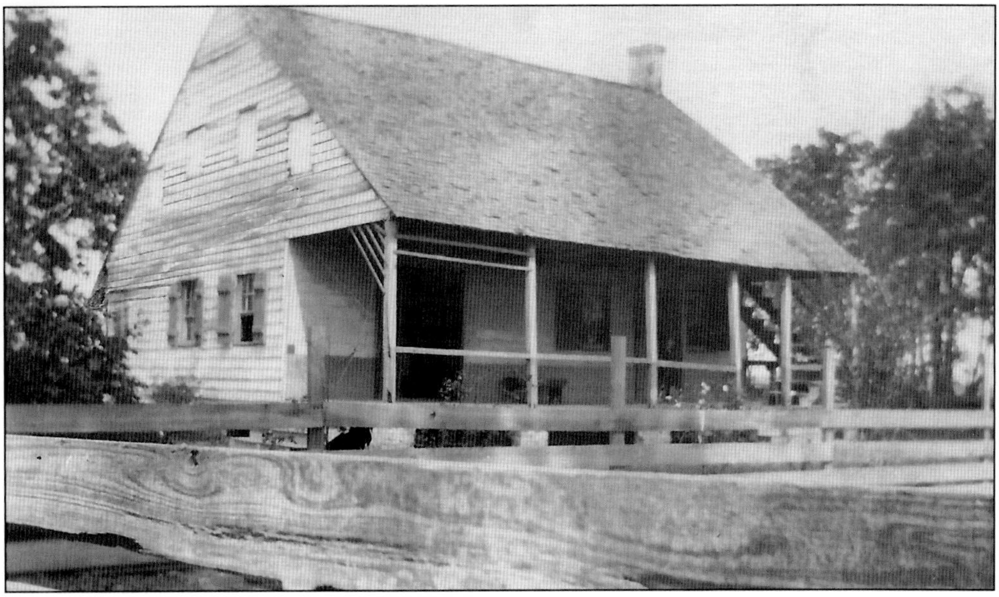

This house originally belonged to Cyril Sonnier and was later owned by Jean Batiste "Nonc Jean" Sonnier's family. It was insulated with *bousillage*, a mud and moss mixture, and was once moved using horses and logs. The Sonnier children stayed in the house while it was moved. (Courtesy of Anne Bourgeois.)

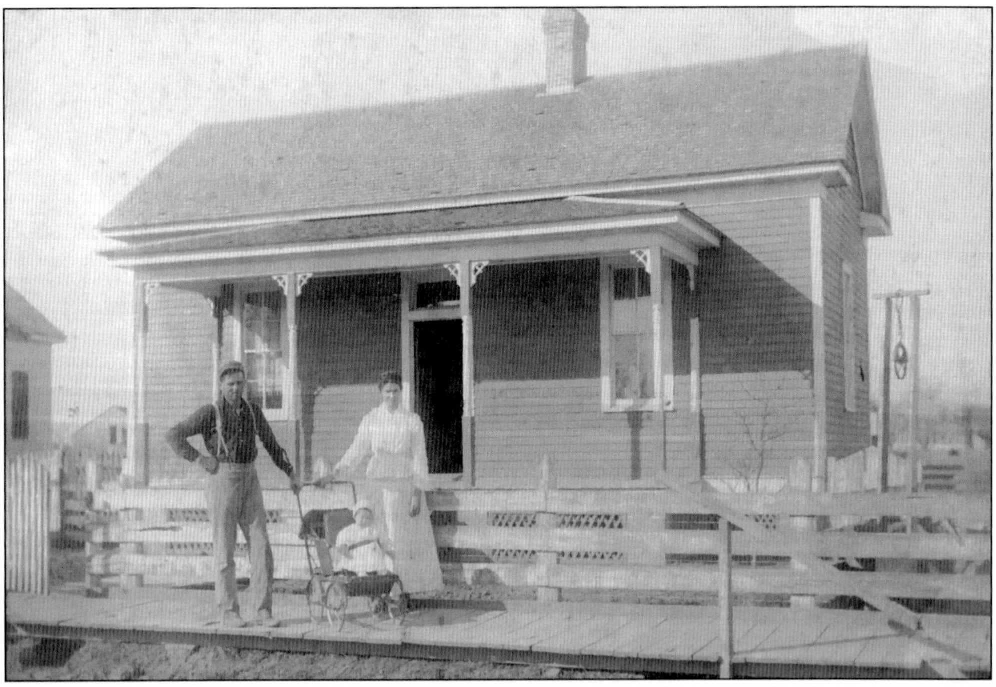

Zephirin Olivier "O.Z." Boudreaux, his wife Ita, and daughter Rhena stand before one of Scott's oldest houses, which O.Z. built in 1909. An engineer and mechanic, he owned a blacksmith shop, worked for the betterment of the community, and crafted the iron gates of Sts. Peter and Paul Catholic Church Cemetery. (Courtesy Mona Stutes Caldwell.)

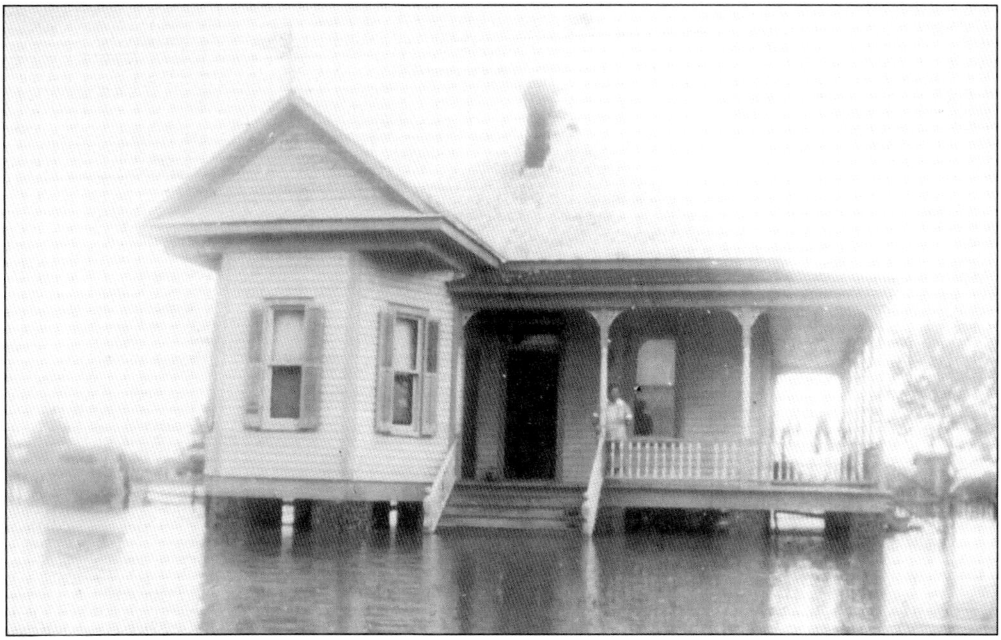

This home, pictured in the 1940 flood, was built by Victor Dugas around 1914. Standing on the porch is Anita Billeaud Sonnier. It was common for houses to be constructed on pillars to prevent water from entering during heavy rains. Claude Hebert, the agriculture teacher at Scott High School, purchased the house in the 1940s and planted vegetable gardens and fruit trees and raised hundreds of chickens. Dennis and Pam Carr are the current owners. (Courtesy of Judy and George Ardoin.)

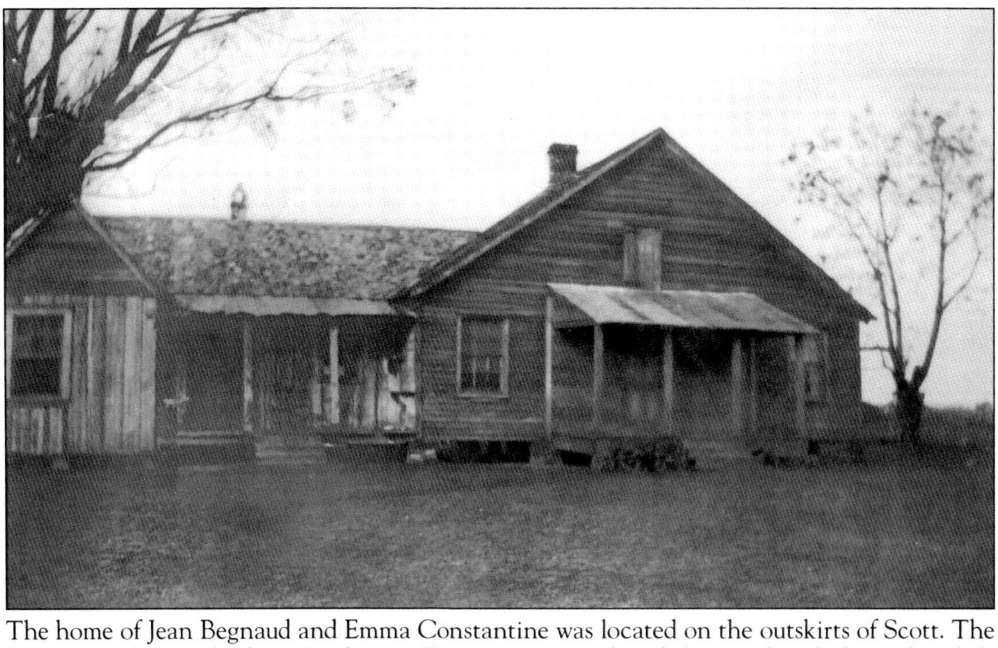

The home of Jean Begnaud and Emma Constantine was located on the outskirts of Scott. The couple raised seven children: Cecile, Ava, Regina, Gaston, Theophile, David, and Theo. Theophile inherited the property and raised his family there. Raymond and Gertrude Martin currently inhabit a home at this site. (Courtesy of Pearl Provost Guidry.)

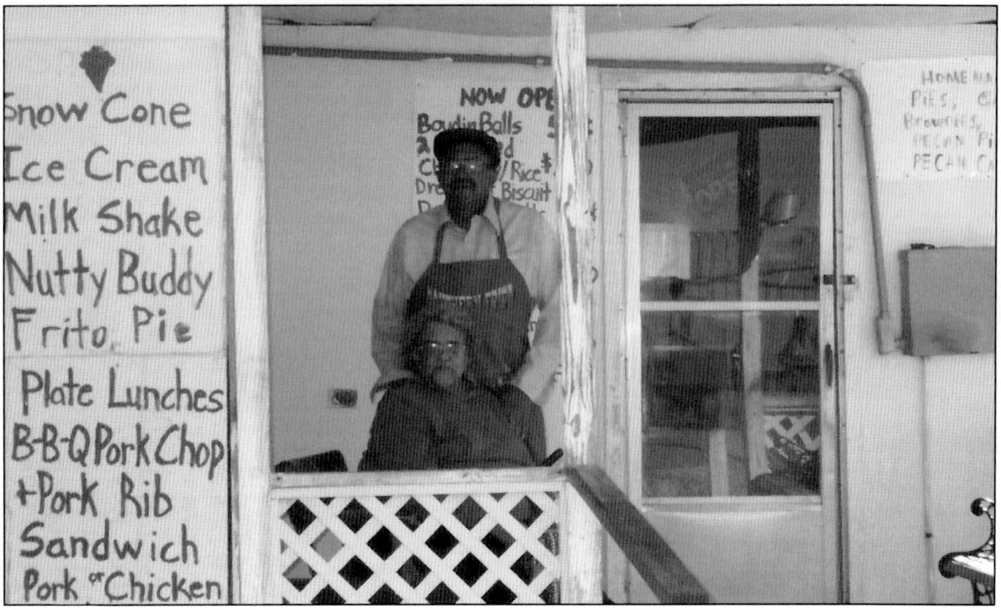


Joseph Willis Morrison opened a small grocery store in the 1950s. He married Mary Grace in 1959, and together they worked in the store. The business had been running for 25 years when they opened a snack bar that served plate lunches, desserts, ice cream, and the best homemade pies in the area. (Courtesy of Purvis Morrison.)

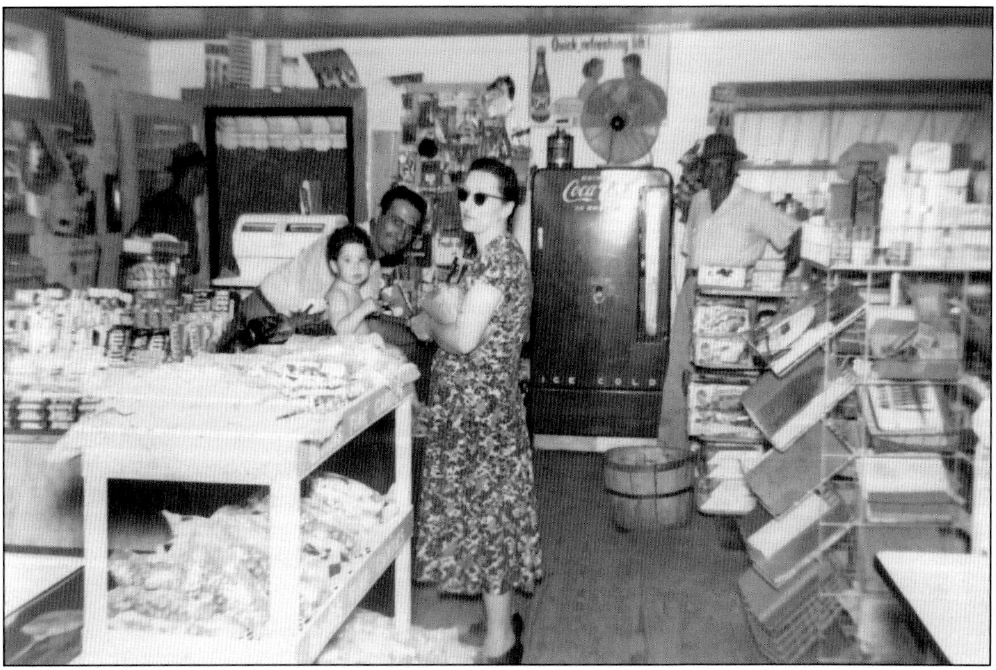

Chester Domingue stands at the counter, and Annie Mae LeBlanc Broussard holds a baby as she shops in "Mr. Chess's" store; shopping in back are Leonce Domingue (left) and Andre Falcon. Customers knew that they could find almost anything in this mom-and-pop store. The building still stands today and has an advertisement for Evangeline Bread on the screen door. (Courtesy of James Domingue.)

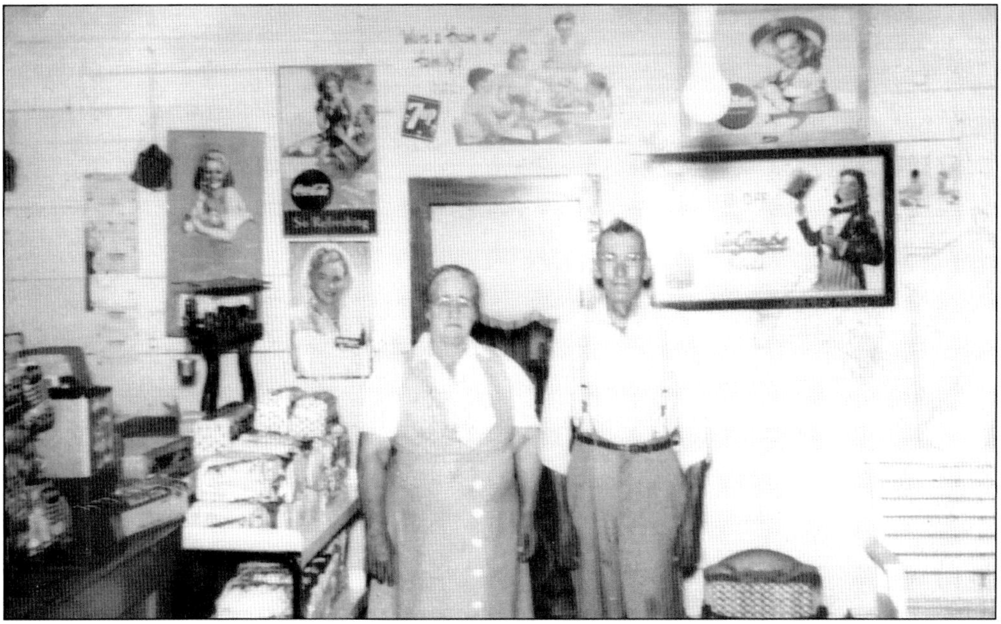

Jacques and Cecile Ancelet Dugas stand in their store across from Sts. Peter and Paul Catholic Church. The Dugases were well known to the Scott-area children, many of whom shopped at their store during recess for candy, hamburgers, and other treats. Dugas was a janitor at La Tit Ecole, switched the mail at the depot, and rang the church bell faithfully every morning and evening. (Courtesy of Rudelle Dronet.)

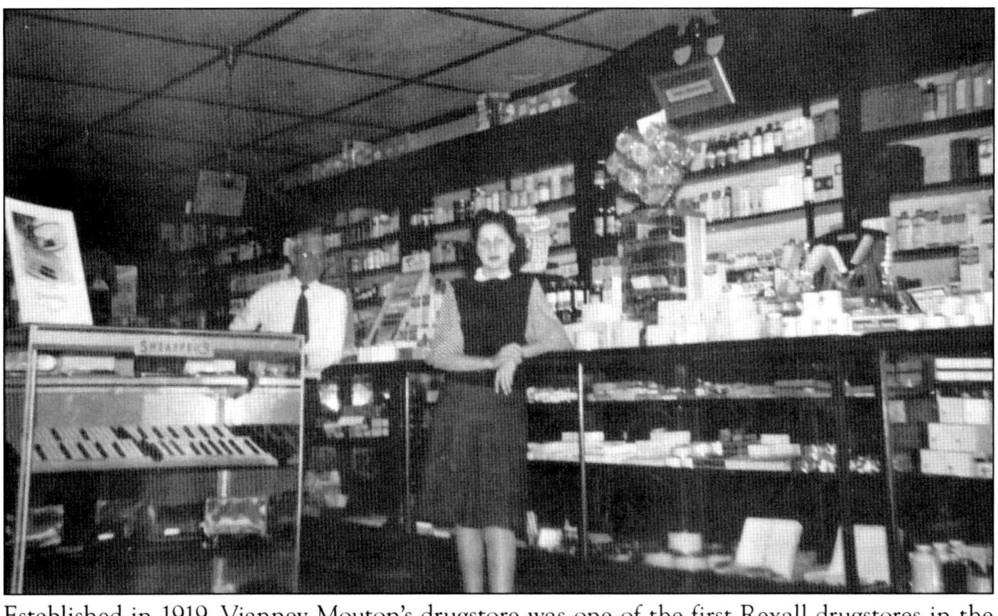

Established in 1919, Vianney Mouton's drugstore was one of the first Rexall drugstores in the state. Mouton (left) and Enola Domingue Lantier (right), a longtime employee, were commonly seen working inside. Larry Hebert, a pharmacist at the drugstore for over 50 years, now owns Mouton's business, currently named Scott Pharmacy and located in the newer building beside where Mouton's drugstore used to be. His daughter Jo-Ann Tanner, also a pharmacist, works in the store. (Courtesy of Larry Hebert.)

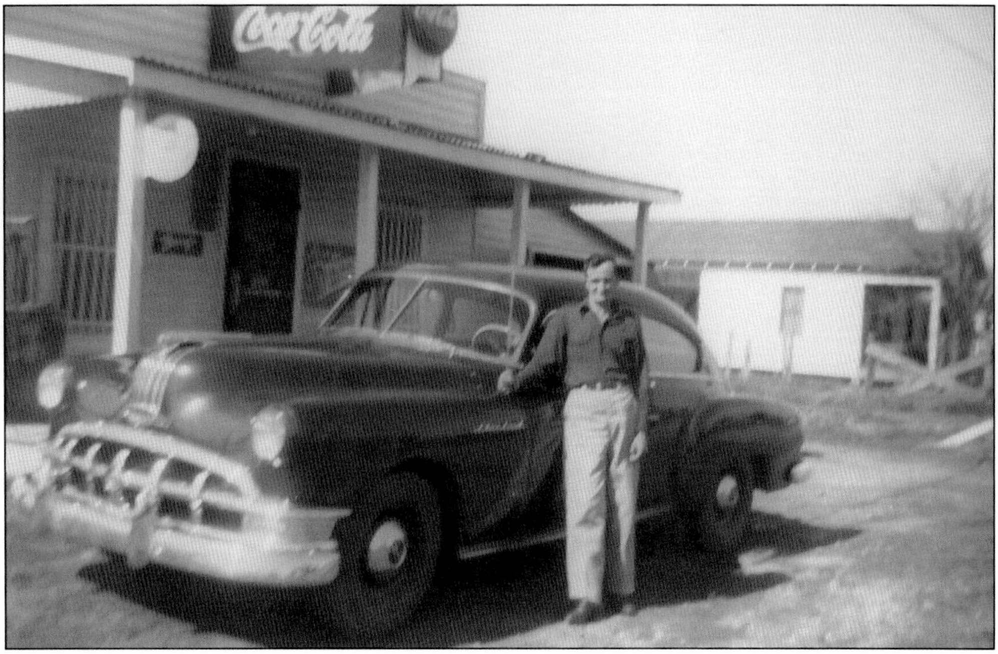


Claby Dugas owned and operated a neighborhood grocery in the front of his house. The store was located on St. Mary Street, and many neighbors bought their groceries there, as it was within walking distance. (Courtesy of Hazel Myers.)

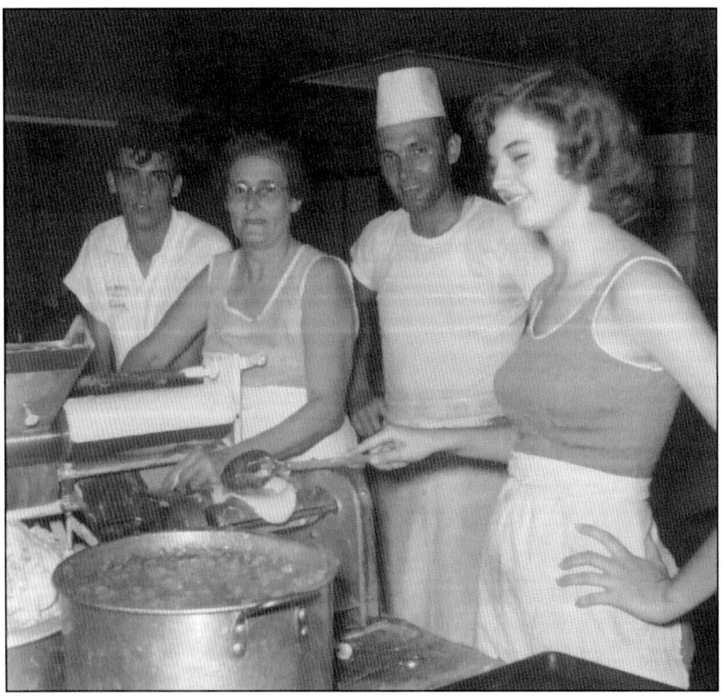

Owners and employees of Bergeron's Bakery seen here in 1956 are, from left to right, Harris Bergeron, Marie Trahan Bergeron, Andrus Bergeron, and Joyce Bergeron. The bakery was located on St. Mary Street and was owned and operated by Marie and Andrus. Many people enjoyed the bakery's specialty, doughnuts. (Courtesy of Joyce Bergeron Mire.)

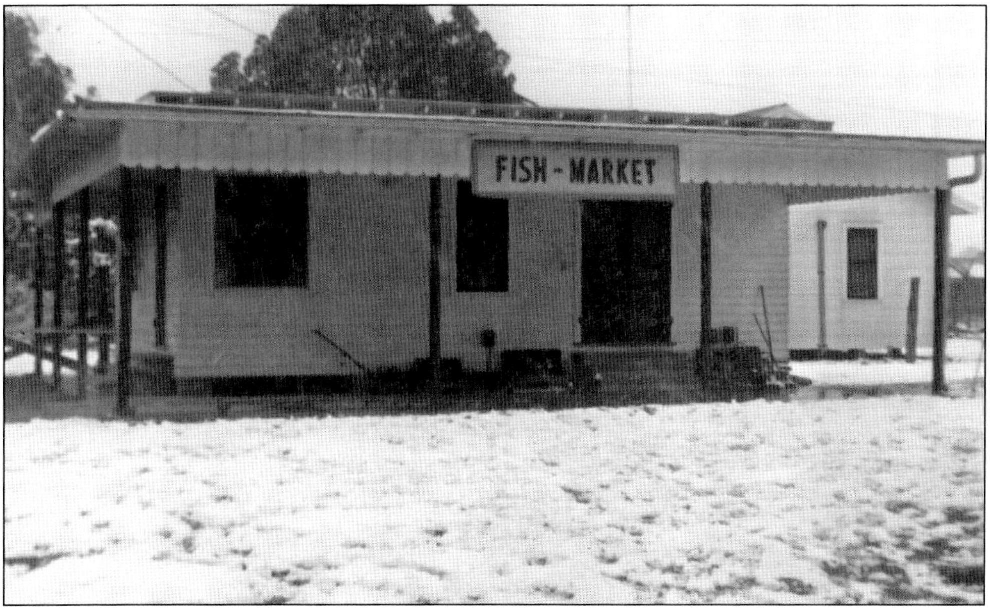


The Mire Meat and Fish Market was owned by Lyman and Sybil Mire. To ensure that everyone knew what he sold, Mire had a fish market sign on one side of the building and a meat market sign on the other side. Scott was a heavily populated Catholic area so they sold fish on Fridays and during the season of Lent. (Courtesy of George Martin.)

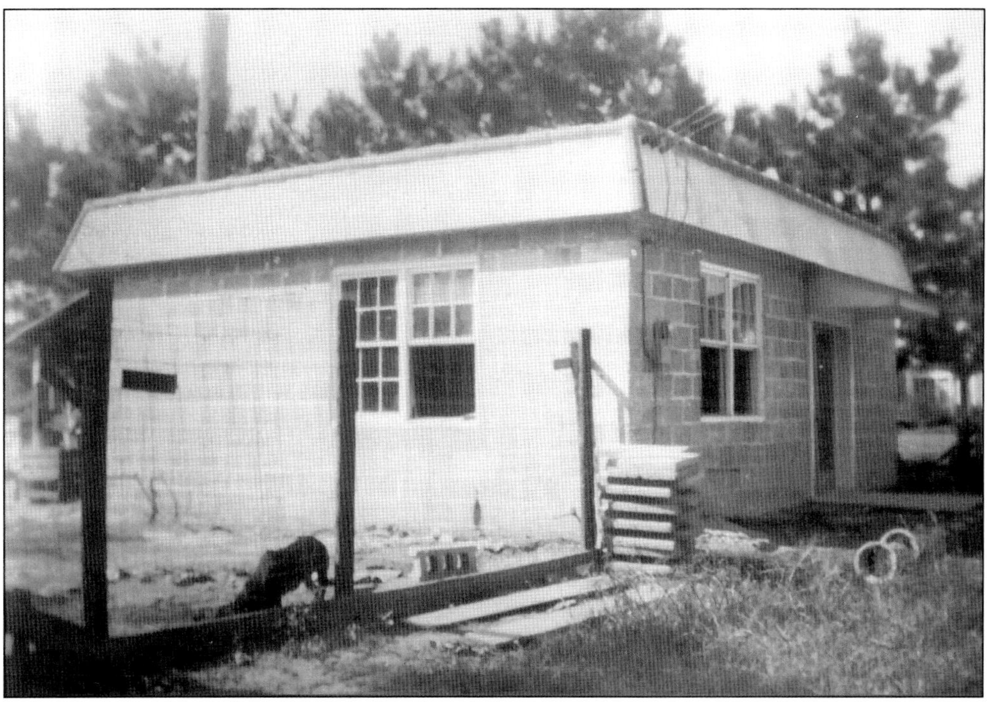

Wilson "T-Will" and Louise Knight owned the first cleaners in Scott, located on Delhomme Avenue. The neighborhood children had many stories about the noise and the steam when they walked by; some thought there might be a dragon that lived in the building. After looking inside, they were fascinated with the steam coming from the machines. (Courtesy of Marguerite Fontenot.)

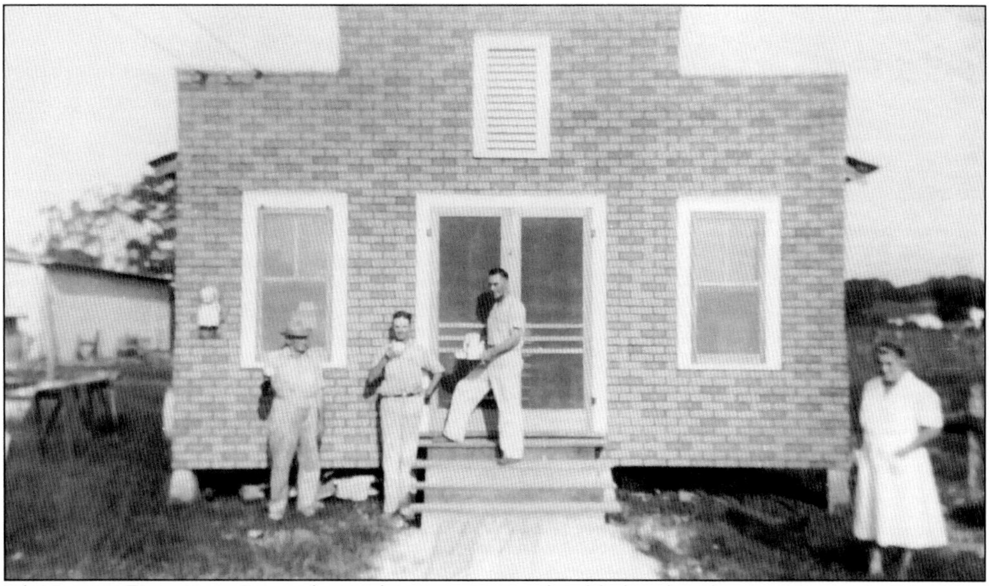

The Ignace Domingue Diner, located on Sunset Road, sold plate lunches to area residents as well as the railroad workers. Pictured from left to right are Pierre Martin, Freddie Sonnier, Ignace Domingue, and Rose Domingue. (Courtesy of Steve Hebert.)

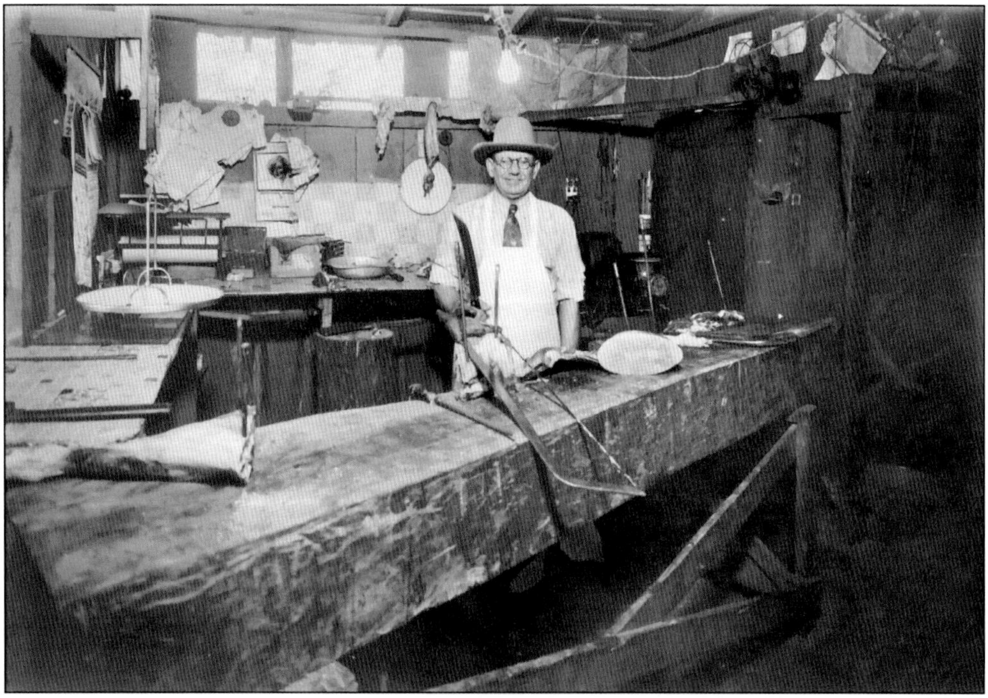

Pete Martin, known as "Nonc Pierre," opened the first meat market in Scott. He partnered with Paul Doucet to slaughter beef on Wednesdays and Saturdays so everyone would have fresh meat during the week. Martin also sold ice he purchased in bulk in Lafayette and kept in his icehouse. He donated meat to the school soup kitchen and was known for his generosity and lagniappe. In this 1923 photograph, he is surrounded by all the tools of the trade in his shop. (Courtesy of Steve Hebert.)

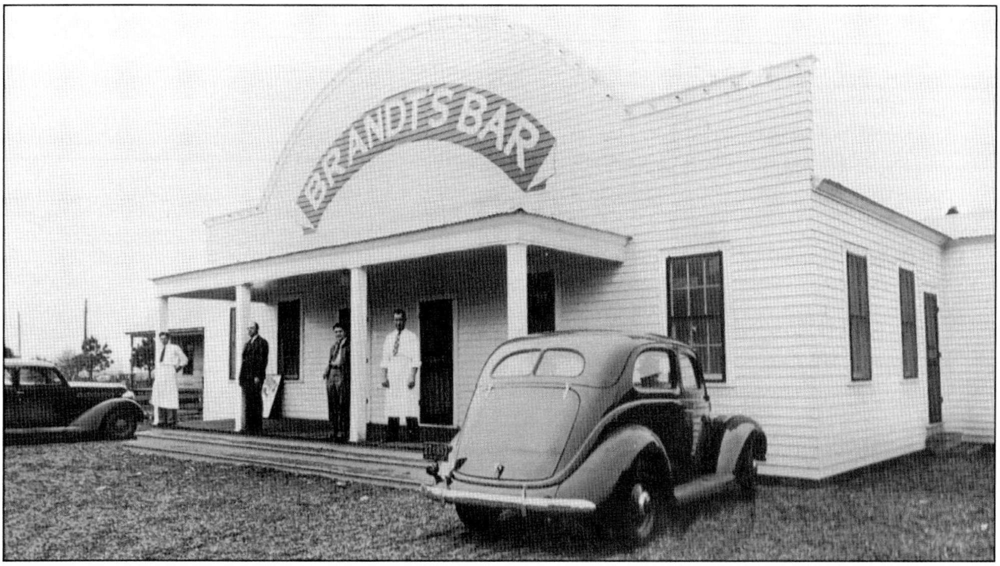


Brandt's Bar, owned by James Orrin Brandt, was located on Cayret Street. In this 1938 photograph, are, from left to right, Ray Pellisier, Brandt, Clebe "Snooks" Begnaud, and Louis Provost (bartender). Martin Begnaud's 1936 car is parked in front of the bar. (Courtesy of Pearl Provost Guidry.)

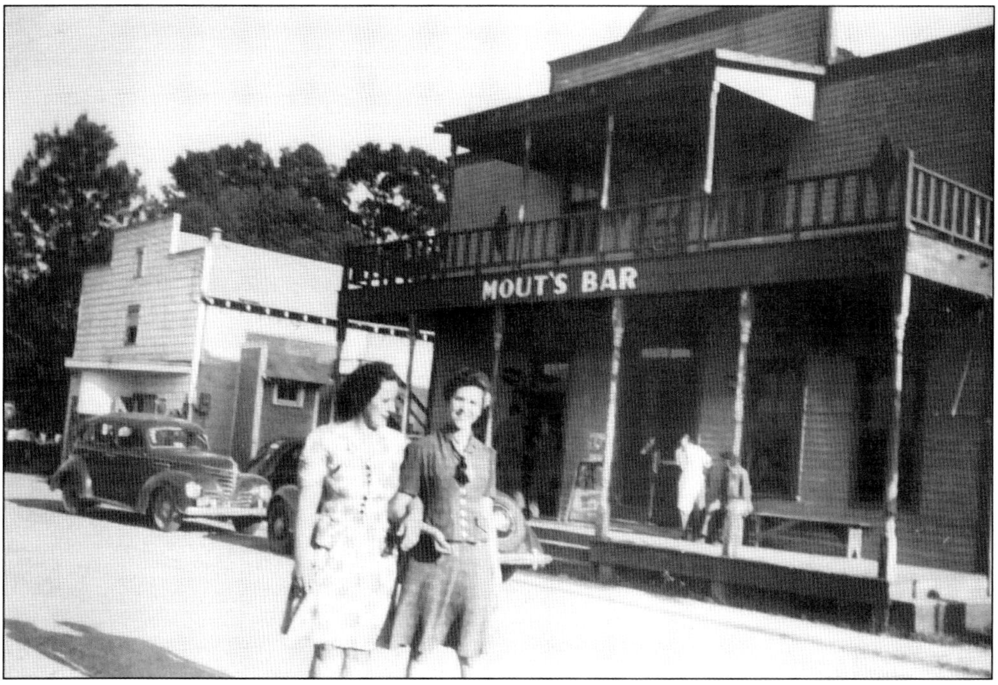


Mout's Bar, owned by Nathan Mouton, was a popular place to go after the movies. This 1942 photograph shows Jessie Leblanc Greig (left) and Vern Domingue Patin walking in the street. The building was remodeled into a one-story structure that still stands today and operates as Critters Spa, a pet grooming and boarding business. The building on the left is the old Joy Theater that burned in the late 1950s. Marshal Prejean and J.B. Shepard ran the movie projector, Bertha Sonnier sold popcorn for 5¢ a box, and Letha Begnaud worked the ticket booth. (Courtesy of Cassie Richard Blair.)

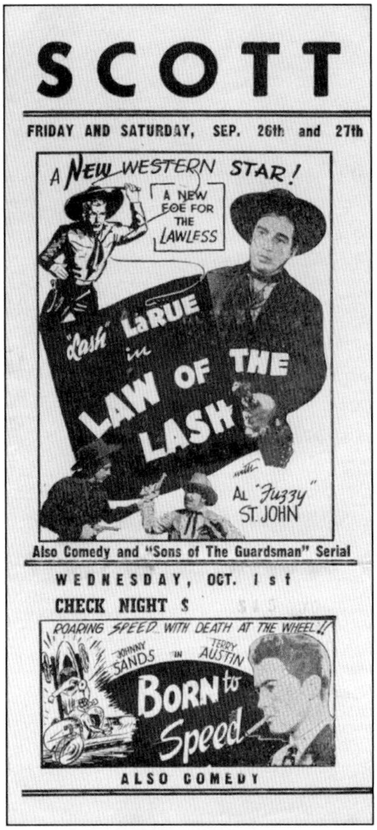


This 1947 movie poster promotes upcoming attractions at the Joy Theater, formerly located on Cayret Street directly south of the railroad tracks. The Joy Theater not only showed movies but also held live performances by popular celebrities of the time, such as Lash LaRue. (Courtesy of Scott City Hall.)

Lash LaRue (left), a Louisiana native, was well known for his bullwhip expertise. He made personal appearances and gave live performances at small-town movie theaters that were showing his films. In this photograph, he poses with George Arceneaux after a live performance at the Joy Theater. (Courtesy of Joyce Arceneaux.)

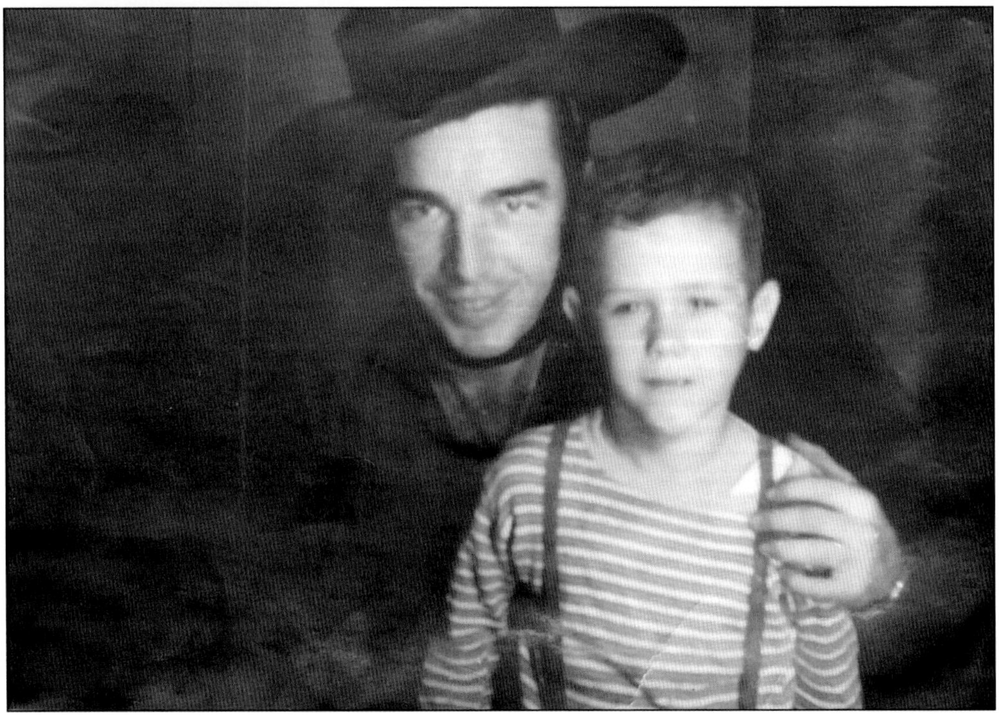

Lidley "Pick-a-boo" Prejean drives the delivery truck for his father's bakery. Prejean's Bakery was located across from Brandt's Bar on Cayret Street. Owner Joe Prejean sold pies, sweets, breads, and specialty cakes. (Courtesy of Carolyn Stutes.)

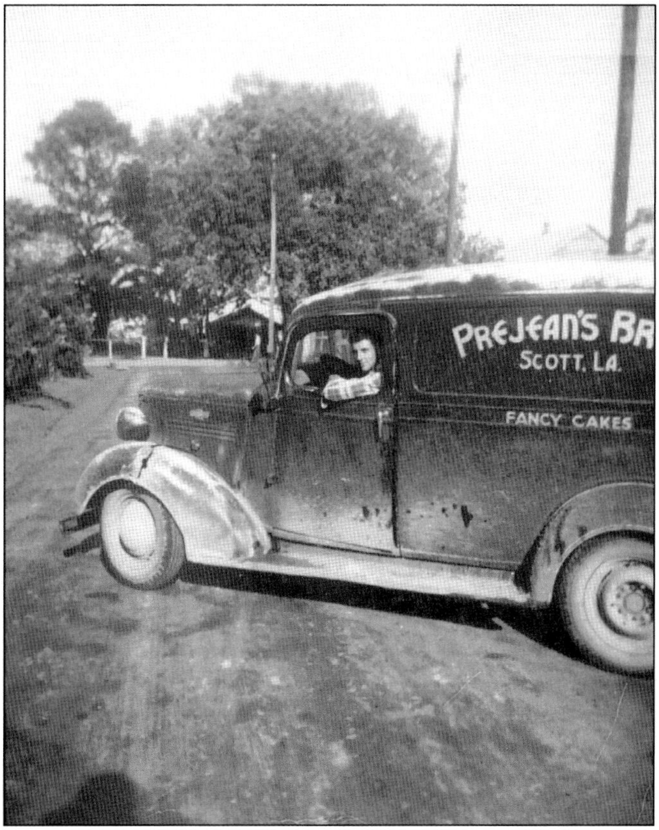


Doucet General Merchandise Store was located just west of the home of its owner, Perez Doucet. He and his wife, Eula, established the business together in 1934. They sold everything from cold cuts to feed and seed and from fabric and shoes to canned goods. After Doucet's death, Eula closed the store in 1948. (Courtesy of Elia Mouton.)

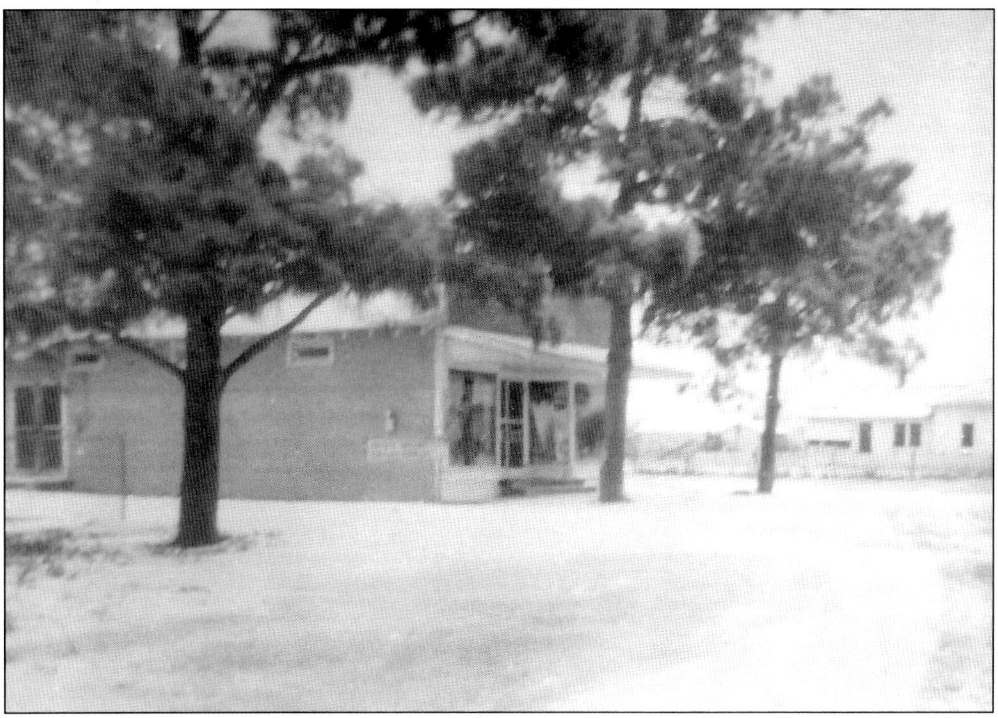

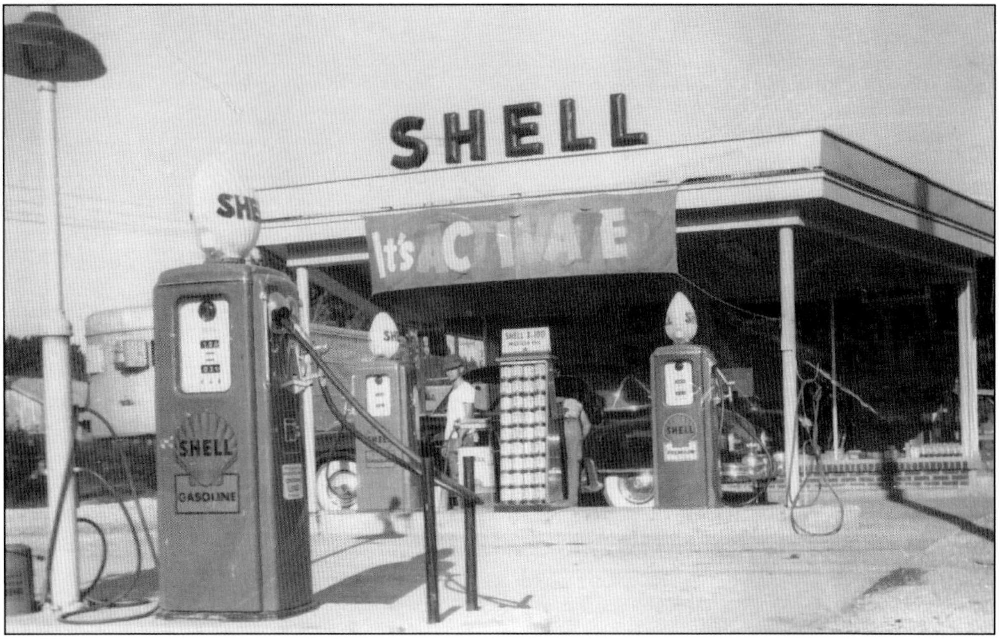

Leon "Doc" Sonnier owned and operated this full-service Shell station. The attendant would pump customers' gas, check their tires, oil, and water level in the radiator, and clean the windows. (Courtesy of Louise Sonnier.)

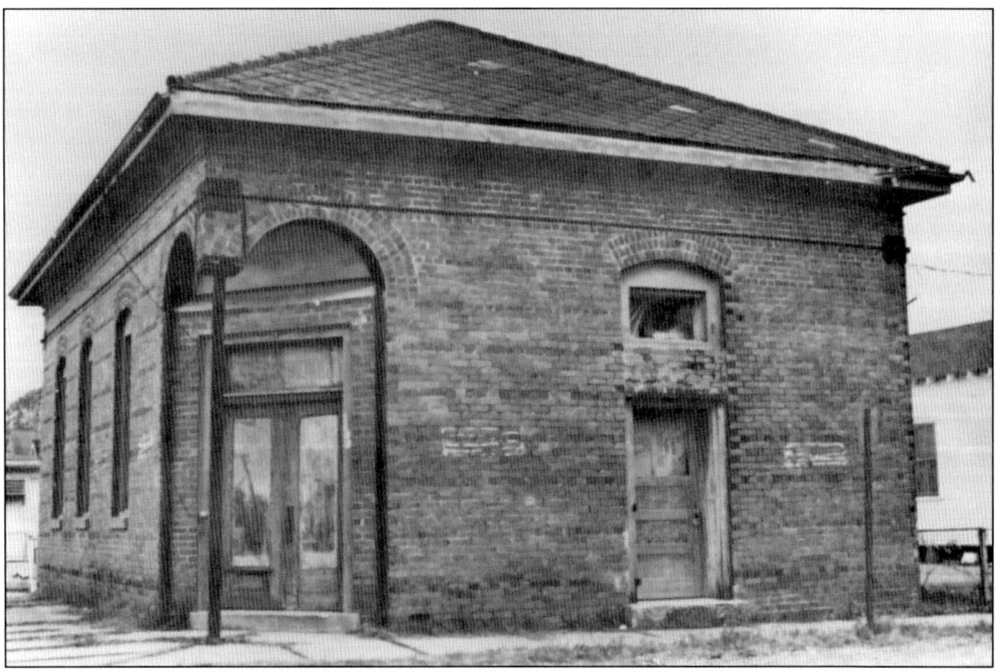
The Bank of Scott was established in 1911 with $17,000 in capital from the sale of 350 bank shares at $50 each. Death notices were nailed to the big post outside the bank. After closing, the building became the post office with Lucille Arceneaux as postmistress. Paul H. Begnaud bought the building to convert into his residence, maintaining the Italianate features and using the old bank vault as his kitchen. (Courtesy of Lafayette Parish Clerk of Court.)

# *Three*

# School Days

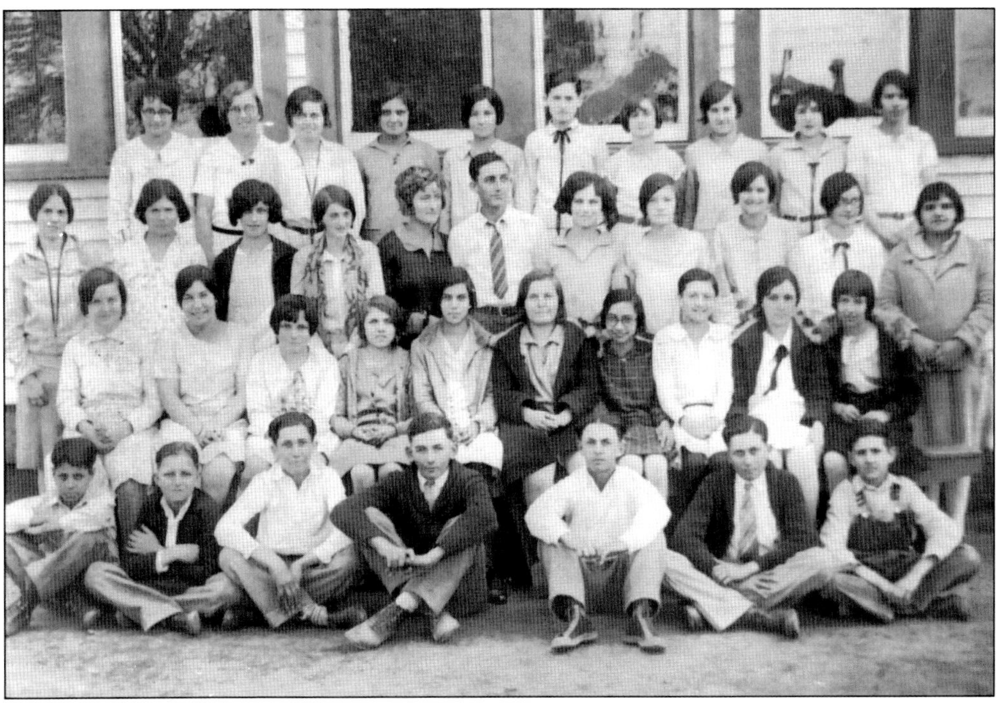

Pictured in 1928, this eighth-grade class was taught by Miss Barry and had 37 students. They actually attended their classes in Scott's new high school building. (Courtesy of Lafayette Parish Clerk of Court.)

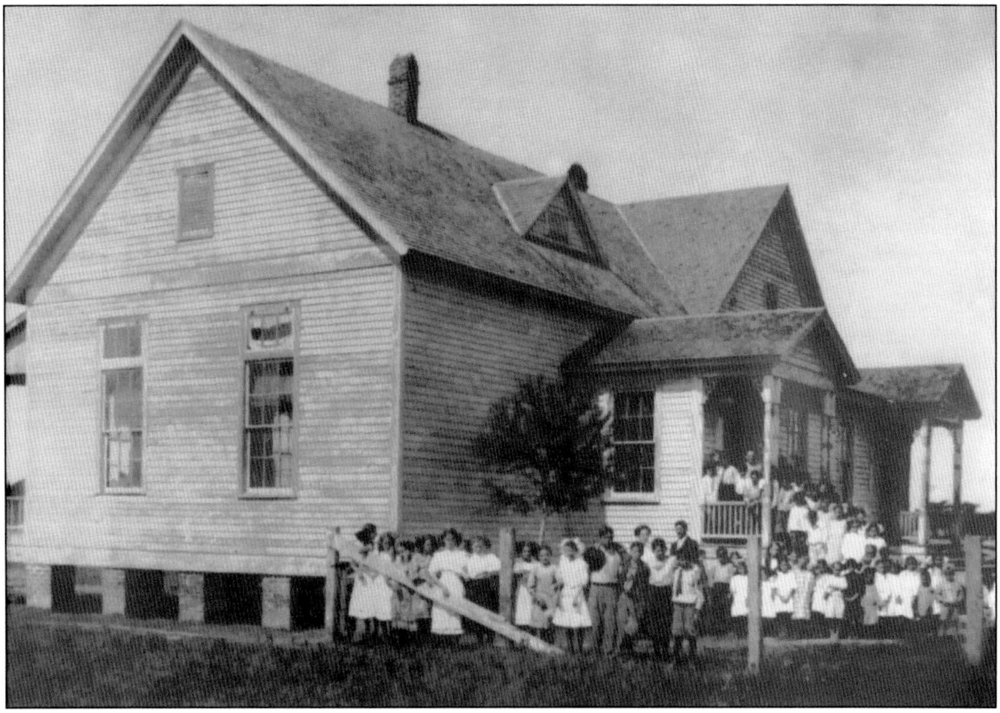

The first Alex Martin School was a tenant house built in the late 1800s or early 1900s. Partitions in the house were torn down to create a one-room school. The first schoolteacher was Phillipe Martin. Alex Martin School closed in the summer of 1923, and the students were transferred to Scott School by horse-drawn wagons. (Courtesy of Annadine Credeur.)

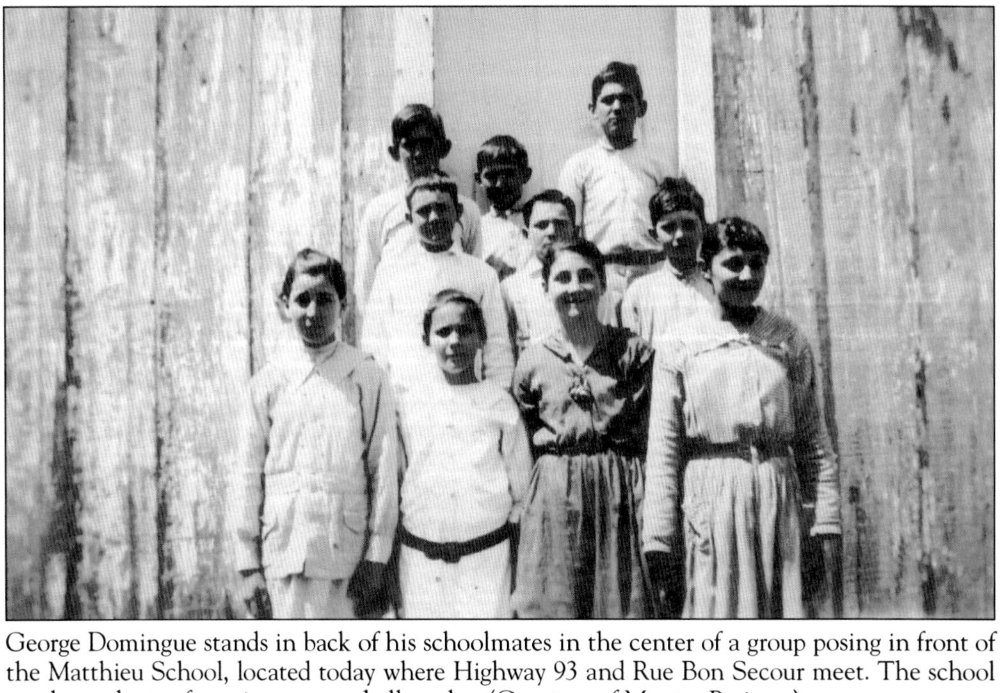

George Domingue stands in back of his schoolmates in the center of a group posing in front of the Matthieu School, located today where Highway 93 and Rue Bon Secour meet. The school taught students of varying ages and all grades. (Courtesy of Montez Prejean.)

Louis Gustave Breaux (pictured), a landowner, police juror, deputy sheriff, and Confederate War veteran, donated land for the first public school in Scott in 1895. It was located on the present-day corner of Old Spanish Trail and Breaux Street. Children of various ages from grades one through five attended. T.R. Simmons was the teacher. (Courtesy of Annadine Credeur.)

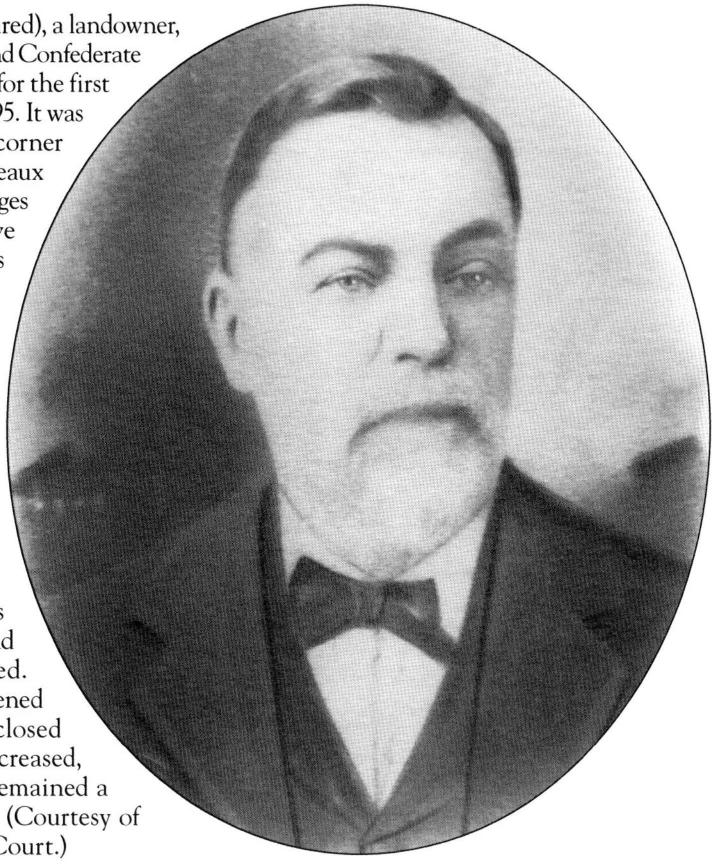

This Scott School began with two rooms in 1905. As enrollment grew, rooms and a second story were added. Eventually, a new school opened in 1928, and this school closed temporarily. Enrollment increased, and it was reopened and remained a primary school until 1951. (Courtesy of Lafayette Parish Clerk of Court.)

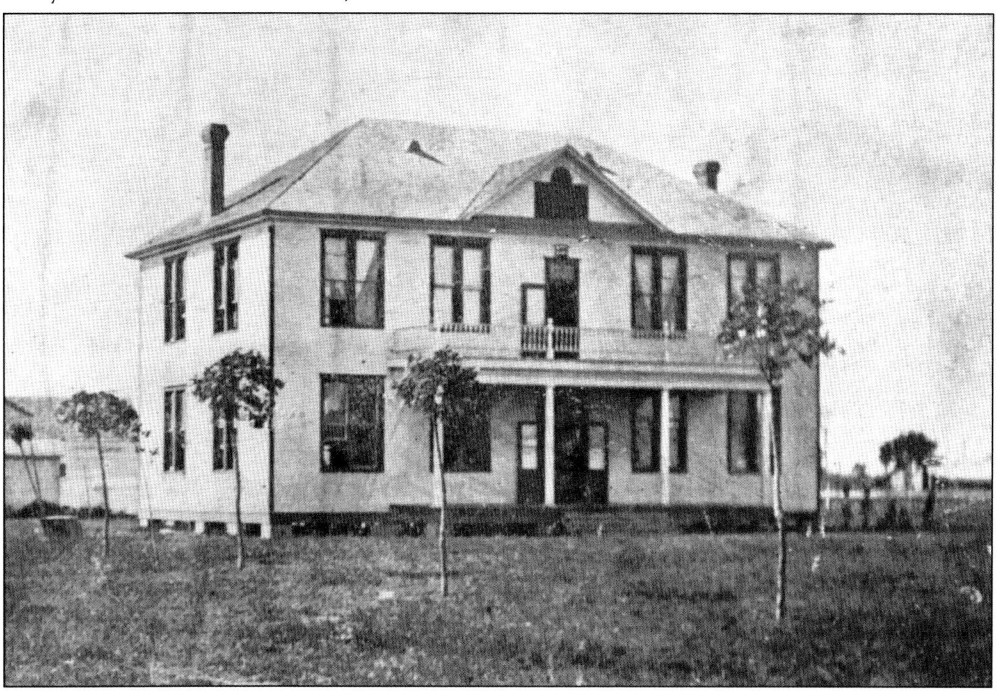

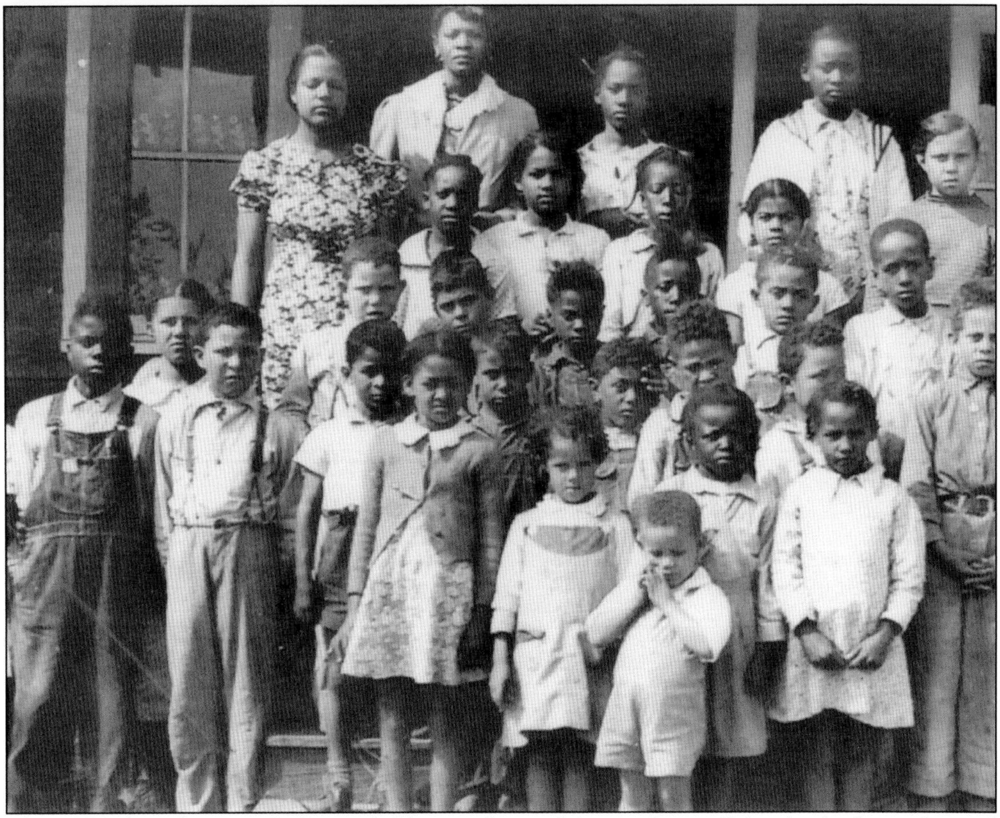

This 1938 class photograph shows children in front of the Anderson School, which was located in the Scott community. Louis "Deh Deh" Anderson, a prominent African American landowner, was dedicated to improving educational opportunities for black children. His efforts resulted in the Anderson School. (Courtesy of Leana Miller.)

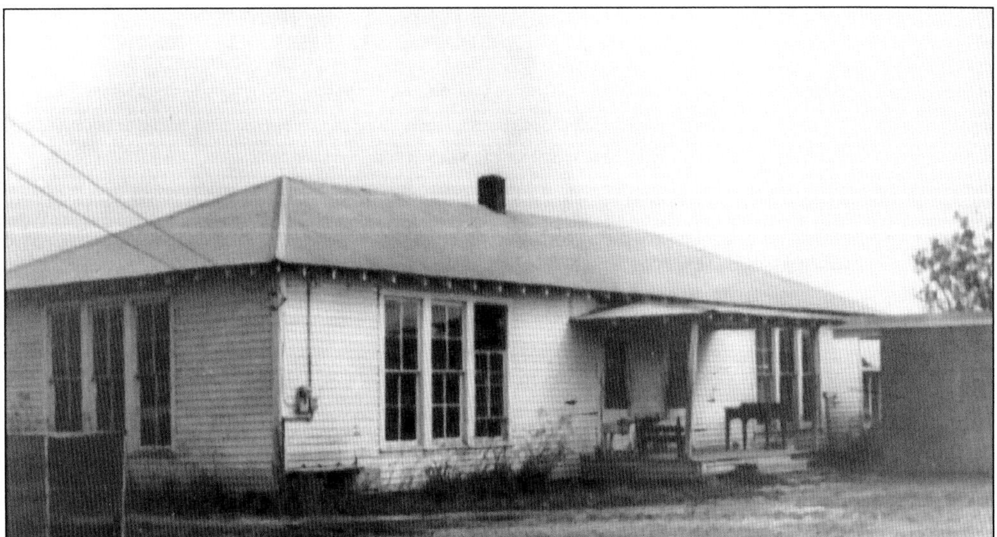

The building, located on Delhomme Avenue, was referred to as the Scott Negro School. It predated Westside Elementary, which opened in 1965. (Courtesy of Lafayette Parish Clerk of Court.)

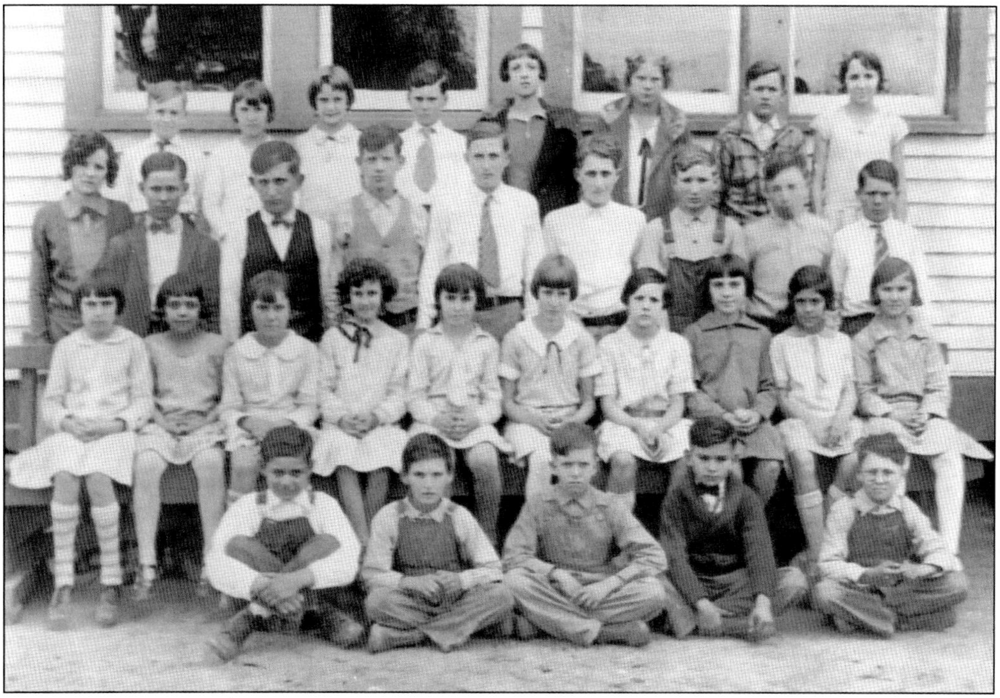

Thirty-two fifth graders pose at Scott School in 1928. (Courtesy of Lafayette Parish Clerk of Court.)

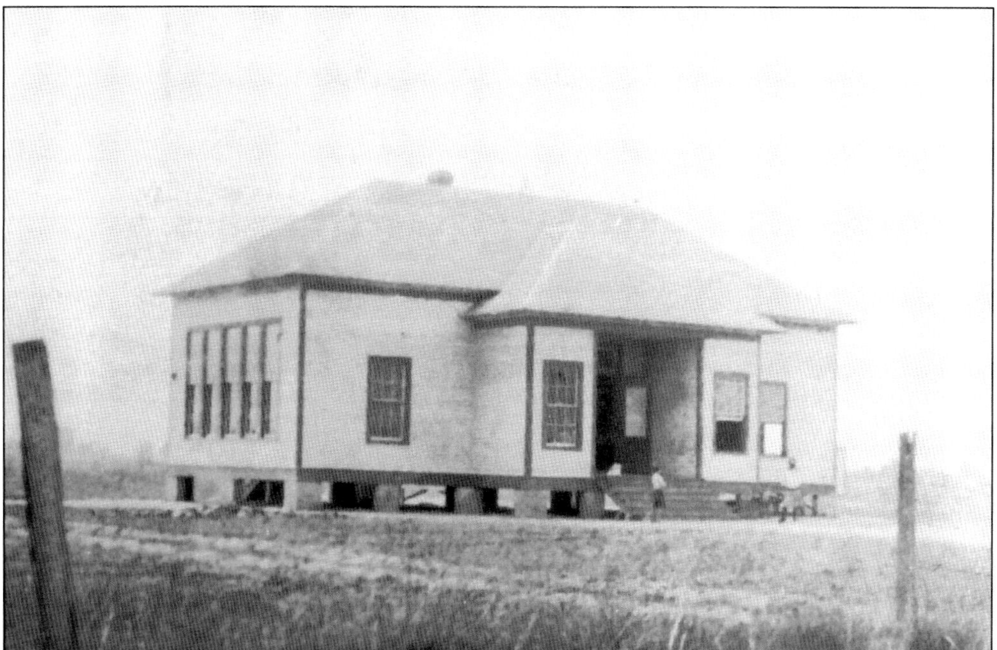

Ossun Elementary opened in 1915 and served as a school for children in that area. It was located near the current Rue Scholastique. (Courtesy of Lafayette Parish Clerk of Court.)

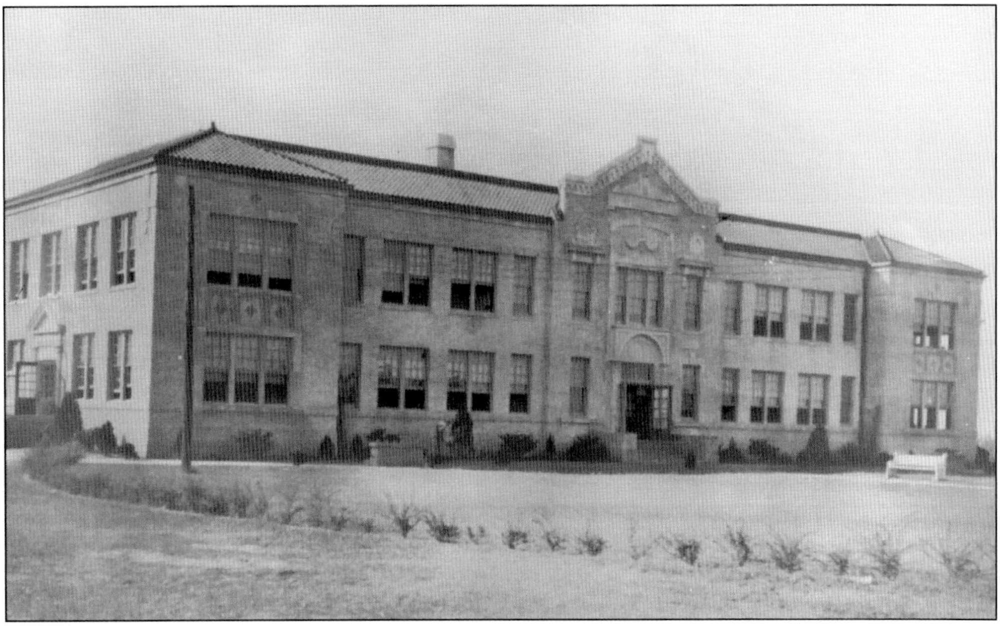

Scott High School opened in 1928 on 10 acres of land donated by Amelia Breaux. The school had several buildings, including a gymnasium with an auditorium, a home economics building, and an agriculture building. When Acadiana High School opened in 1970, this became a middle school. It was closed in 1984 and eventually razed. (Courtesy of Lafayette Parish Clerk of Court.)

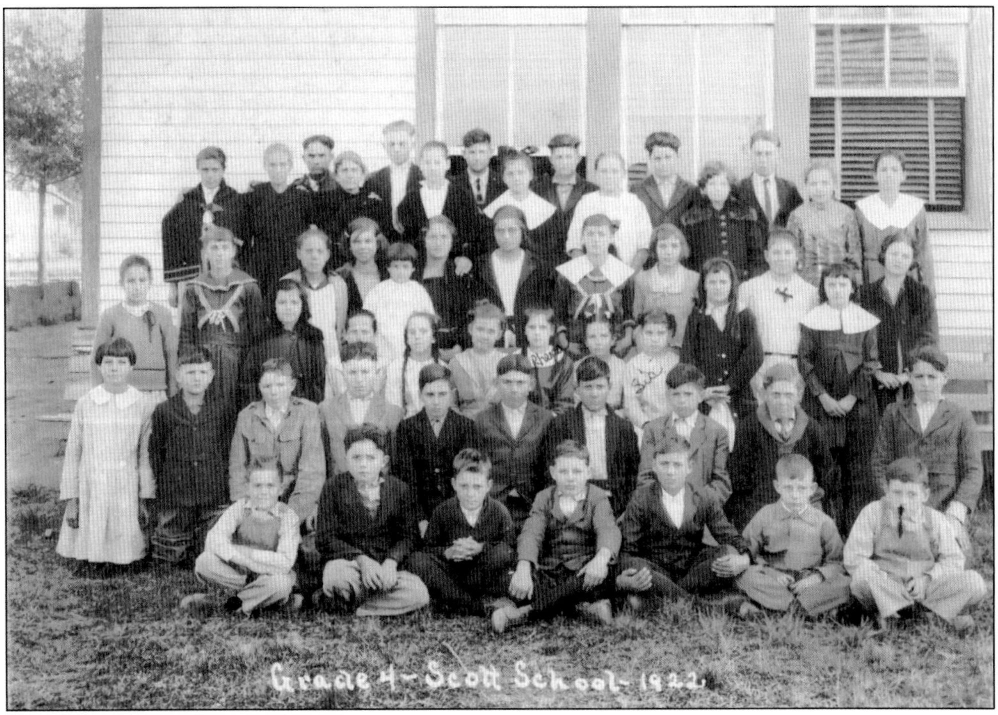


Sisters Rhena (third row, fifth from left) and Ita "Sis" Boudreaux (third row, seventh from the left) pose with other fourth-grade students in this 1922 Scott School photograph. (Courtesy of Mona Stutes Caldwell.)

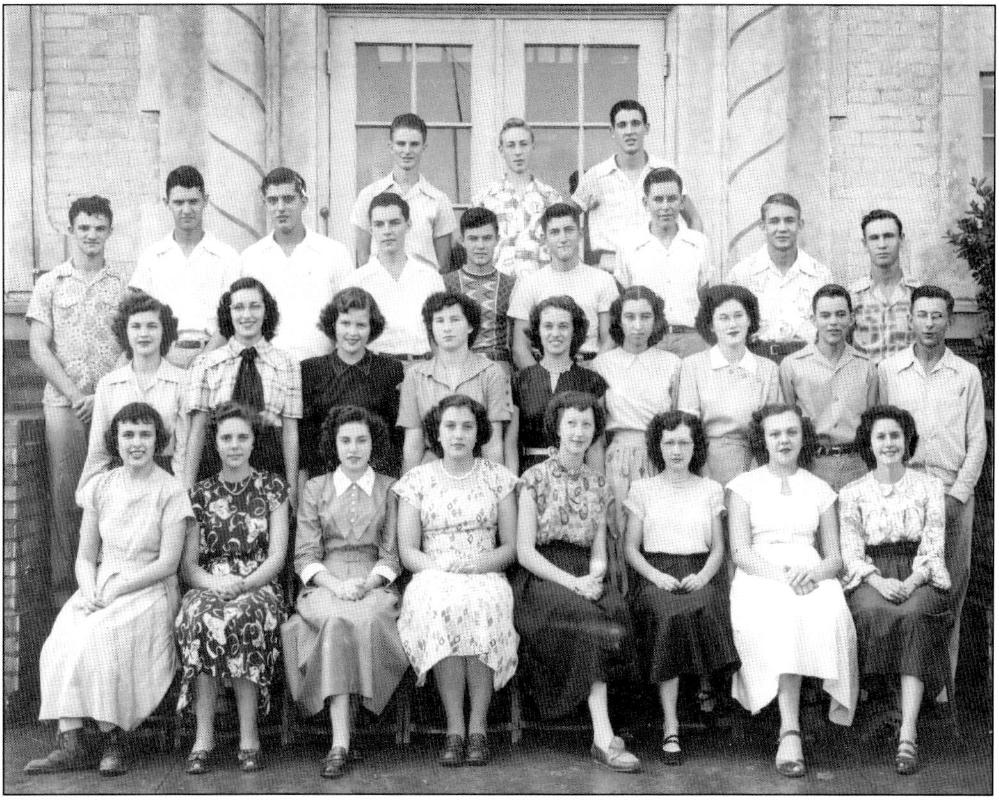

These 29 seniors from Scott High School in 1950 were the first students to attend the new school for 12 years; previous classes only attended for 11 years. In the 1948 yearbook, these students are listed as sophomores, and there was no junior class listed. (Courtesy of Cheri Norton Broussard.)

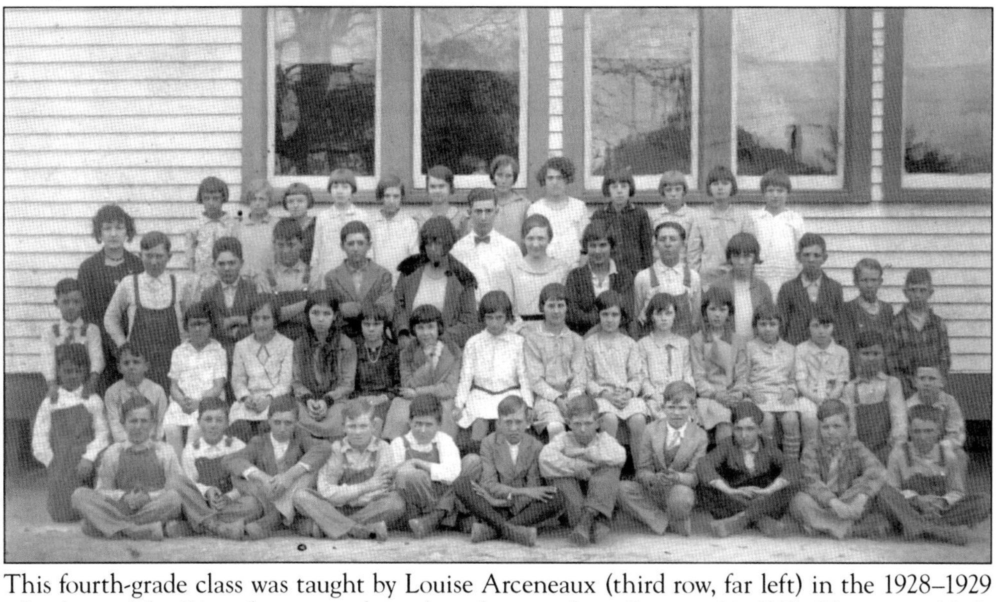

This fourth-grade class was taught by Louise Arceneaux (third row, far left) in the 1928–1929 school year. The 54 students pose for a class photograph on January 24, 1929. (Courtesy of Judy and George Ardoin.)

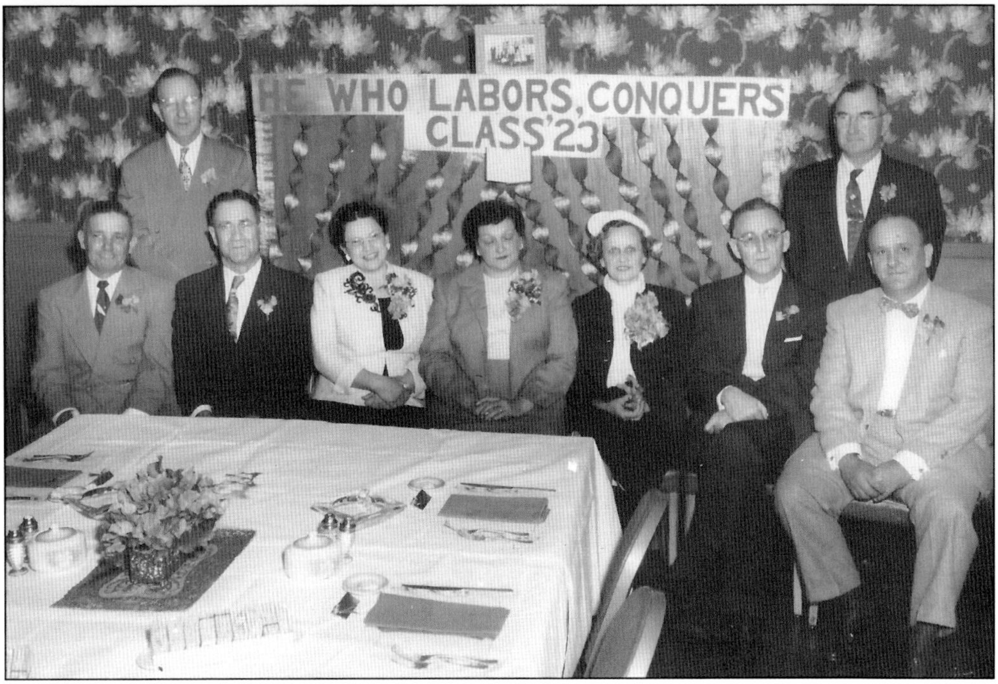

A reunion of the first graduating class of Scott High School is seen here in the late 1940s or early 1950s. The classmates pose proudly under their motto: "He Who Labors, Conquers." Kit Carson was the principal when this class graduated. (Courtesy of Lucille Sonnier.)

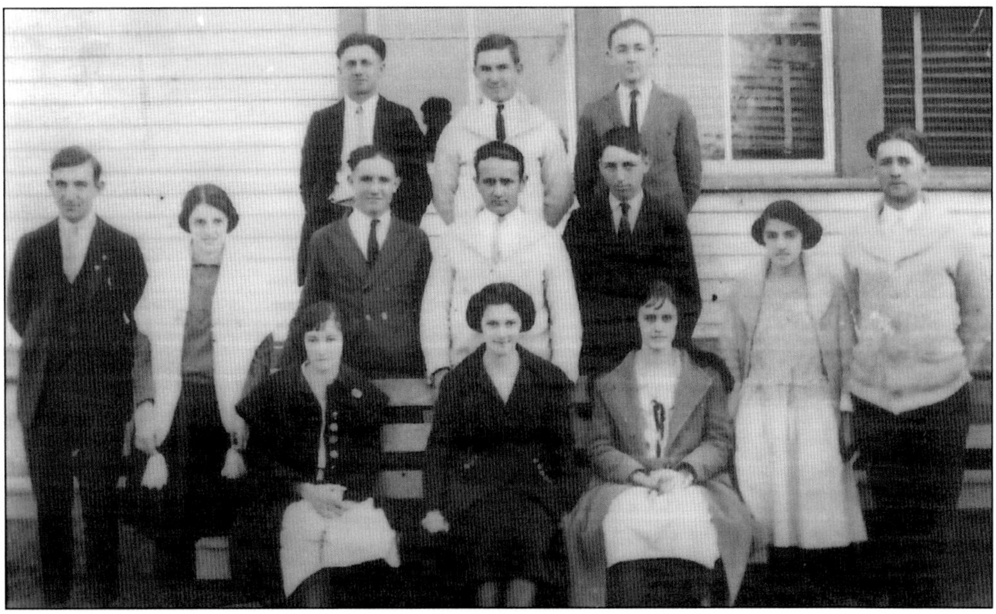
Scott High School's same graduating class poses with the principal for this 1923 photograph. Pictured from left to right are (first row) Mercedes Dugas, Beulah Mouton, and Leota Chaisson; (second row) principal Kit Carson, Ada Martin, Frank Sonnier, Hector Sonnier, Mayo Weber, Lillian Montet, and Essie Prejean; (third row) Louis Sonnier, Murphy Greene, and Darwin Briggs. (Courtesy of Lafayette Parish Clerk of Court.)

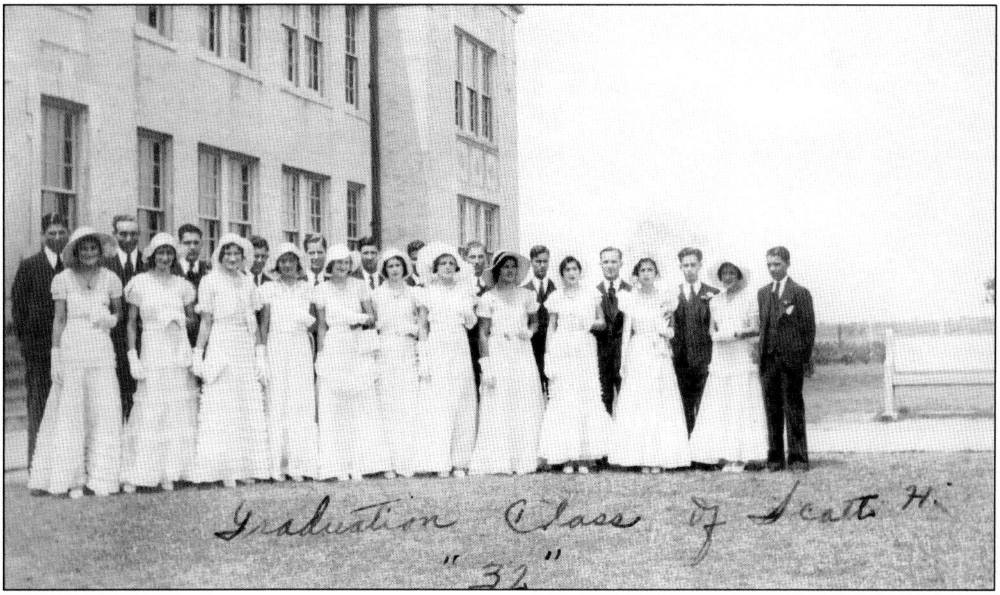


Scott High School's class of 1932 poses for its graduation photograph. The students are, from left to right, (first row) Effie Hebert, Irene Hernandez, Mary Arceneaux, Mabel Boudreaux, Mabel Guidry, ? Broussard, Martha Boudreaux, Mabel Raggio, Mabel Ancelet, Jeanette Begnaud, and Eunice LeBlanc; (second row) Eddie Sonnier, Lloyd Boudreaux, Saul Sonnier, Lee Broussard, Nathan Ancelet, Irby Arceneaux, Johnnie Domingue, Raoul Lagneaux, Nason Guidry, Caffery Domingue, Oday Trahan, and Aaron Domingue. (Courtesy of Mary Stutes.)

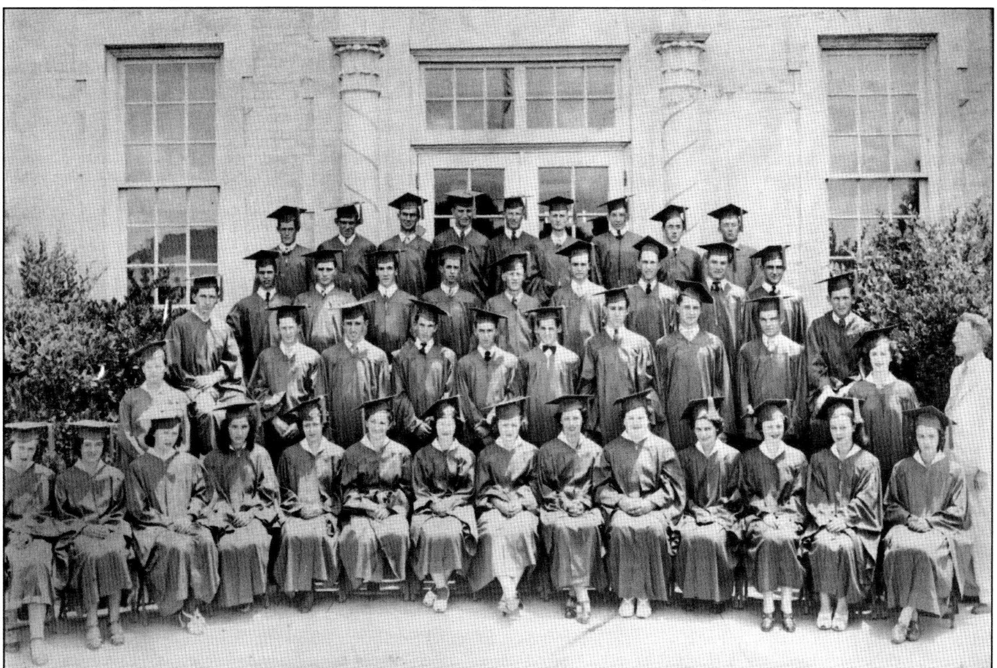

The 1939 class of Scott High School graduated 46 students, the largest class in the school's history. At the time, graduation ceremonies were held in the high school auditorium. Principal Sidney J. Durand (far right in the white suit) presided over the event. (Courtesy of Cassie Richard Blair.)

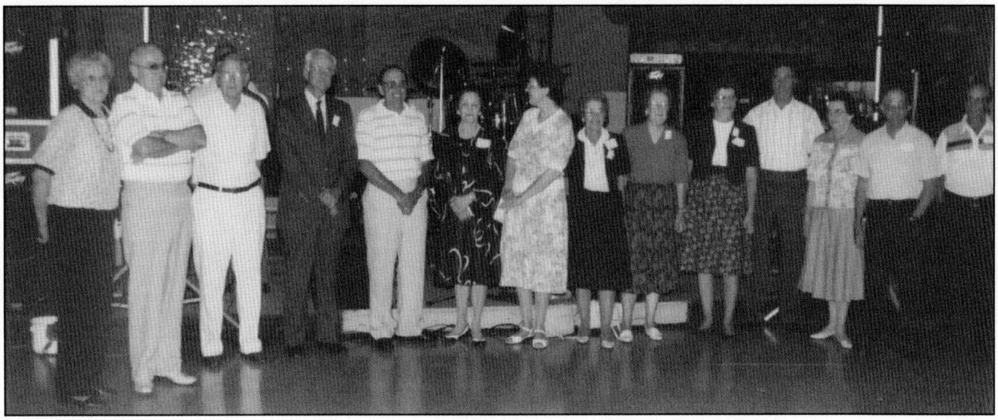

These former teachers from Scott High School gather at a class reunion. Pictured from left to right are Francis Prejean, Eloi Comeaux, Gene Martin, Charles Delana, Malcolm Lacy, Noelie Provost, Peggy Roy, Emily Raggio, Hazel Alpha, Ena Domingue, John Glenn Boudreaux, Mary Ann Dugas, Luther Jenkins, and unidentified. Delana became the Lafayette Parish superintendent, and Lacy, Boudreaux, and Comeaux served as principals. (Courtesy of Annadine Credeur.)

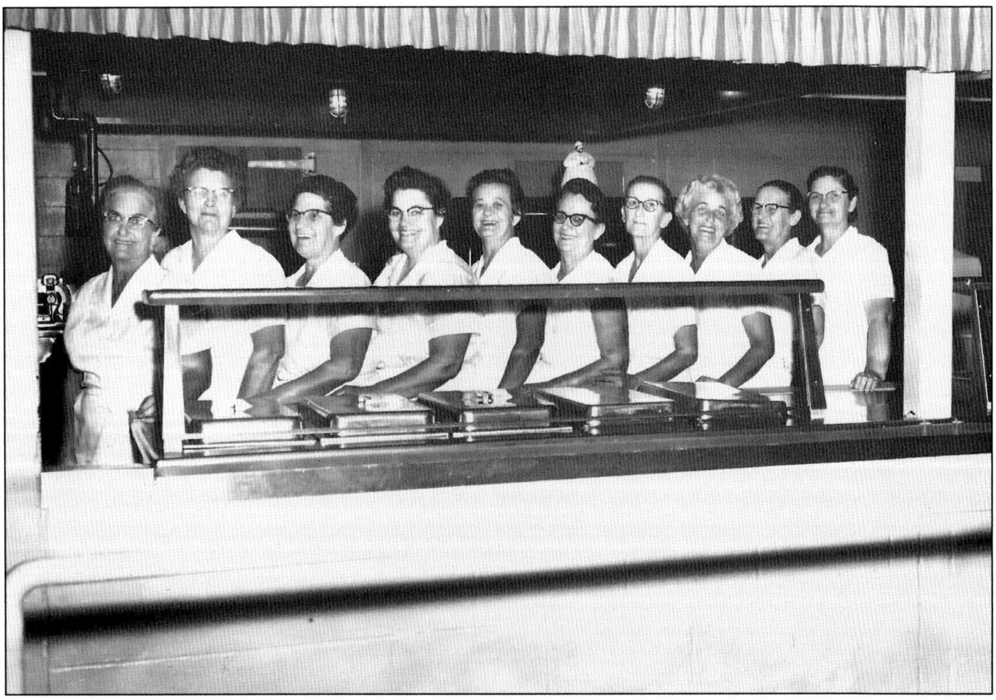

The "lunch ladies," who cooked and served the Scott High School students' food, were a vital part of the school community. A mutual love existed between these cafeteria workers and the children they served. Seen from left to right are Roberta Prejean, Maria Domingue, Hilda Simon, Effie Hollier, Lonnie Lacy, Mathilde Mire, Letha Begnaud, Aline Stutes, Edith Alleman, and ? Robin. (Courtesy of Carolyn Stutes.)

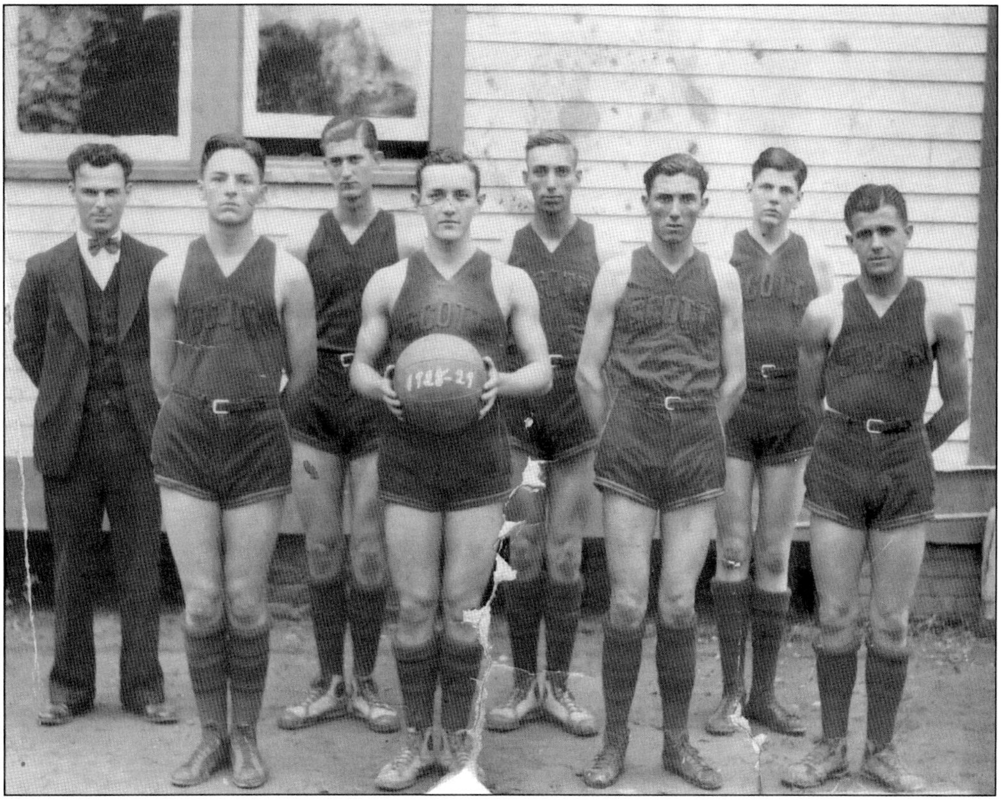


Basketball was an important sport in Scott schools, with several of the men's teams winning championships. These seven members of the 1928–1929 Scott High School basketball team pose with their coach (left). (Courtesy of Steve Hebert.)

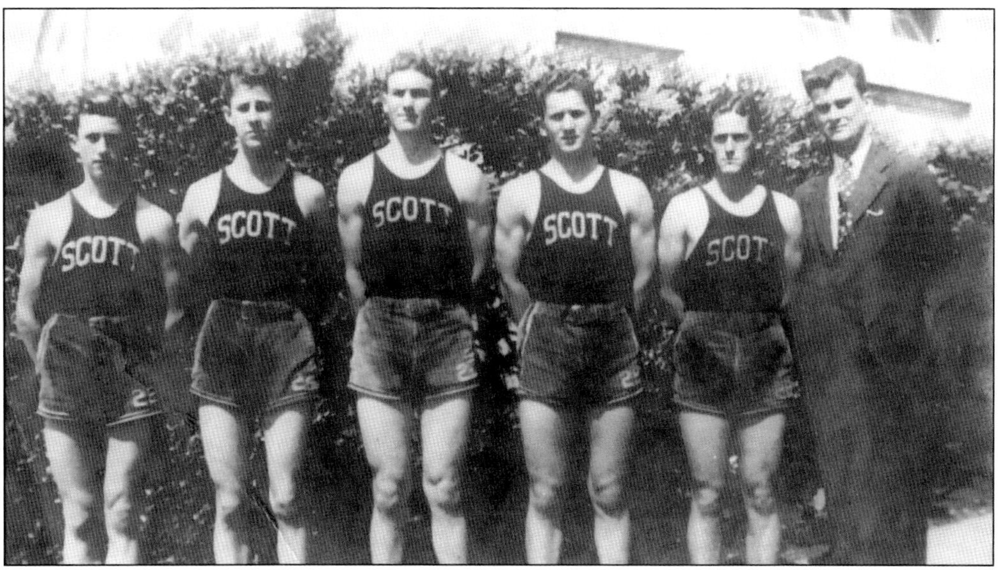


Coach Charlie Delana (right) poses with his basketball team, the Scott High Eagles. From left to right are J.B. Richard, E.G. Begnaud, Sam Foreman, Paul Duhon, and Joe Prejean. (Courtesy of Cassie Richard Blair.)

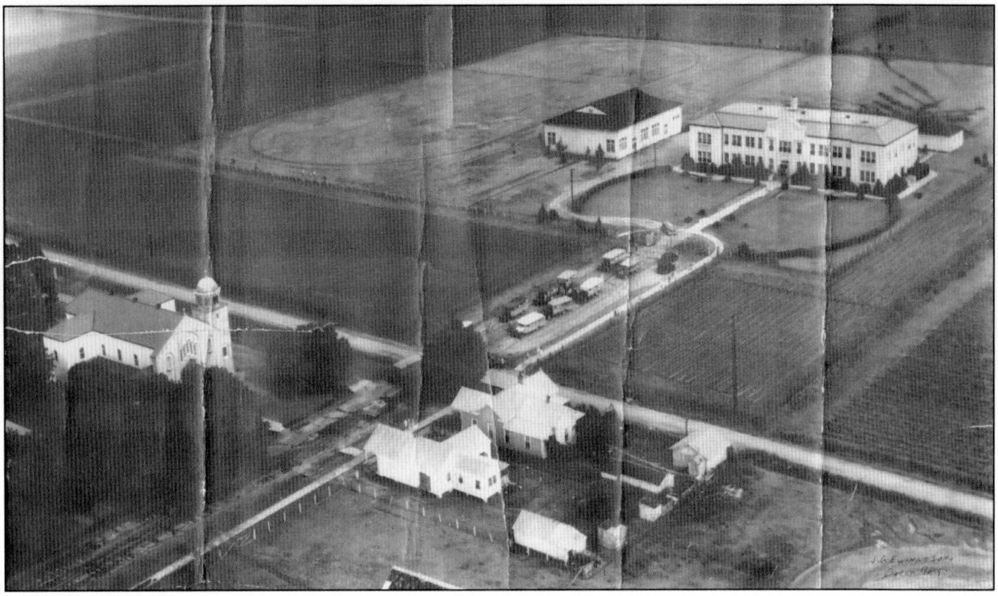

Sts. Peter and Paul Catholic Church, on the far left, and Jacques Dugas's home and grocery, in the front center, are seen in this aerial photograph. Next door, behind the Dugas home, is Joe Boudreaux's home and Andre Boudreaux's hamburger stand. In the back right are the school and gymnasium. School buses are lined up to take the students home. The home economics building (not pictured) and its facilities were used by residents at specified times to can and preserve fruits and vegetables. (Courtesy of Donald Arceneaux.)

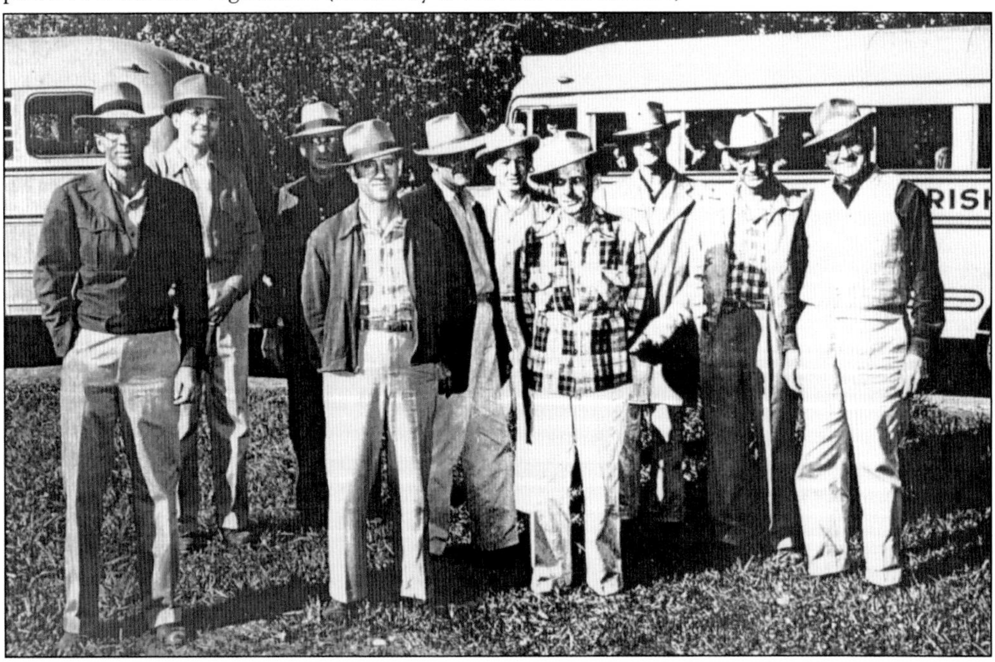

School bus drivers for Scott seen here in 1950 include, from left to right, (first row) Dudley Guilbeau, Eucharist Hernandez, Jean Vileor, and Davis Arceneaux; (second row) Esta Labbe, John Begnaud, Pierre Mouton, Raoul Guilbeau, "Une" Begnaud, Pavie Prejean, and Edward Alleman. (Courtesy of Lafayette Parish Clerk of Court.)

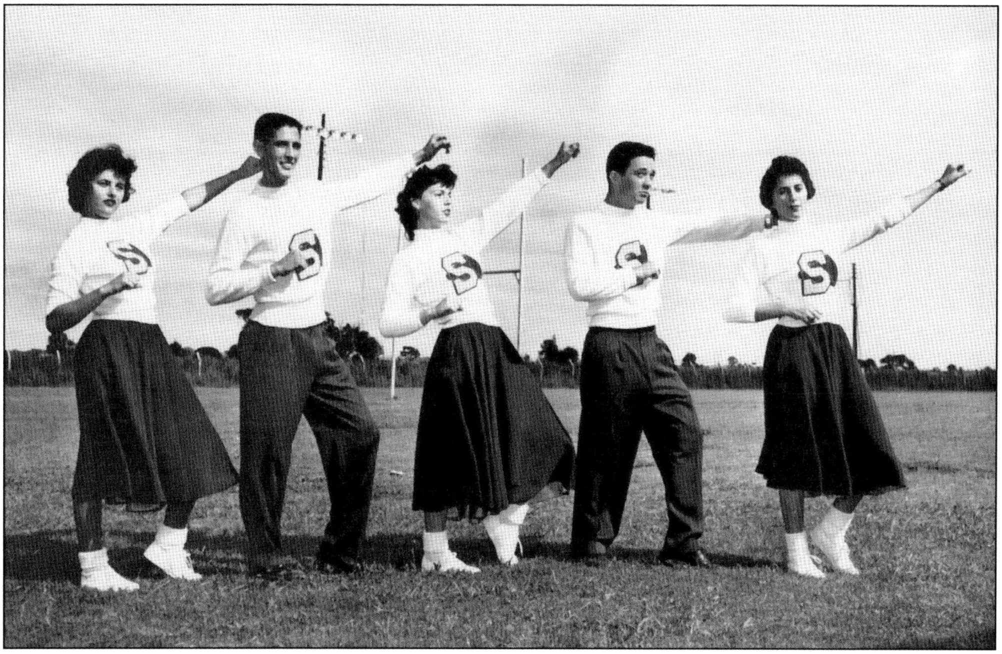

These 1959 high school cheerleaders are, from left to right, Anna Marie Boudreaux, Larry Stutes, Louella Breaux, Henry Martin, and Joyce Arceneaux. They did their part to get the fans excited and cheer for their team. (Courtesy of Becca Begnaud.)

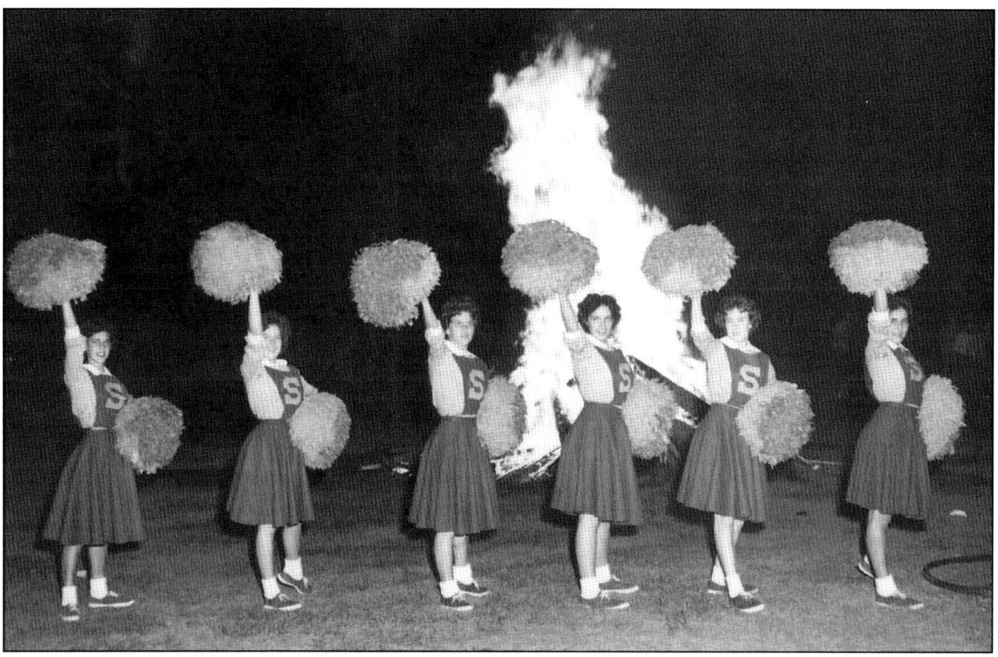

The cheerleaders pictured here from left to right are Audrey Breaux, Delores Miller, Lucille Fontenot, Cynthia Simar, Jacquelyn Owers, and Arlene Richard. They are getting the crowd involved during the 1961 homecoming bonfire. The efforts of the team, the crowd, and the cheerleaders ensured that the Scott football team beat the Northside High Vikings 12-6. (Courtesy of Annadine Credeur.)

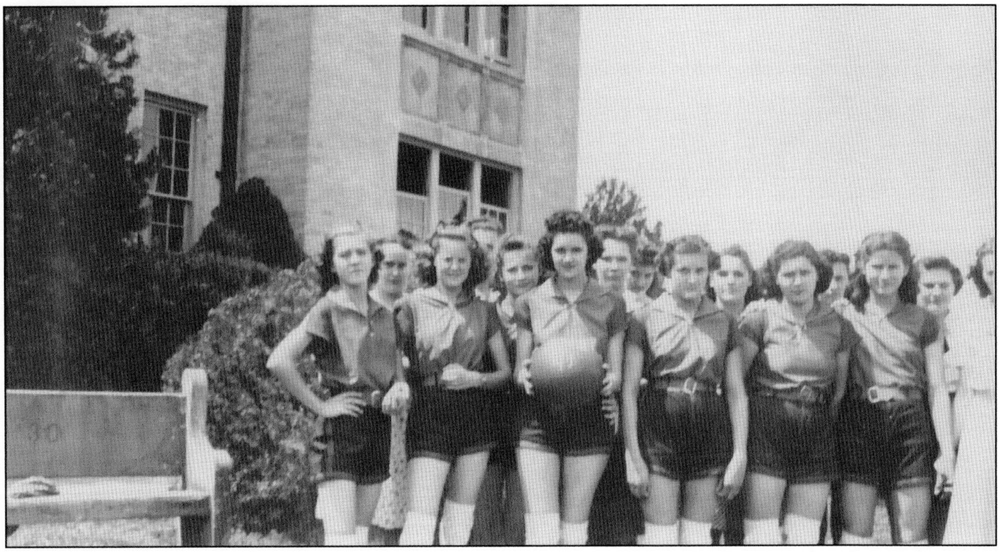

The 1941 Scott High School girls' champion basketball team poses with some of its fans. The team members are, from left to right, Edna Mae Martin, Joyce Sonnier, Ann Broussard, Masil Lagneaux, Frances Hutchinson, and Verna Domingue. Each team had six players, and only the forwards could score points. The girls' teams only played on half the court. (Courtesy of Glen Courville.)

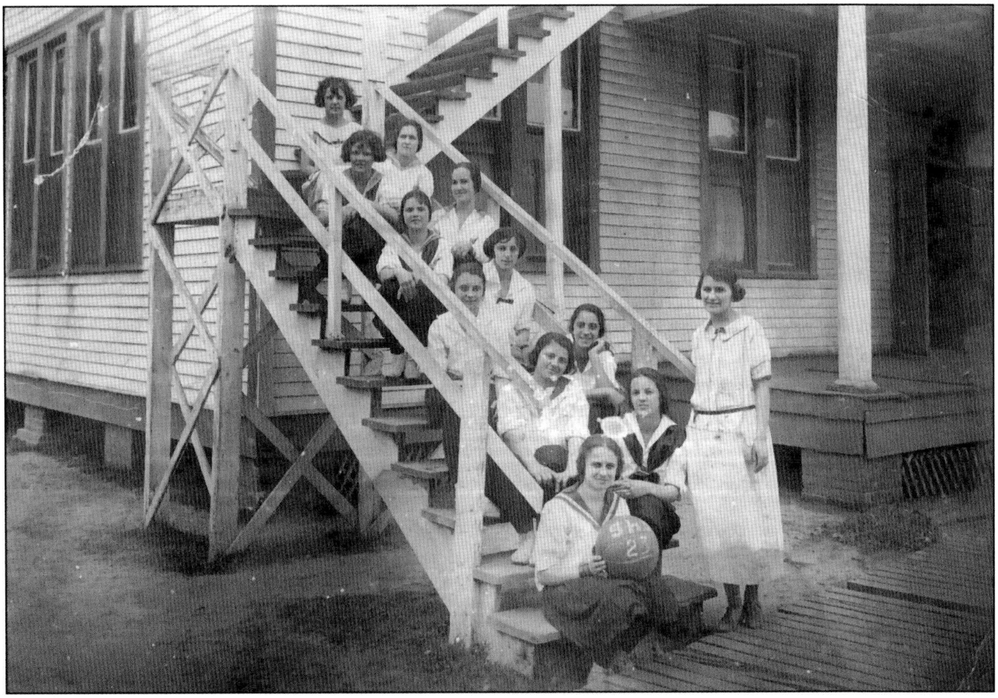

Pictured is the Scott High 1923 state champion girls' basketball team. Members seen here include, from top to bottom, coach Freshie Dupuis, Monique Raggio, Uniford Deshotels, Roberta Doucet, May Sonnier, Nola Martin, Mae Pellesier, Azema Martin, Marie Mouton, Bernice Foreman, Blanche Martin and coach Gussie Broussard. Five of the team members were born in 1907, the year Scott was incorporated: Blanche Martin, Marie Martin, Mae Pellesier, Nola Martin, and Monique Raggio. (Courtesy of Cheri Norton Broussard.)

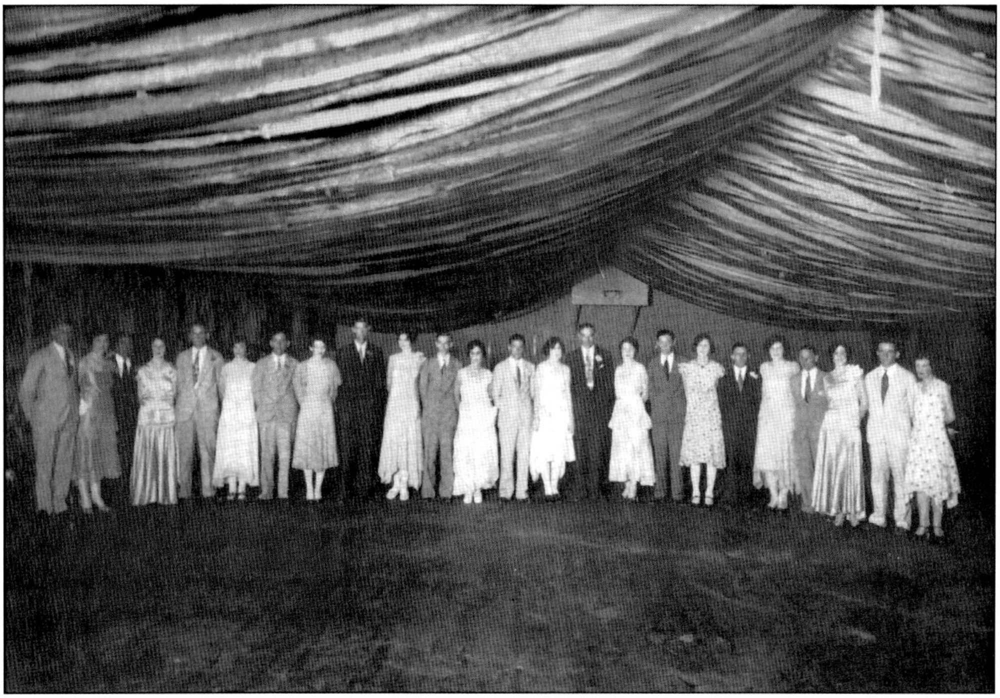

The 1930 senior class is dressed for the prom in its decorated gymnasium. (Courtesy of Mona Stutes Caldwell.)

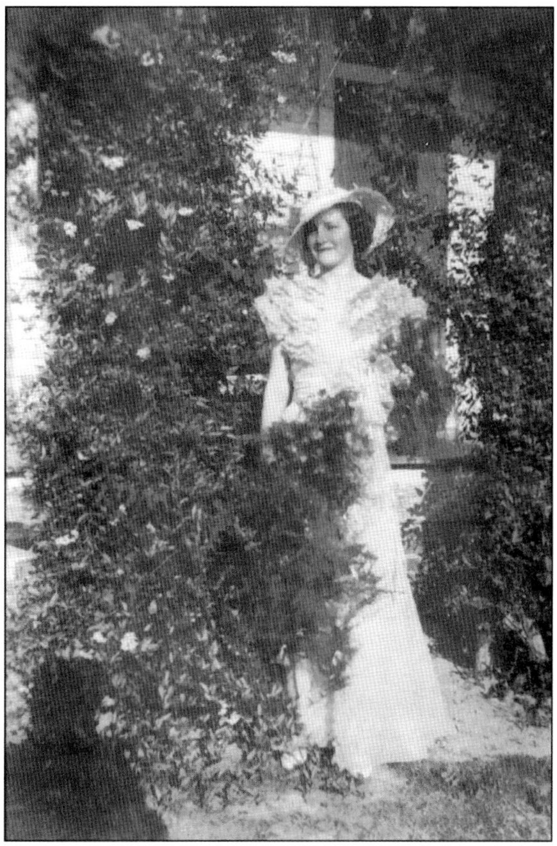

Noelie Martin, the 1934 class valedictorian, is pictured in her graduation dress and hat. In the early 1900s, graduates did not wear caps and gowns but wore formal dresses and suits. (Courtesy of Annadine Credeur.)

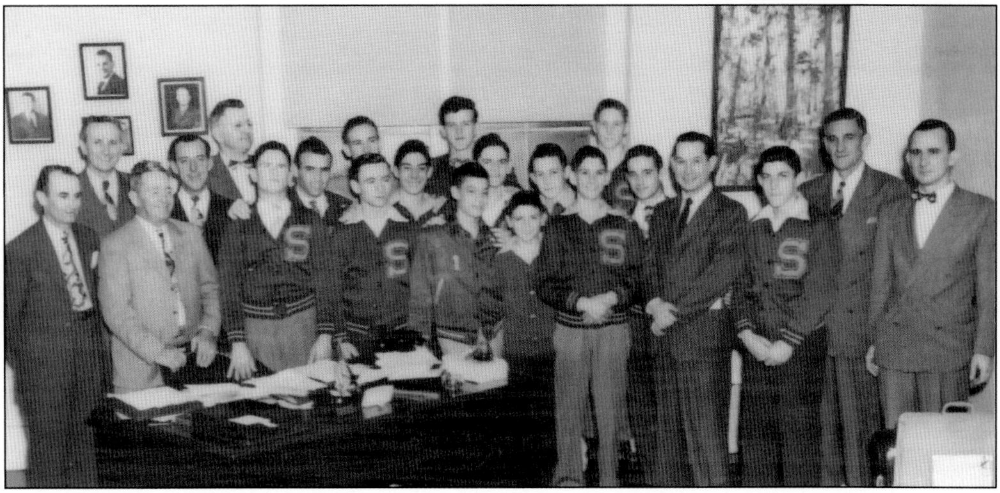

Boxing was an important team sport in Scott for many years. Various teams won regional, state, and national honors. This 1948 team won the national boxing championship in Charlottesville, Virginia, and visited the White House in Washington, DC. The national championship was refereed by Jack Dempsey. (Courtesy of Lafayette Parish Clerk of Court.)

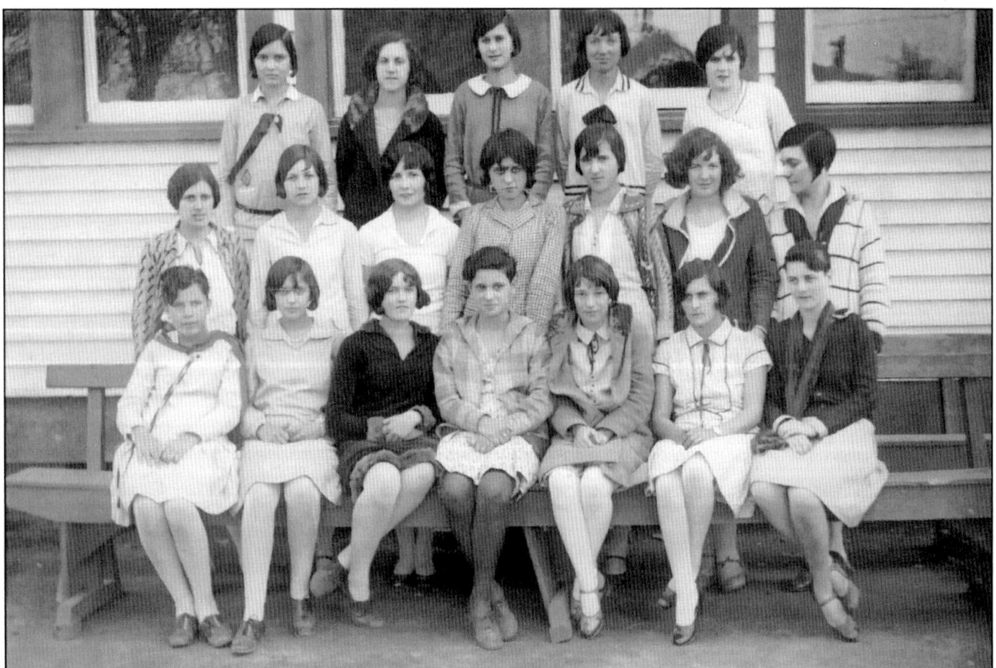

Home economics was a female-only course that taught the basics of sewing and cooking as well as canning and preserving fresh fruit and vegetables. (Courtesy of Mona Stutes Caldwell.)

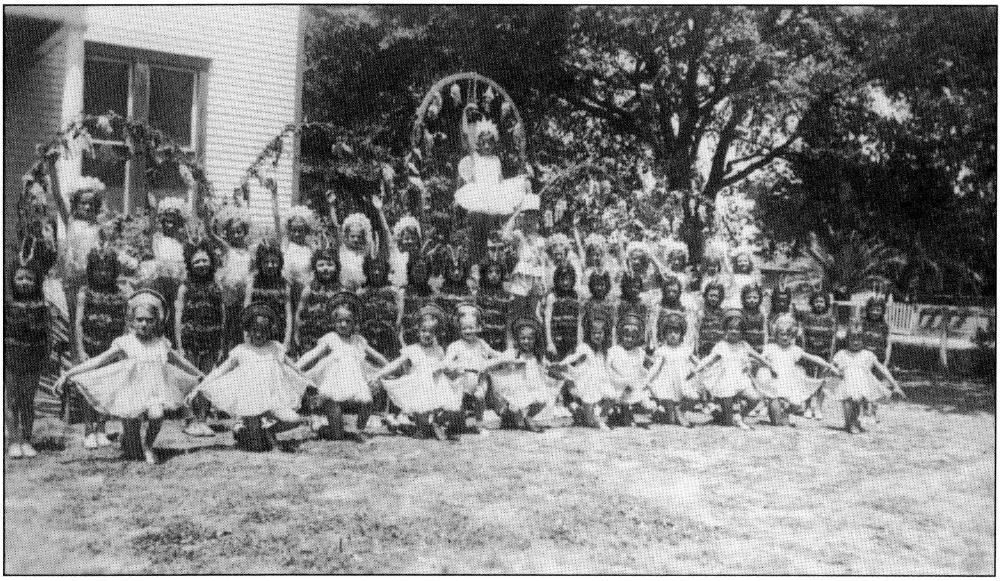

The youngest dancers, seen here in the front row, curtsey during the climactic close of the annual Scott High School class play in 1937. (Courtesy of Carolyn Stutes.)

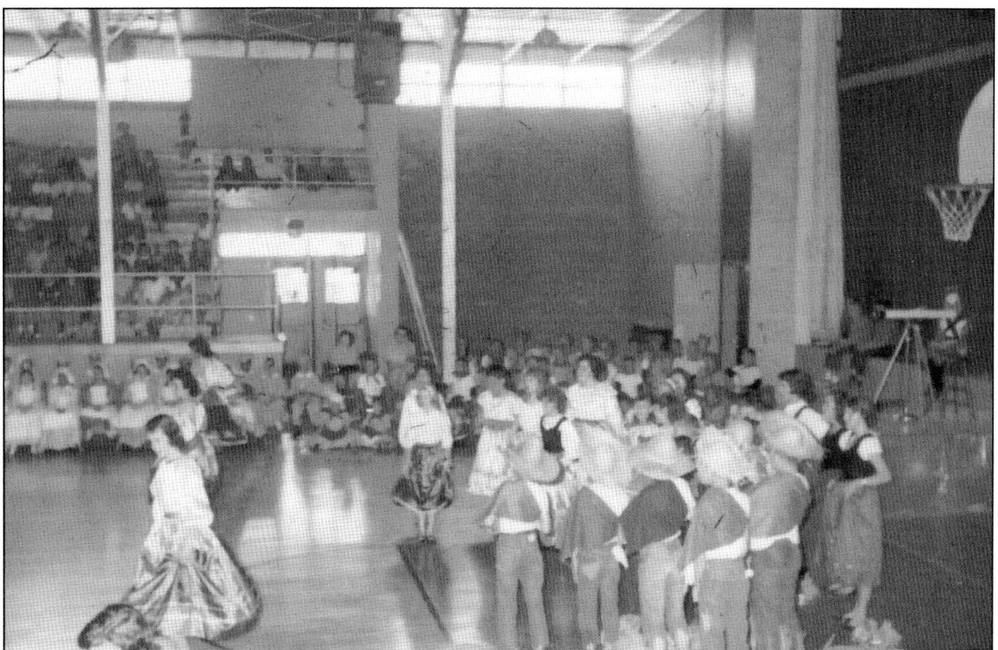

Student actors and actresses gather in the Scott High School gymnasium for the opening of the 1964 class play as family and friends await the show. (Courtesy of Earlene Carriere.)

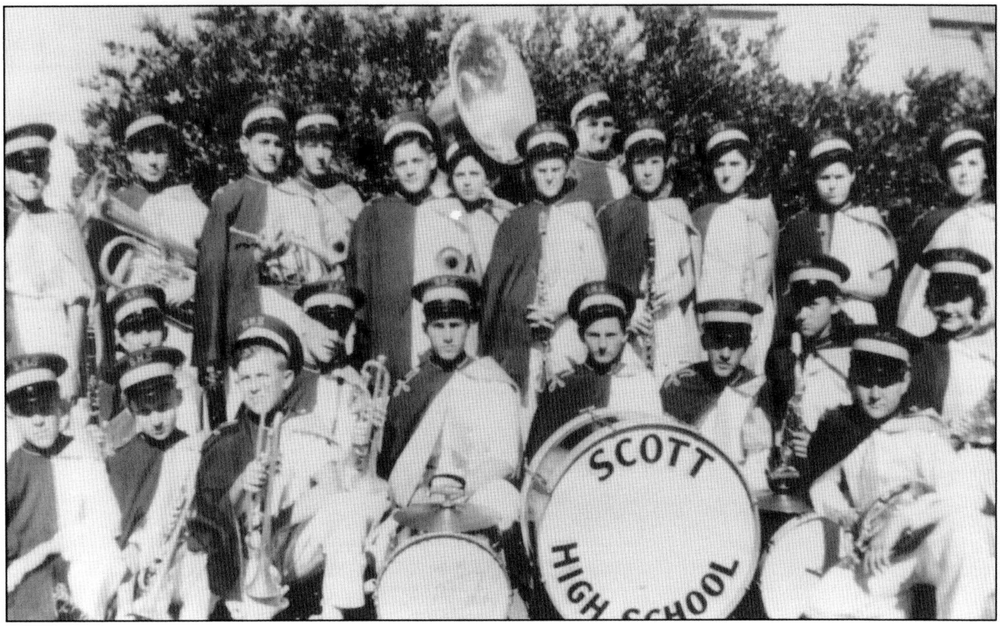


The 1939 Scott High School Marching Band included, from left to right, (kneeling) Jimmy Neef, Milton Guilbeau, Billy Neef, Curtis Ellis, Ravis Ancelet, Pearl Blanchard, Paul "Potout" Begnaud, Beryl Guillot, Stephen "Doo" Arceneaux, and Catherine Arceneaux; (standing) Woodley Credeur, Gertrude Domingue, Lauly Credeur, Chester Duhon, Milton Lagneaux, Rita Boudreaux, Joyce Sonnier, Lee Louis Martin, Winnie Guilbeau, Mary Frances LeBlanc, Lois Trahan, and Jessie LeBlanc. (Courtesy of Lafayette Parish Clerk of Court.)

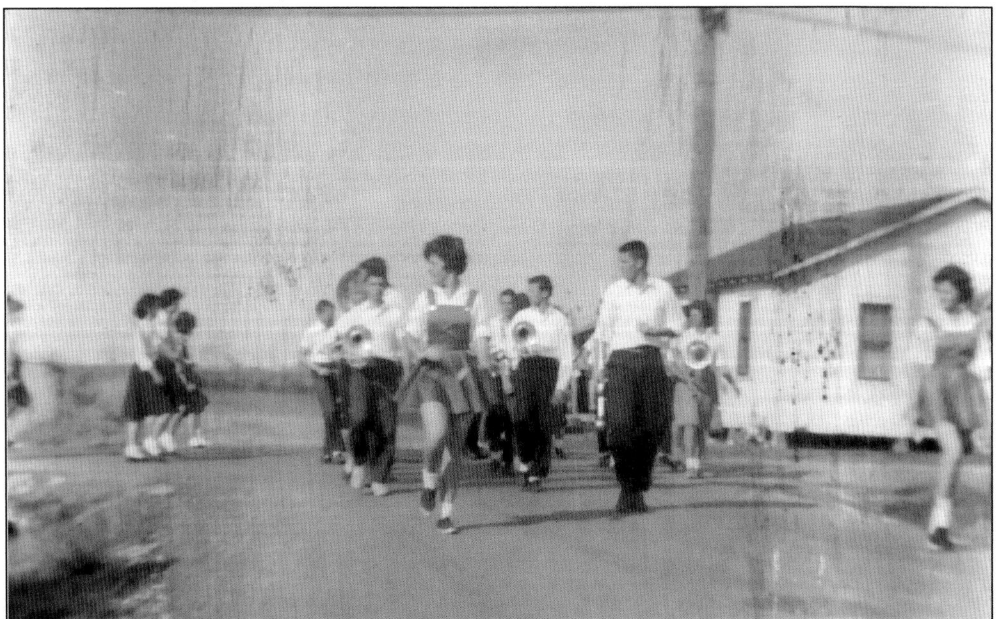

Scott High School homecomings included a bonfire, a parade, and a big game. In this 1950s parade, at the corner of St. Louis and Alfred Streets, the band marches south to the high school. (Courtesy of Earlene Carriere.)

*Four*

# Our Faith Defines Us

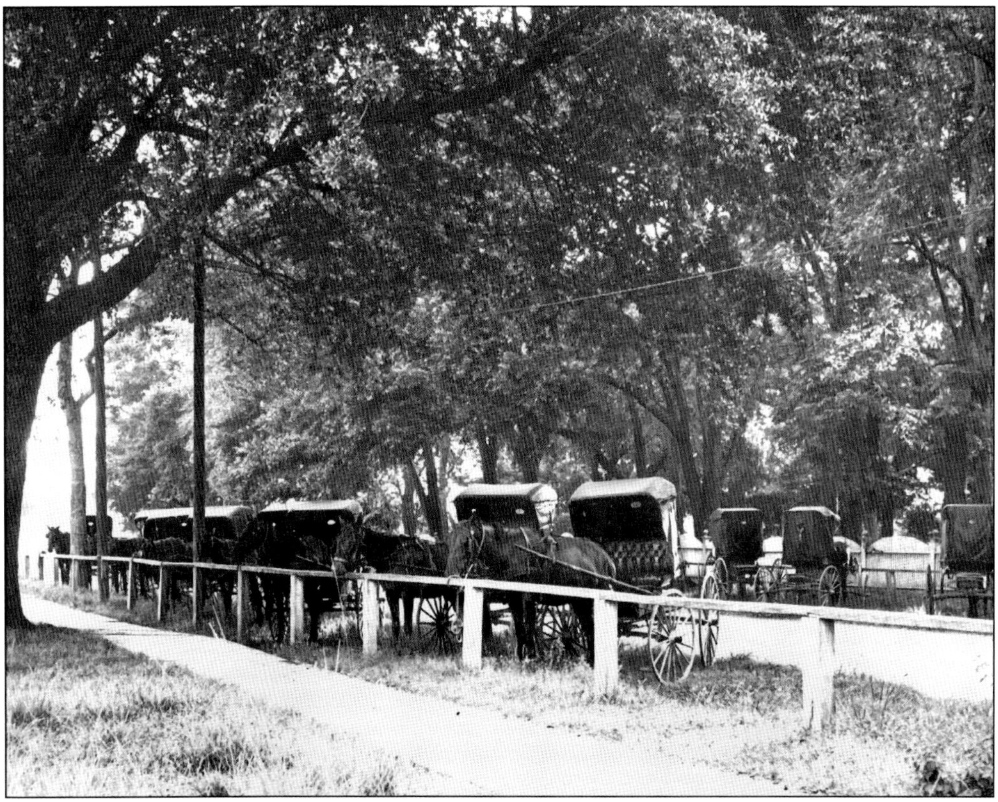

All modes of transportation were used to bring families to church. The horses and buggies could be seen for several blocks as they lined up on both sides of the road. This scene is in front of Sts. Peter and Paul Catholic Church on Paul Street. (Courtesy of Nelwyn Prejean Babineaux.)

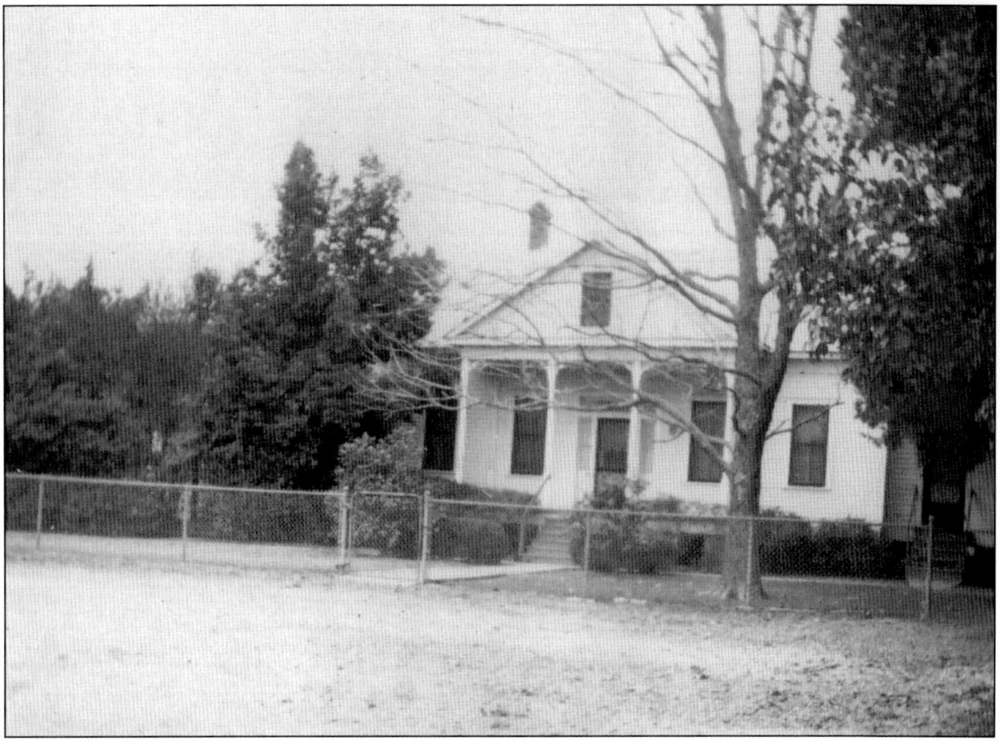

The first church rectory for Sts. Peter and Paul Catholic Church was built in 1905 by Father Durand. It was constructed on land that had been donated by the Alcide Judice family. This building remained in use for over 50 years until a bigger one was constructed in 1962. The new rectory included extra bedrooms to accommodate visiting clergy and friends, office space, and storage areas. (Courtesy of Lucille Sonnier.)

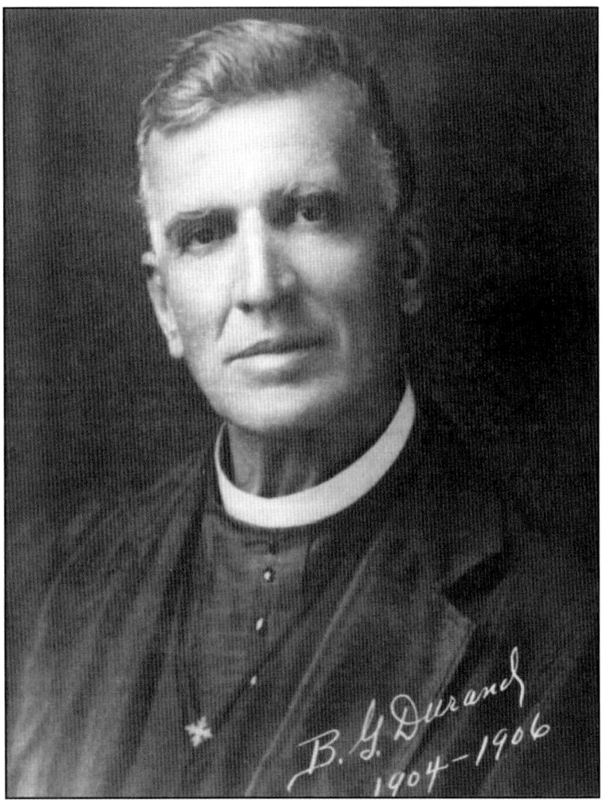


Fr. Benjamin Gabriel Durand came to Scott in 1904 as the first resident priest for Sts. Peter and Paul Catholic Church. He established the first choir with Amelia Breaux as the first organist. Father Durand helped to organize the oldest parish organization, the Cemetery Society, with Basile Sonnier as the first president. (Courtesy of Fr. Tom Voorhies.)

Fr. Joseph Victor Monteillard was born in France and served as priest in Scott from 1919 to 1928. During his tenure, the Ladies Altar Society was established in 1919 with Maude G. Prejean as the first president. He commissioned O.Z. Boudreaux to build the iron gates for the entrance to the cemetery. In 1921, the Holy Name Society was organized with Sebastian Hernandez as the first president. (Courtesy of Fr. Tom Voorhies.)

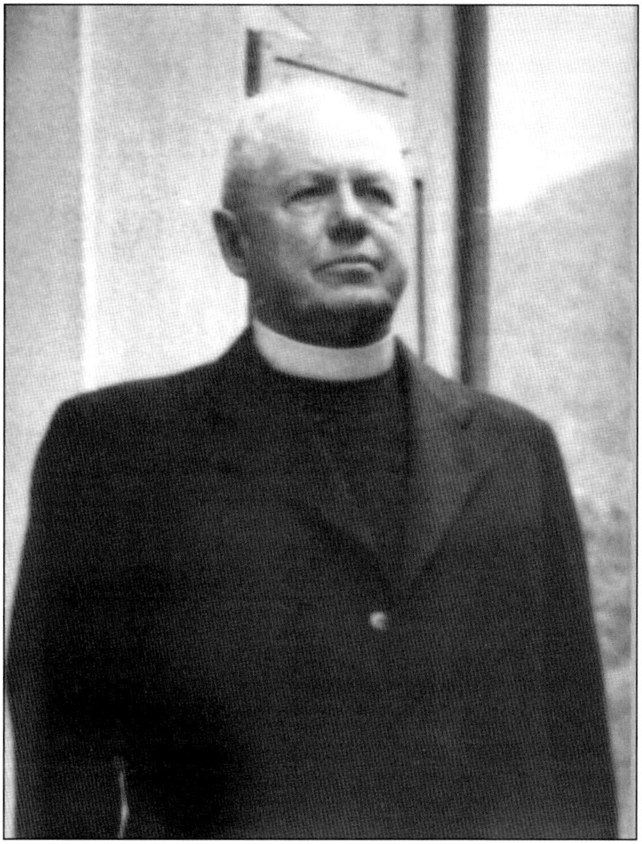

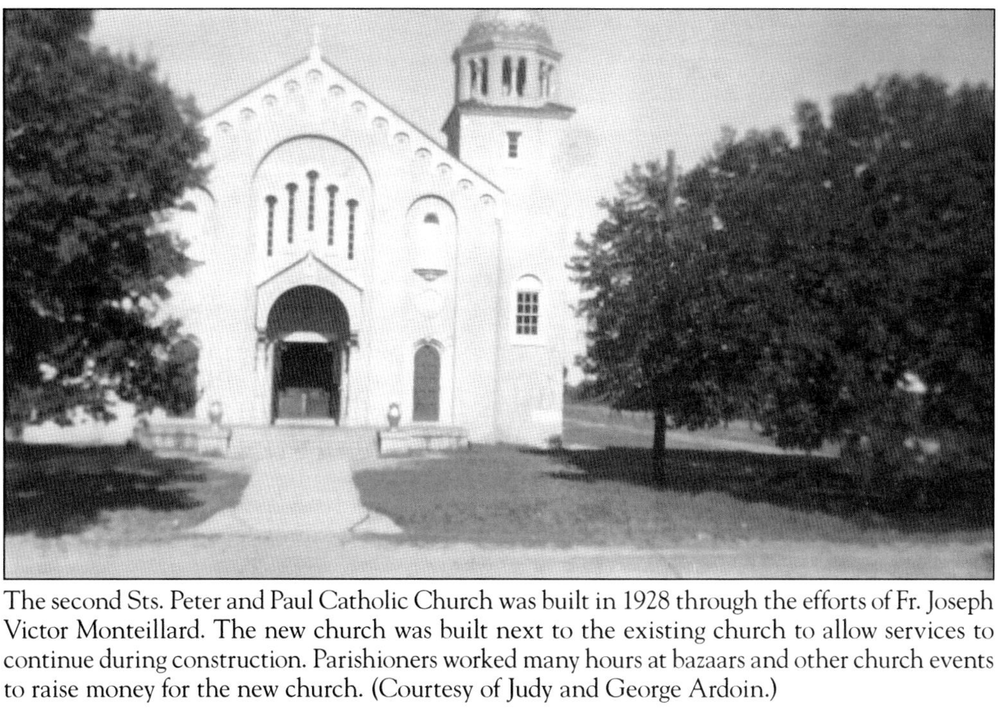

The second Sts. Peter and Paul Catholic Church was built in 1928 through the efforts of Fr. Joseph Victor Monteillard. The new church was built next to the existing church to allow services to continue during construction. Parishioners worked many hours at bazaars and other church events to raise money for the new church. (Courtesy of Judy and George Ardoin.)

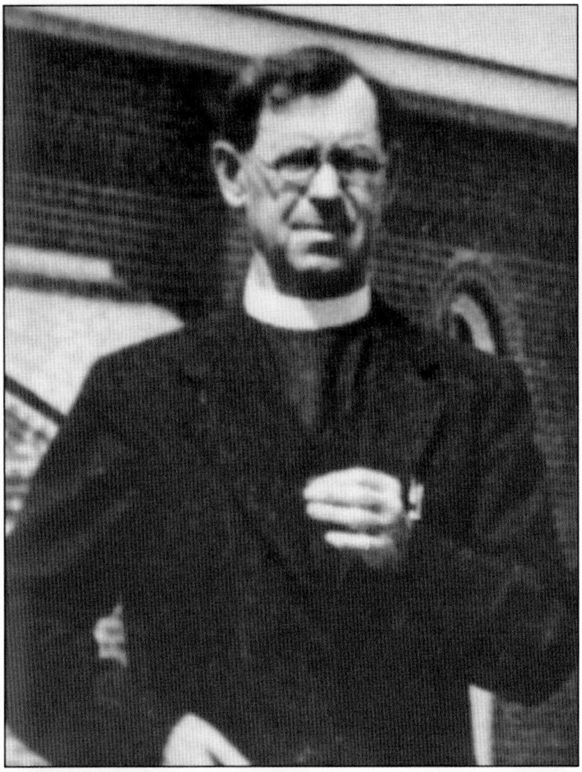

Fr. Alexander Chaslas was born in France in 1876 and ordained in Galveston, Texas. He served as resident priest in Scott from 1929 to 1938. He was responsible for completing the interior of the second Sts. Peter and Paul Catholic Church. (Courtesy of Fr. Tom Voorhies.)

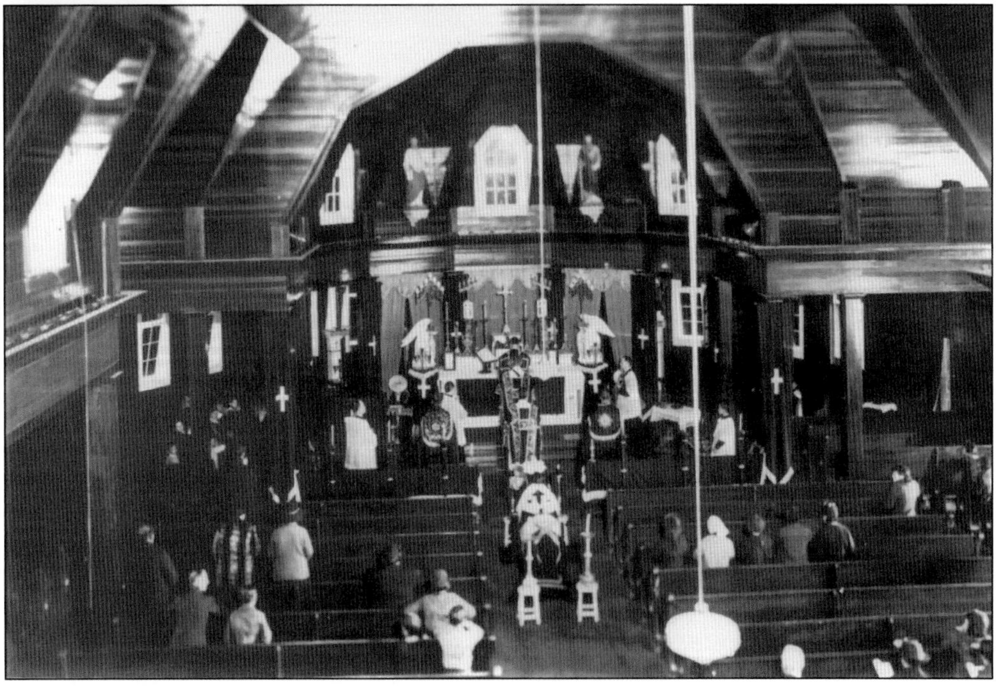

The altar and statues of the interior of the second Sts. Peter and Paul Catholic Church were purchased new and are still in use today in parts of the current church. (Courtesy of Pearl Provost Guidry.)

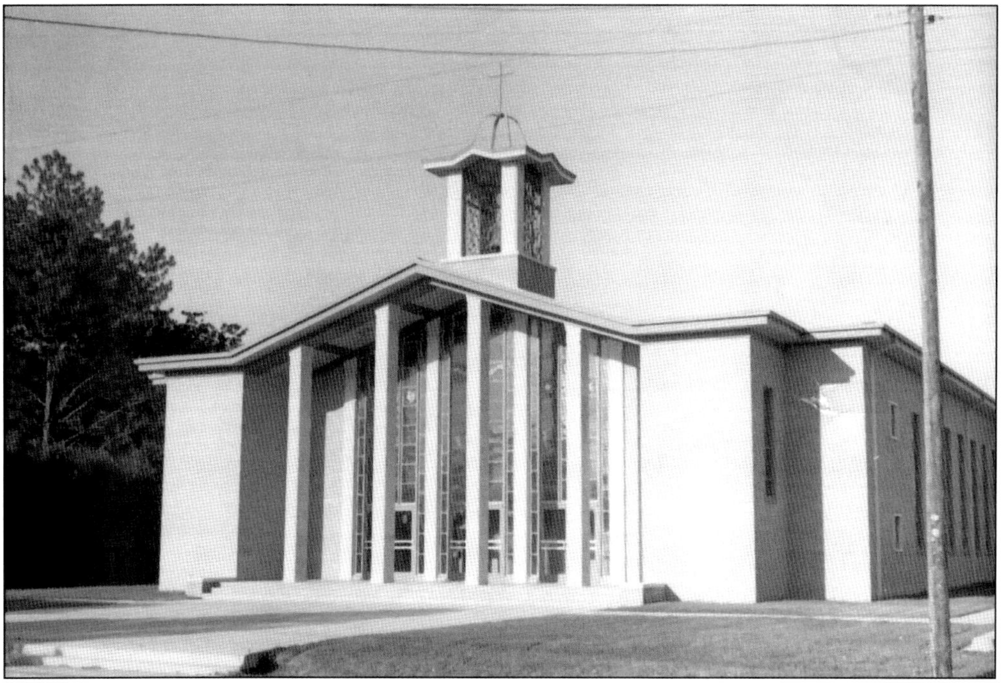

Today's Sts. Peter and Paul Catholic Church, built in 1962, has a contemporary design and a spacious sanctuary. The main altar is composed of multicolored Italian marble with mosaic panel inserts, as are the side altars. Statues from the older church were refurbished and are still being used. Beautiful stained-glass windows adorn the building. (Courtesy of Cheri Norton Broussard.)

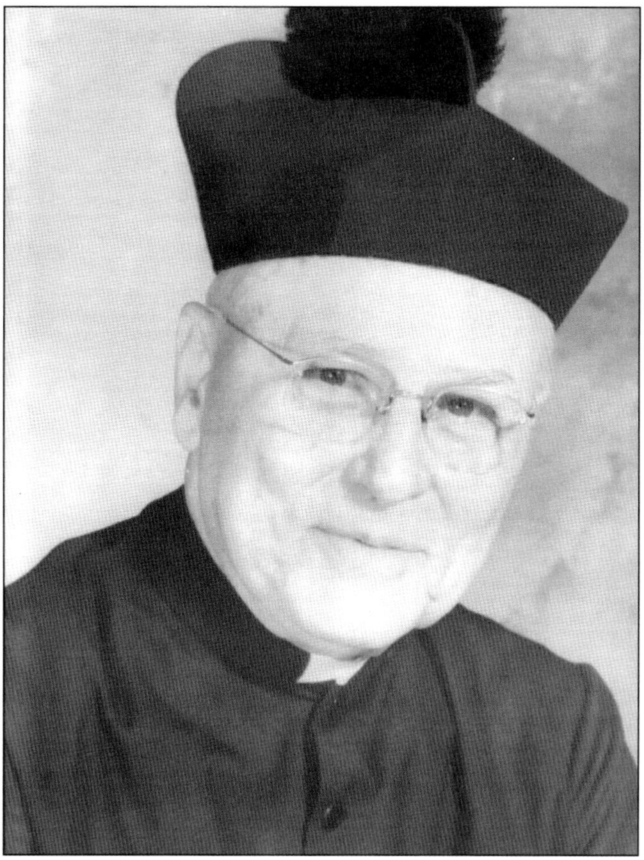

Fr. Lawrence Martin Fournet served as Sts. Peter and Paul Catholic Church's priest longer than any other to date, from 1949 to 1967. He helped guide the building of the present-day church and established a home for the Sisters of the Eucharistic Missionaries. (Courtesy of Fr. Tom Voorhies.)

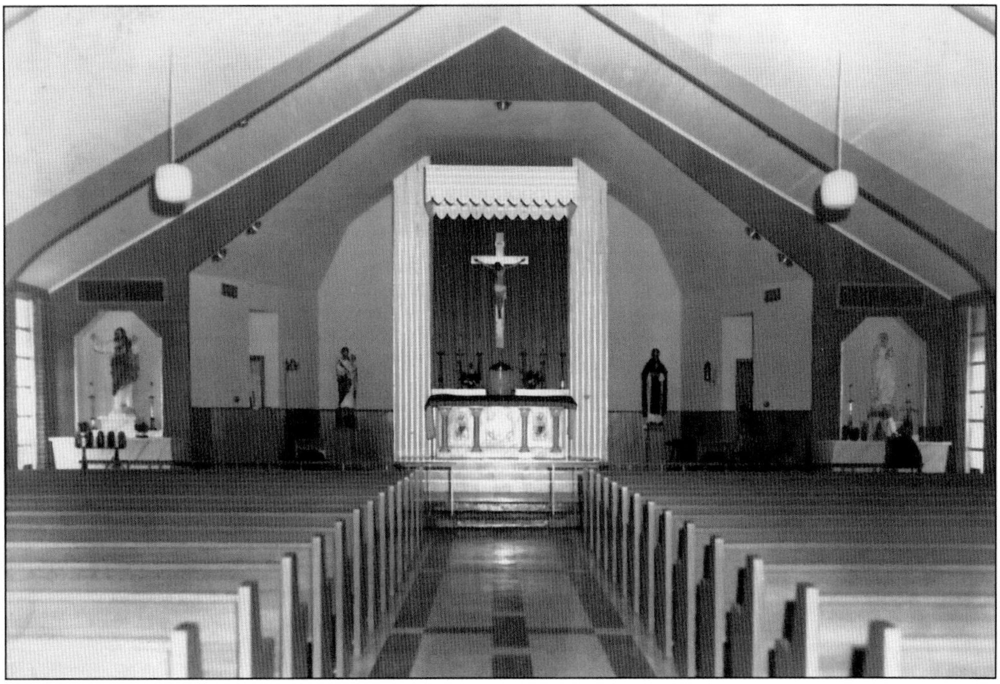

The inside of St. Martin de Porres Church contains a marble altar and statues. The first pastor was Fr. Clarence Howard, SVD. There were many fundraisers held in 1982 to help with the reconstruction of portions of the church that had burned in a fire. (Courtesy of Purvis Morrison.)

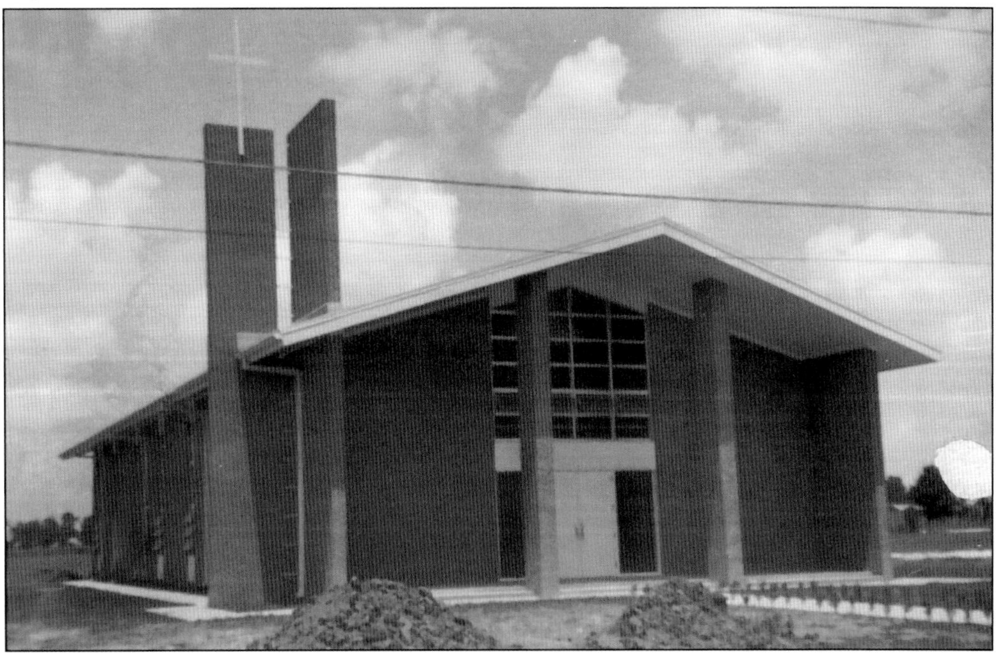

This 1962 photograph is the original St. Martin de Porres Church. It was constructed by Claude and Clifton Anderson. On February 2, 1982, part of the church burned down, rendering the building unsuitable to hold Mass. Sts. Peter and Paul Catholic Church extended an invitation to combine Mass times until a new church could be built. (Courtesy of Viola Mallet.)

The marriage of Marie Breaux and Sidney Provost was the first of 41 weddings in the year Scott was incorporated. They were married on January 3, 1907, by Father Detchemendy. (Courtesy of Annadine Credeur.)

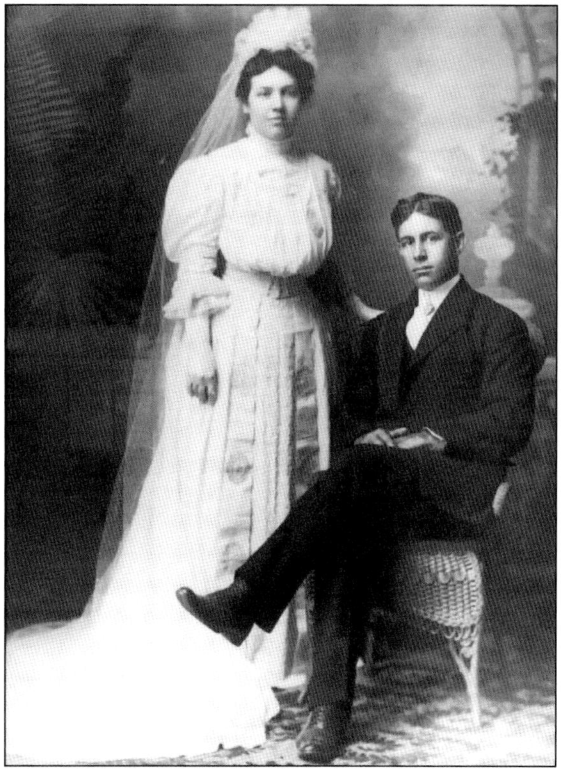

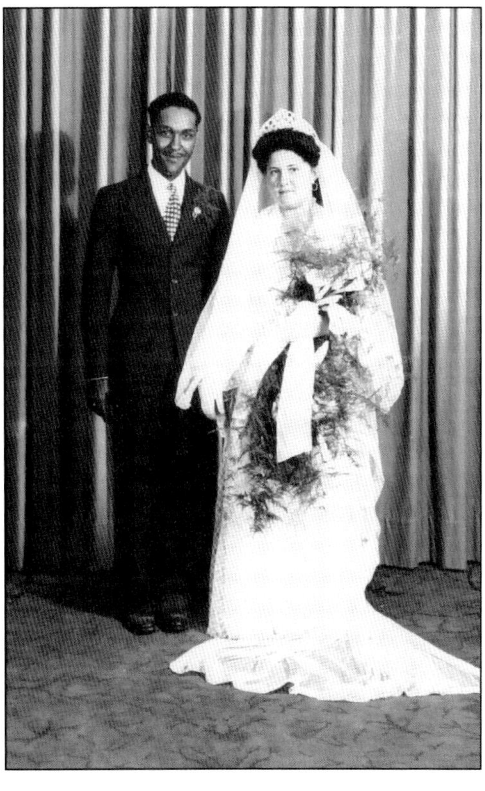

On April 27, 1946, Gumbleton Mallet and Viola Bernard were united in marriage at Blessed Martin de Porres Mission by Rev. Anthony Burgess, SVD, at 9:00 a.m. After the ceremony, members of the wedding party traveled to Lafayette to a local studio to have their photograph taken as there was no appointment required. A reception was held outside of the home of the bride's parents. (Courtesy of Viola Mallet.)

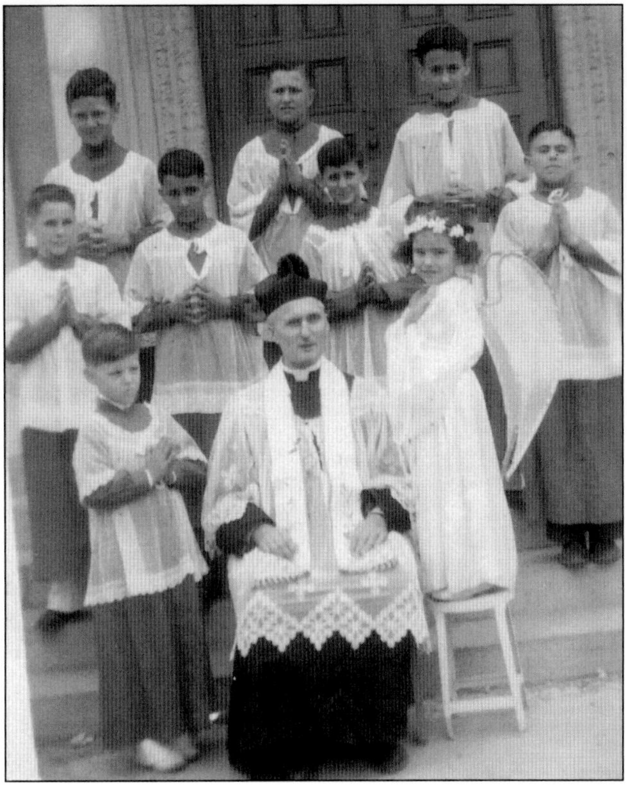

The altar boys and an angel gather with Father Bona in 1940 prior to one of many First Communion services. Pictured are, from left to right, (front row) Warren Trahan, Father Bona, and angel Betty Labauve; (second row) Fred Domingue, J.L. Raggio, Floyd James Guidry, and Dudley Labauve; (third row) Steven Arceneaux, Roy Broussard, and Woodley Credeur. (Courtesy of Marguerite Fontenot.)

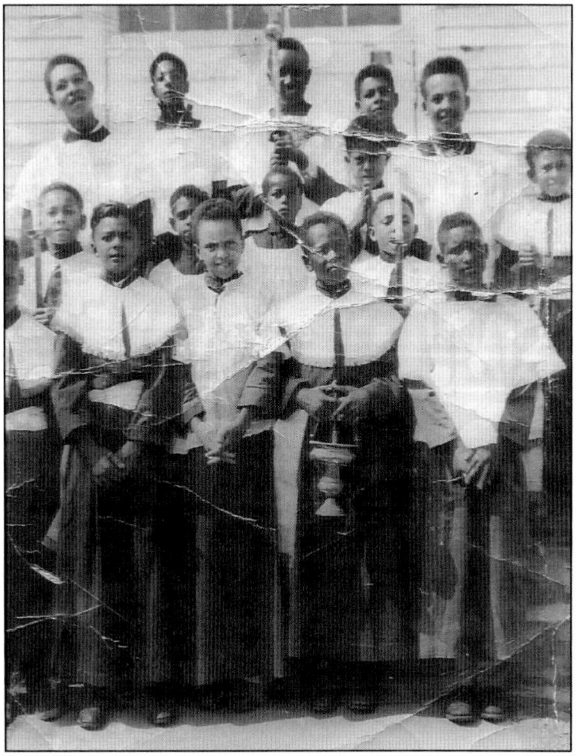

There were 16 boys who were altar servers of the Blessed Martin Chapel, where they assisted the priest during services. (Courtesy of Purvis Morrison.)

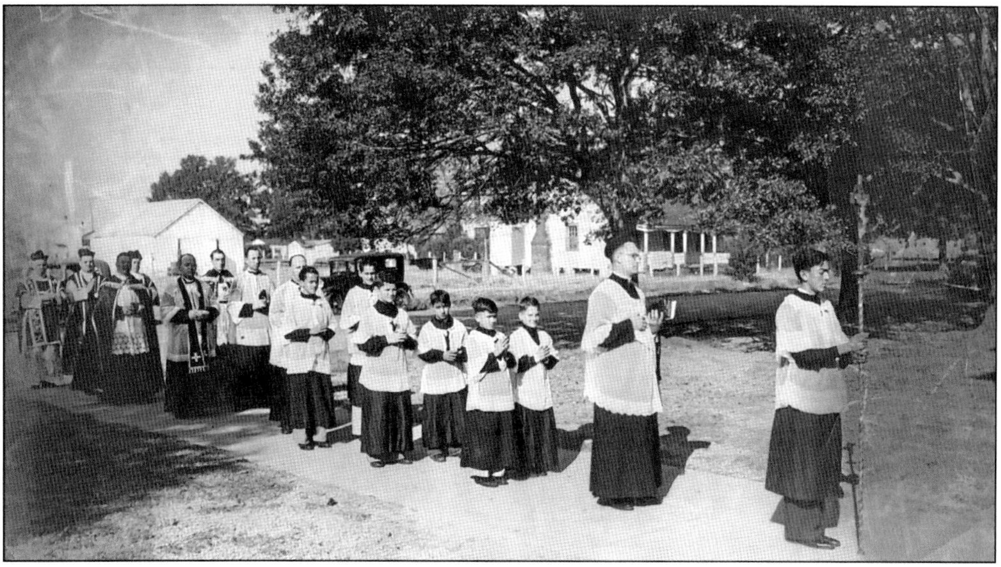

Crossbearer Paul H. Begnaud leads the procession followed by Father Gaudet for a solemn requiem. The altar boys are, from left to right, (first row) Dudley LaBauve and Fred Domingue; (second row) Steven "Do" Arceneaux and J.L. Raggio; (third row) Lauly Credeur and Woodley Credeur. The remaining participants are unidentified. (Courtesy of Pearl Provost Guidry.)

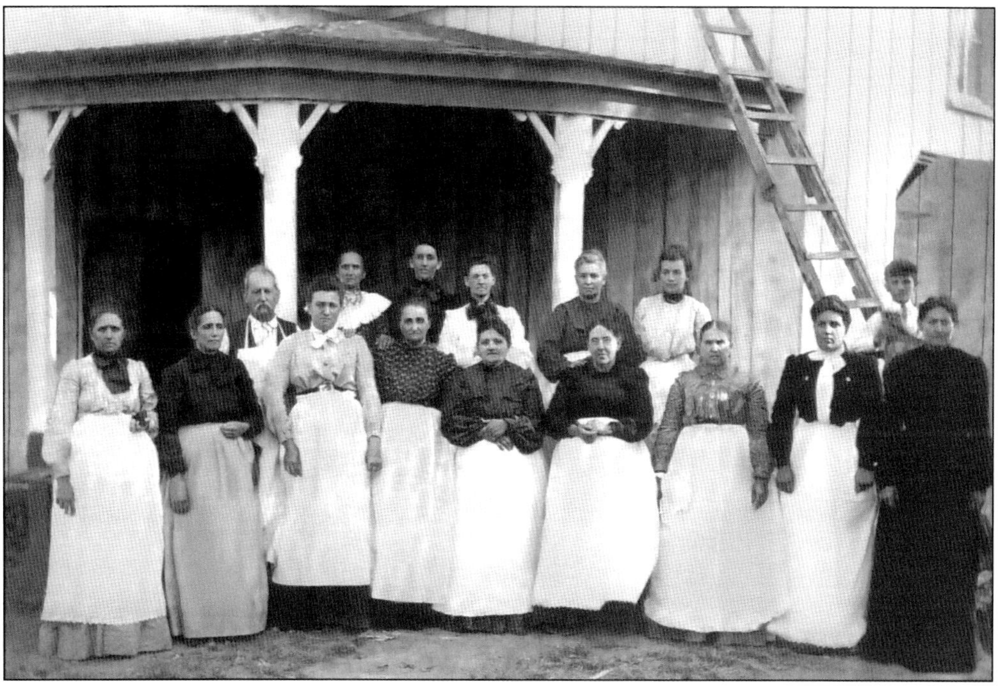

Sts. Peter and Paul Catholic Church bazaar workers are, from left to right, (first row) Mrs. Alex Boudreaux, Mrs. L.A. Boudreaux, Anna Wilkins, Mrs. Charles "Tom" Boudreaux, Mrs. Joe Pelletier, Mrs. Simon Boudreaux, Mrs. Etienne Mouton, Mrs. Dupre Patin, and Mrs. Jack Breaux; (second row) O.A. Boudreaux, Mrs. Felix Bernard, Mrs. Samuel Jenkins, Mrs. Alexander Delhomme Jr., Mrs. Joseph Alexander Begnaud, Mrs. Antoine Hebert, and an unidentified child. (Courtesy of Fr. Tom Voorhies.)

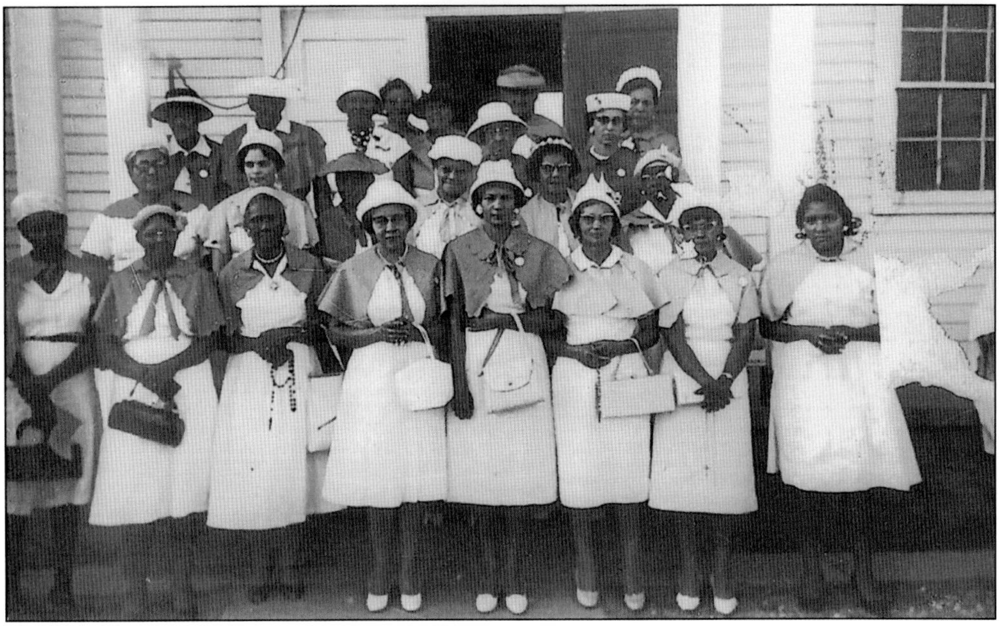

The altar ladies of St. Martin de Porres Church are, from left to right, (first row) Theresa Fox, Agnes Chaisson, unidentified, Bernadette Bernard, Alvenia Chaisson, Arlene Mire, Effie Perkins, and Vivian Dugas; (second row) Angelina Chaisson, Lula Bernard, Marie Anderson, Rita Andres, Mildred Monnette, and Thelma Chaisson; (third row) Alesia Morrison, Odile Arceneaux, Arcenia Williams, unidentified, To-Tout Sinegal, May Livings, Sarah Citizen, Ella Jolivette, and "T-Mae" Prejean. (Courtesy of Leana Miller.)

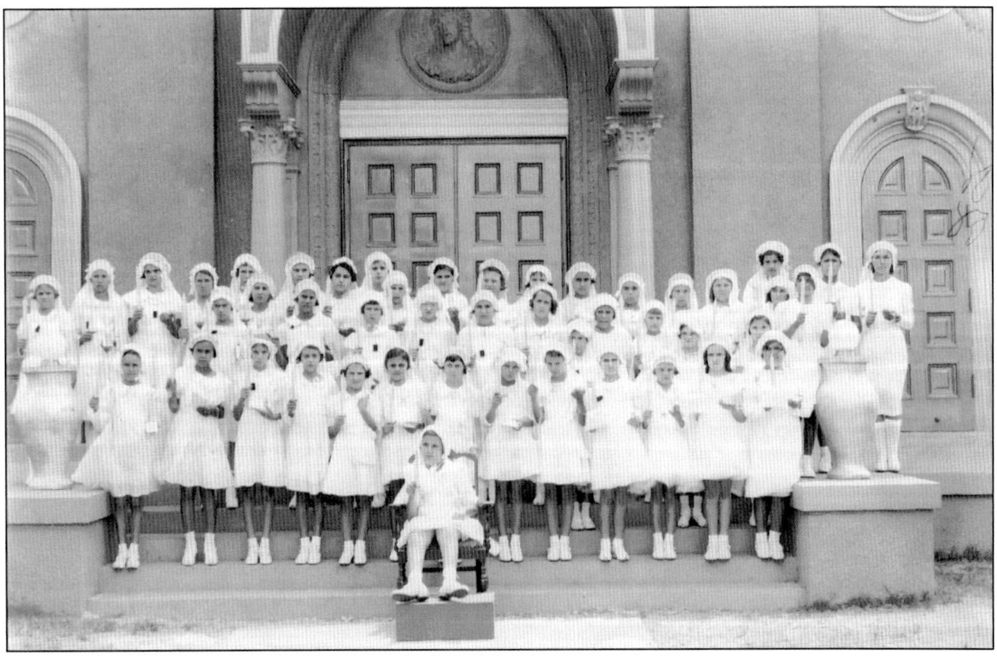

This 1938 First Communion class included 39 girls. They wore white dresses and headdresses and carried candles during the ceremony. Alberta Sonnier is sitting in the chair in the front. (Courtesy of Cheri Norton Broussard.)

Blanche Martin (left) and Ada Martin, daughters of Pierre Martin the local butcher, pose for this Confirmation photograph in 1906. (Courtesy of Jessie Poirrier.)

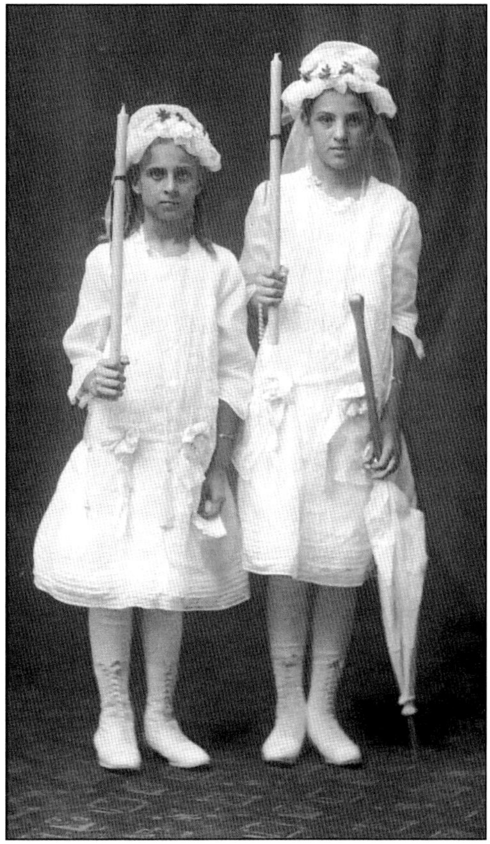

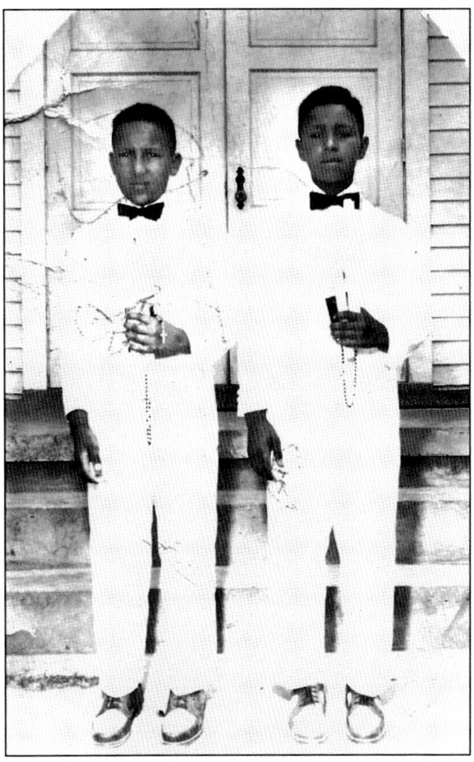

In 1950, Clarence Arceneaux (left) and Milton Arceneaux received the sacrament of First Communion at the Blessed Martin Chapel. (Courtesy of Clarence Arceneaux.)

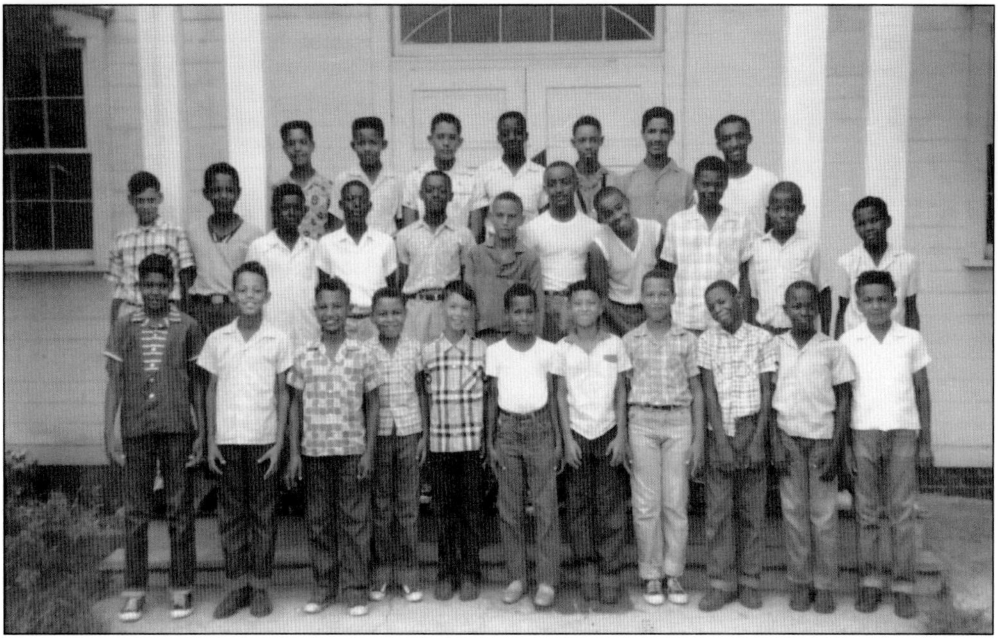

This summer camp and catechism class was held in 1962 at Blessed Martin Chapel and taught by Raymond Mercier. Some of the students include, from left to right, (first row) Case Lee Andres (second), Wilbert Mire (fifth), and Darel Morrison (last); (second row) Weldon Mire (first); (third row) Relond Anderson (next to last) and Russell Chaisson (last). (Courtesy of Viola Mallet.)

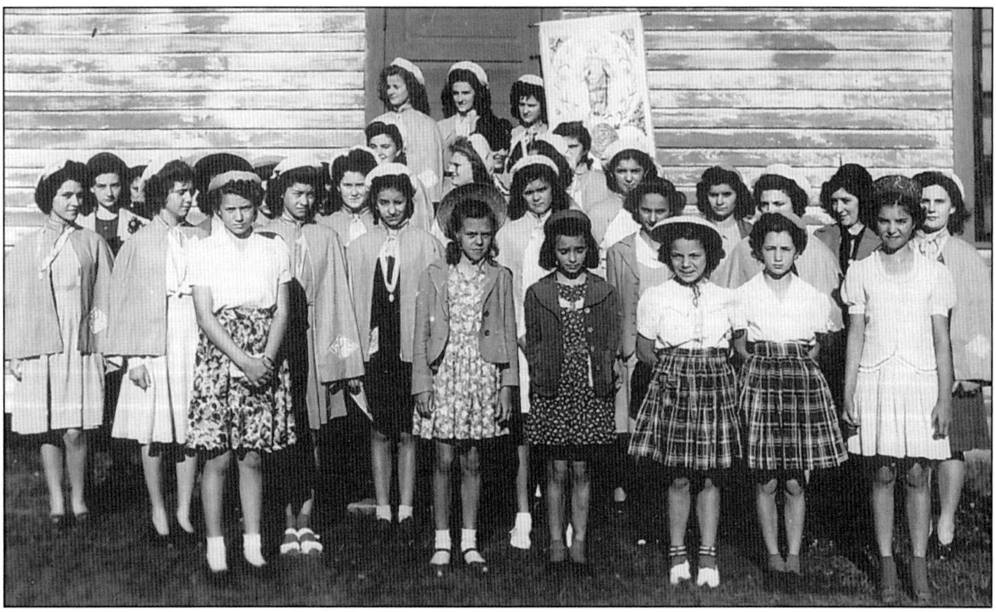

Sodality members at Sts. Peter and Paul Catholic Church attended novenas and had meetings. Some of the members seen here include Verdie S. Guidry, Georgette Knight, Georgie B. Duhon, Louise Sonnier, Ena M. Domingue, Verda B. Prejean, Molly K. Lalonde, Audrey K. Broussard, Mathilde S. Broussard, Rudelle D. Dronet, Jane T. Kemp, Rosie S. Adams, Sara Ann Spence, Pearl P. Guidry, Virginia Prejean, Cerita Potier, Barbara Nell Domingue, and Betty Broussard. (Courtesy of Louise Sonnier.)

The 1962 Blessed Martin Chapel basketball team included, from left to right, (first row) Preston Bernard, Nolan Broussard, Claude Anderson Jr., Wilbert Mire, unidentified; (second row) Charles Gary, Harold Sonnier, Donald Ray Arceneaux, and two unidentified boys. (Courtesy of Viola Mallet.)

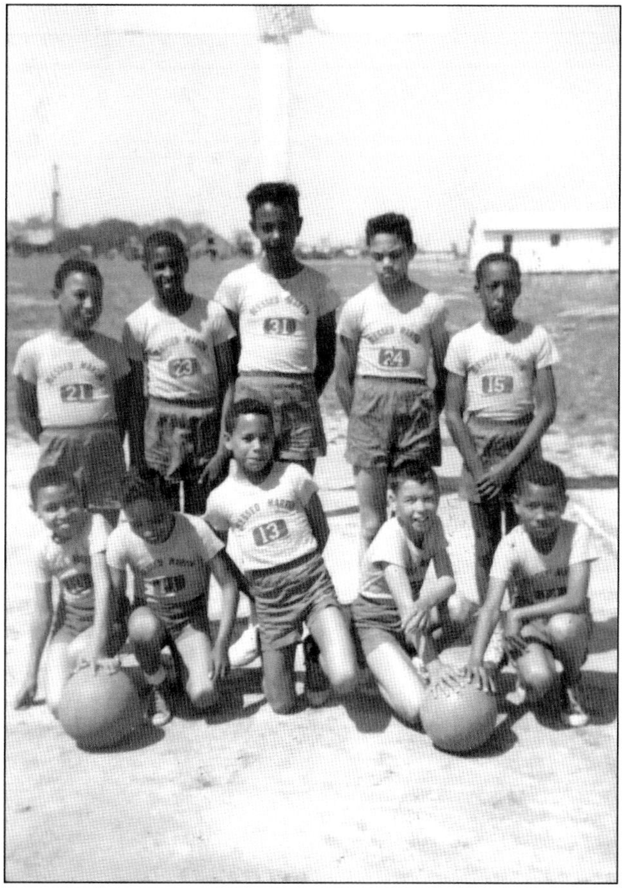

The 1962 Blessed Martin Chapel basketball team's older boys in the second row are, from left to right, Paul Living, Clarence Arceneaux, Donald Chaisson, Wilbert Chiasson, unidentified, and Ronald Chaisson. (Courtesy of Viola Mallet.)

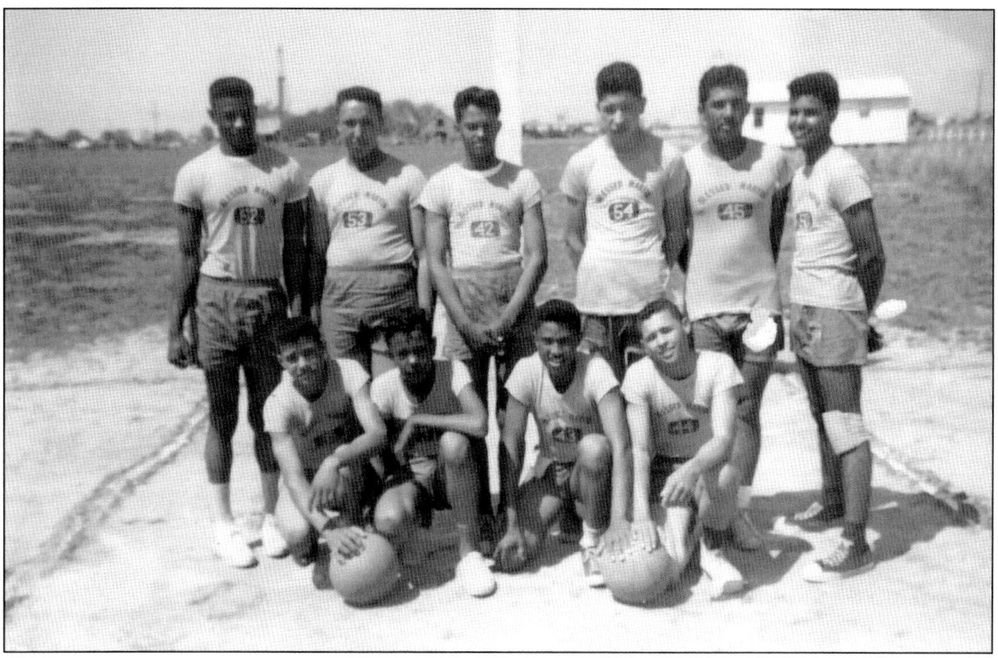

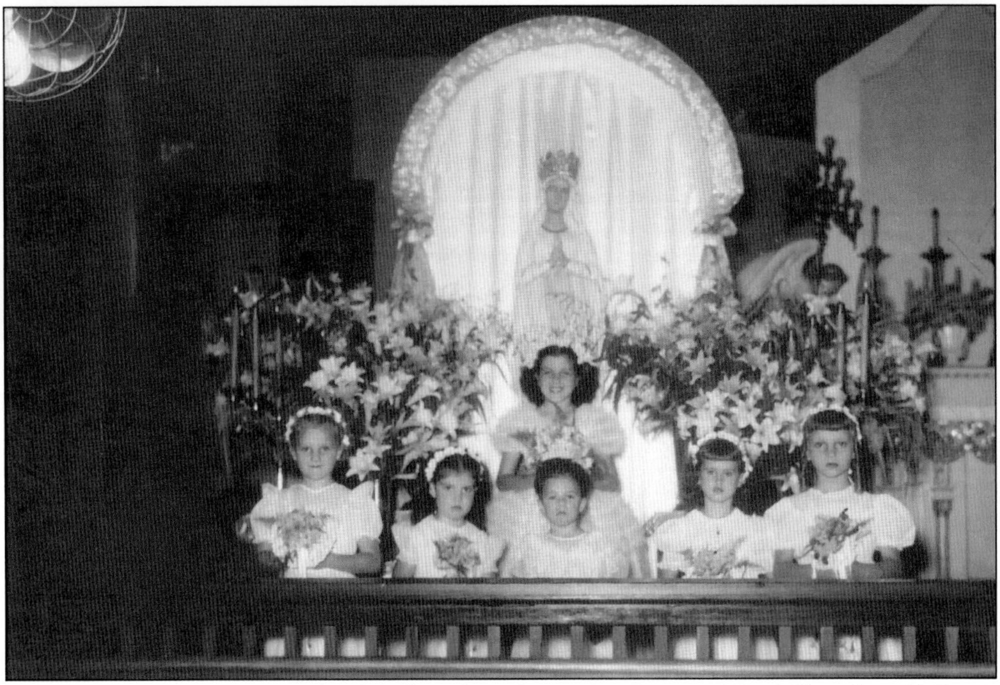

Participating in the Crowning of the Blessed Mother at Sts. Peter and Paul Church in 1949 are, from left to right, (first row) Mary Ellen Broussard, Catherine Bollich, Carole Martinez, Sharon Delana, and Merlene Pellisier; (second row) Claudette Prejean. The crowning was usually celebrated in May. (Courtesy of Becca Begnaud.)

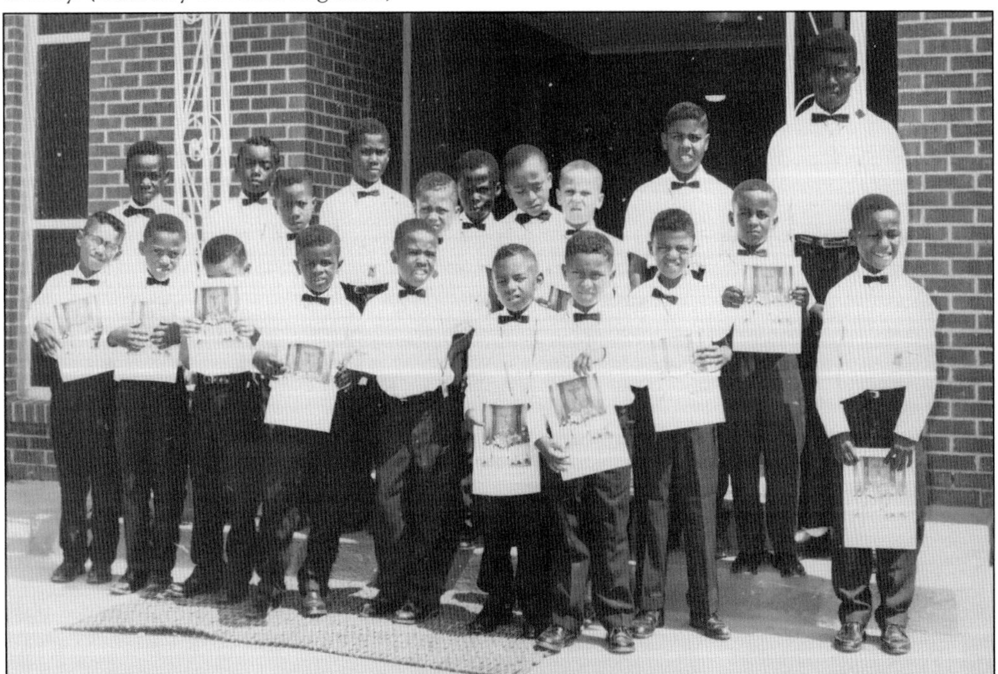

These 19 boys of St. Martin de Porres Church are holding a photograph that shows the group being blessed by the priest. (Courtesy of Viola Mallet.)

# *Five*

# EVERYDAY LIFE

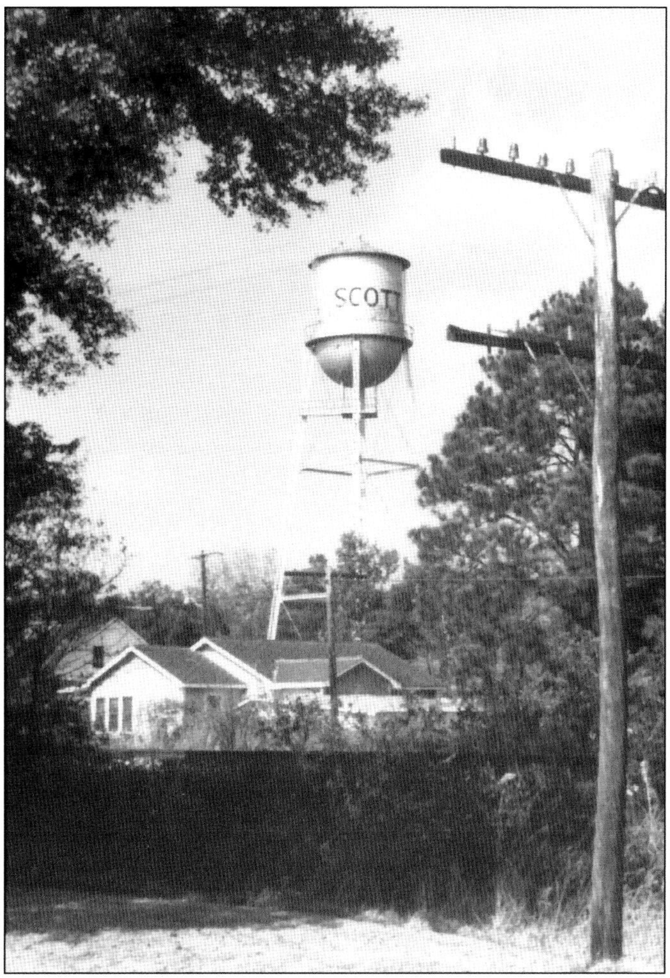


The water tower stood next to Scott's municipal building. Although the tower is gone and the municipal building accommodates a beauty shop, stories still circulate about the escapades of youth who climbed this landmark structure. (Courtesy of Wayne Domingue.)

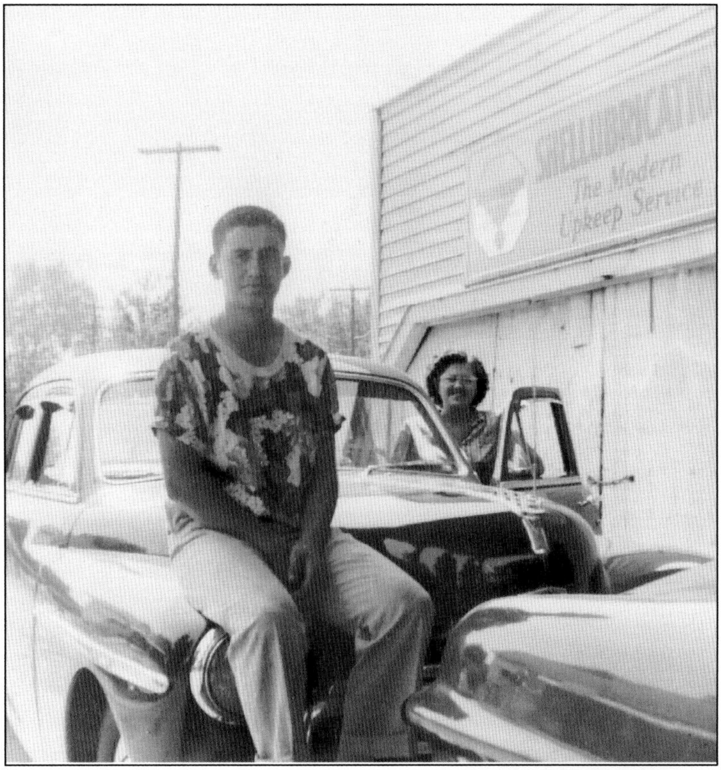


Daniel Roach and Louise Sonnier stand beside "Doc" Sonnier's Shell service station, which promised "modern upkeep service." Local residents depended on the station for gasoline and full-service car care. (Courtesy of Louise Sonnier.)

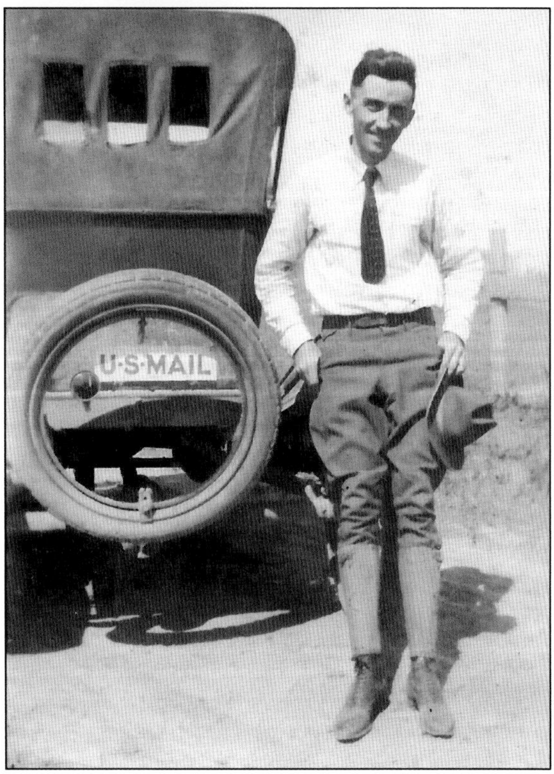


Louis Delhomme was Scott's only rural mail carrier for 44 years. He delivered mail by horse and buggy over unpaved roads and in any weather. In the 1920s, he began using his own car to make deliveries. He went through three personal vehicles before he retired in 1960. (Courtesy of David Delhomme.)

Claude Cinquieme Boudreaux worked in his uncle O.Z. Boudreaux's mechanic and blacksmith shop. In this October 18, 1939, photograph, he is using a drill press that was used to drill holes in some iron works that were made in the blacksmith shop. *Cinquieme* means fifth in French, and Claude was the fifth child of Julie and Andre Boudreaux. (Courtesy of Polly Boudreaux Richard.)

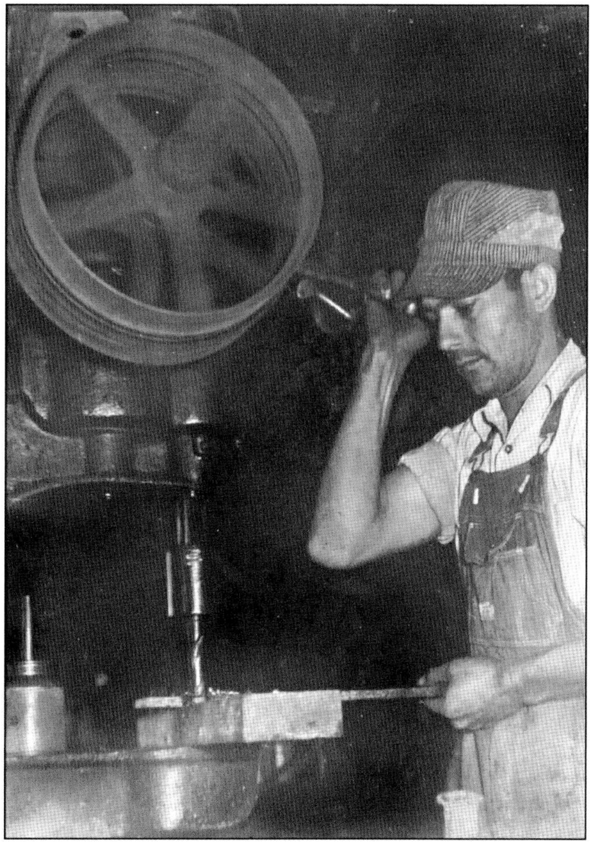

Railroad workers take a few moments to pose for this 1943 photograph. During World War II, the railroad men worked overtime because the trains were a strategic way to transport soldiers, fuel, food, and munitions. Pictured from left to right are (first row) Dallas Broussard, Lee Ray Benoit, E.J. Camelle, and John Muka; (second row) Justilion "Cop" Prejean, William Jenkins, Paul Breaux, Will Hoffpauir, Authur Duhon, and Johnny Schieb. (Courtesy of Lafayette Parish Clerk of Court.)

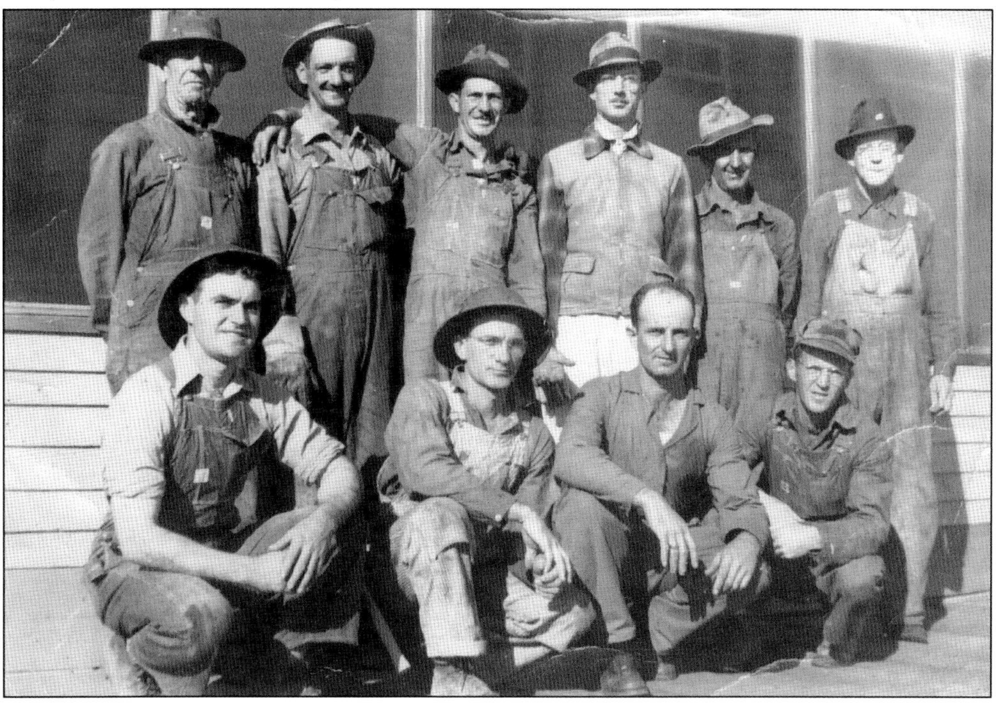

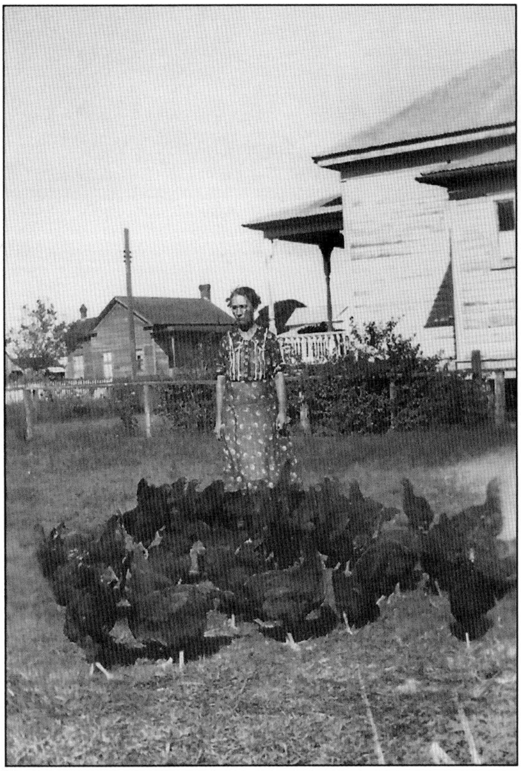

In this 1940s photograph, Leila Boudreaux eyes her chickens in the backyard. Many families raised animals for food and planted vegetable gardens, called "Victory Gardens" during the war. Chickens provided eggs and meat as well as feathers for pillows and mattresses. (Courtesy of Carolyn Adams.)

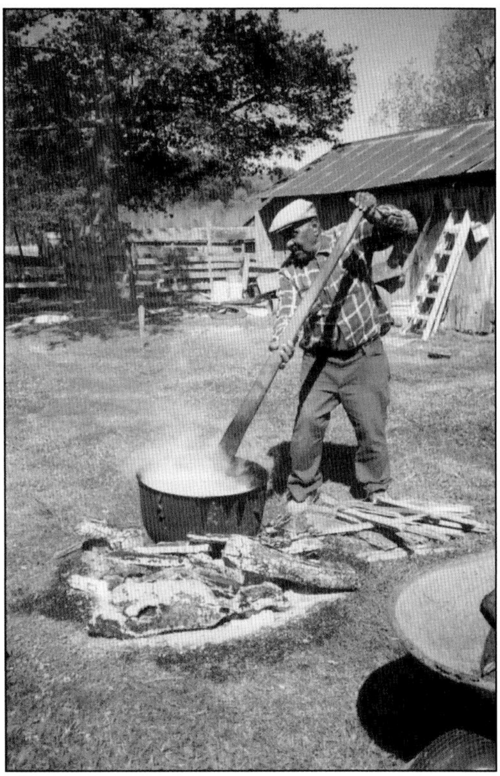

Gumbleton Mallet is working hard tending to his large pot at the *boucherie*, which took place every year during the fall months after farming crops were completed. Nearby family and neighbors came to help one another slaughter the fattest pig. This was an all-day event, and anyone who helped left with a packet of boudin, cracklins, and a pork roast. (Courtesy of Viola Mallet.)

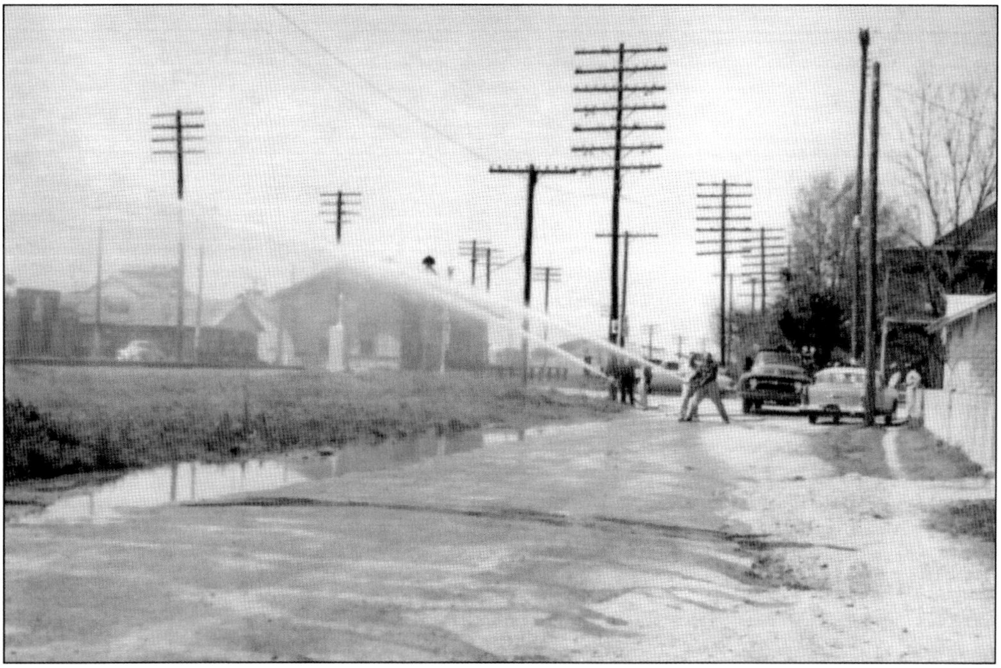

Volunteer firefighters Leon "Doc" Sonnier (left) and Andrus Martinez test the fire hoses as part of a routine safety check. With their backs to the Bernard House, they aim the hoses in the direction of the depot across the street. (Courtesy of Louise Sonnier.)

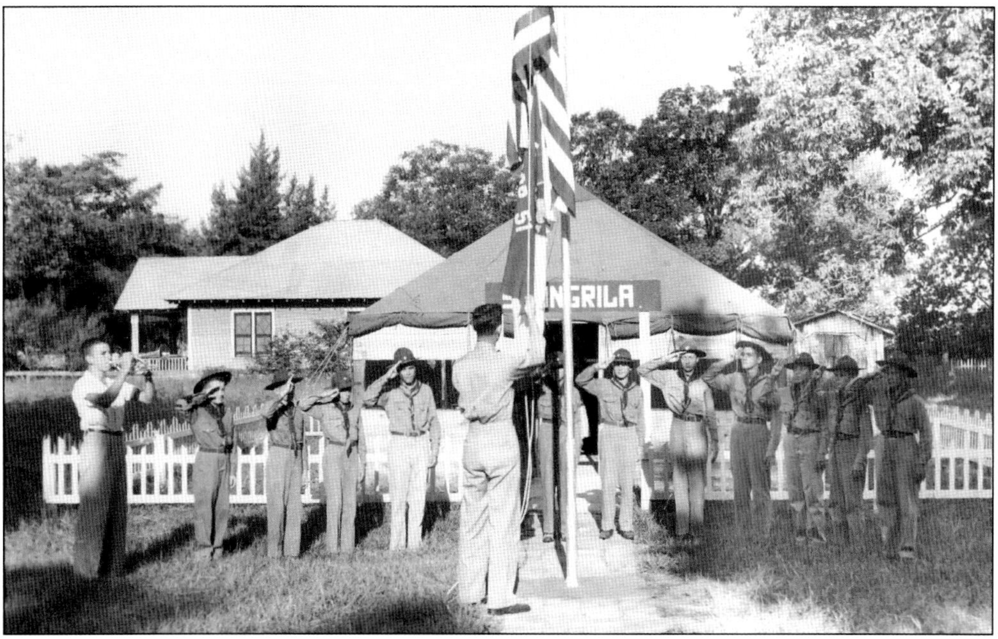

These Scouts (to the right of the bugler) are, from left to right, Wayne Bollich, Robert Sonnier, James Lee Martin, Lindon Lormand, Elmo Broussard Jr., unidentified, Carrol Sonnier, Fred Domingue, Caro Louviere, Raymond Mouton, and Ned Boudreaux. They are saluting as Scoutmaster Leroy Gouradron raises the flag at Shangrila, a Boy Scout camp used in the late 1940s for den meetings, campouts, and activities needed to earn Eagle Scout badges. (Courtesy of Elmo Broussard Jr.)

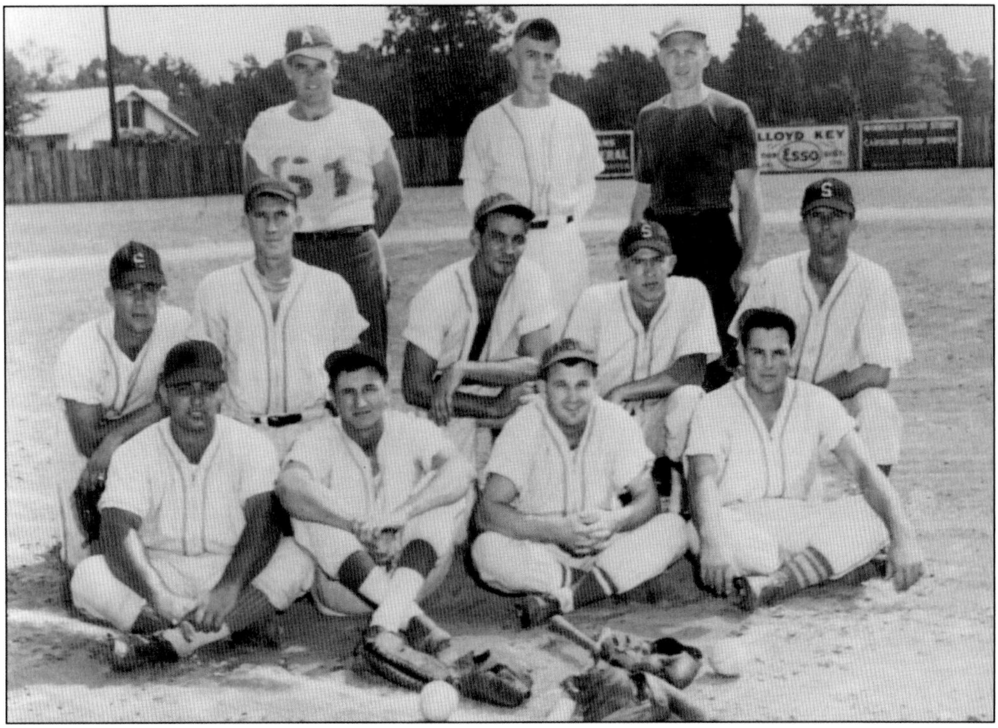

These young men were runners-up in the 1949 state fast-pitch softball tournament. Shown here are, from left to right, (first row) J.L. Raggio, Roy Broussard, Roy Dugas, and Curley Guidry; (second row) C.J. Comeaux, Alvin Hoffpauir, Eddie Logan, Bill Neef, and J.B. Richard; (third row) "Tiny" Touchet, Jimmy Neef, and Warren "Buddy" Landry. The team began in 1940 through the initiative of Andrus Martinez. Richard later played professionally. (Courtesy of Marguerite Fontenot.)

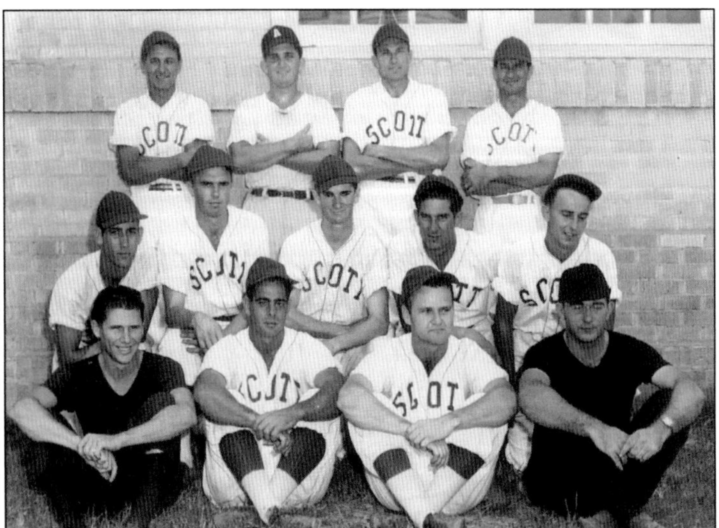

The 1941 Scott fast-pitch softball team members are, from left to right, (first row) Leroy Dugas, Paul "PeeWee" Broussard, Steve "Do" Arceneaux, and Warren Duhon; (second row) C.J. Comeaux, Eddie Richard, Kermit Kilchrist, Autrey "Chank" Boudoin, and Warren Landry; (third row) Roy Broussard, Lee Martin, Andrus Martinez, and Curtis Broussard. (Courtesy of Marguerite Fontenot.)

Claudette Prejean (front) and her aunt Rhena Hebert Begnaud huddle in front of the train depot during a rare Scott snowfall. (Courtesy of Claudette Prejean LeBlanc.)

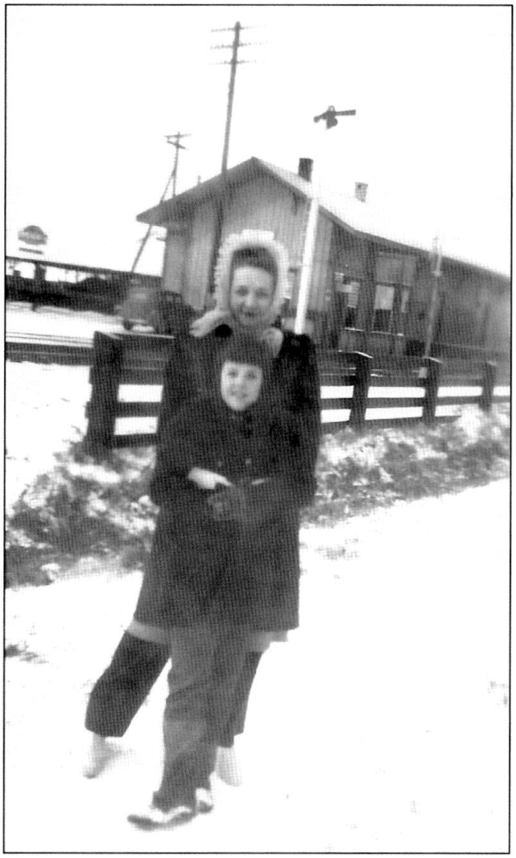

Social gatherings, Sunday drives, and photography were part of everyday life and weekend activities in Scott during the 1960s. Note the license-plate holder on the Ford Fairlane is celebrating Louisiana State University's centennial. Enjoying their day are, from left to right, Jeanette Anderson (with Brownie Hawkeye camera), Rita Anderson (in the background), Helen Joyce Mire, Bernadette Anderson, unidentified, and Dorothy Mire. (Courtesy of Leana Miller.)

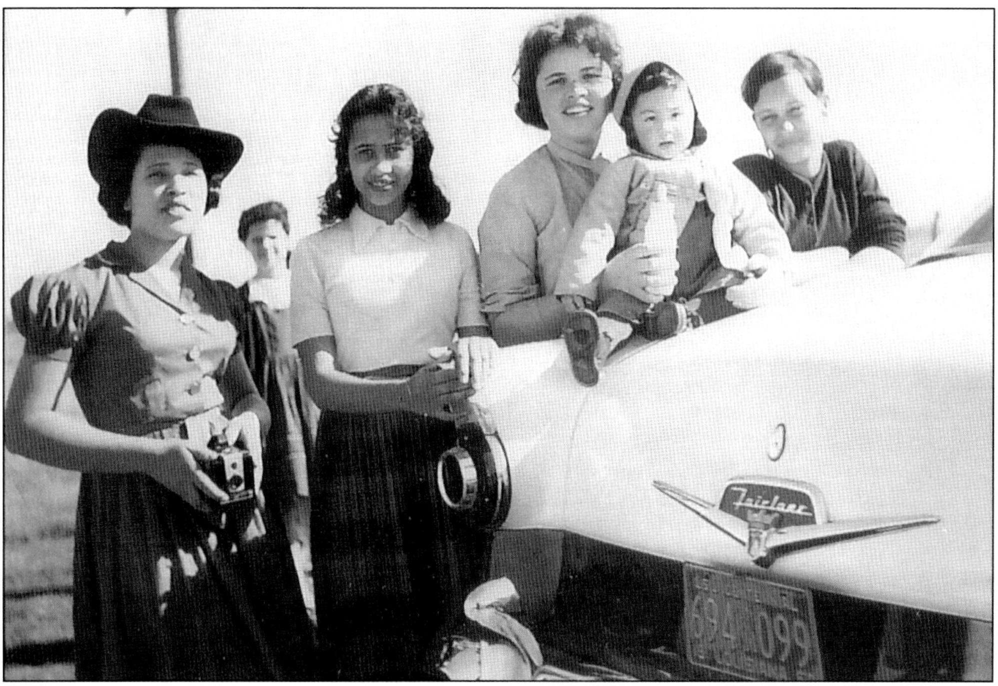

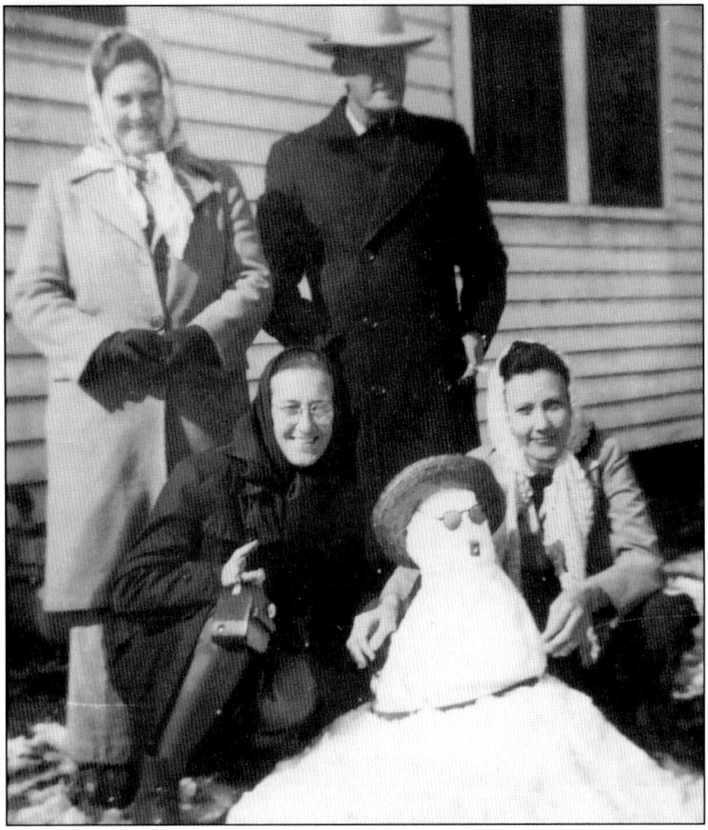

Pictured from left to right are (first row) Letha Martin Begnaud (holding a camera) and Marie Therese Begnaud; (second row) Bertha Sonnier and Elphia Martin. They are proving that it takes only a little snow to make a snowman in Scott. (Courtesy of Louise Sonnier.)

Anytime it snowed in Scott, everyone wanted to make a snowman. In this 1950 photograph are, from left to right, Jude Arceneaux, Joyce Arceneaux, Betty Labauve, Pearl Provost, Gerry Bollich, and George Arceneaux, who have gathered around their creation. (Courtesy of Pearl Provost Guidry.)

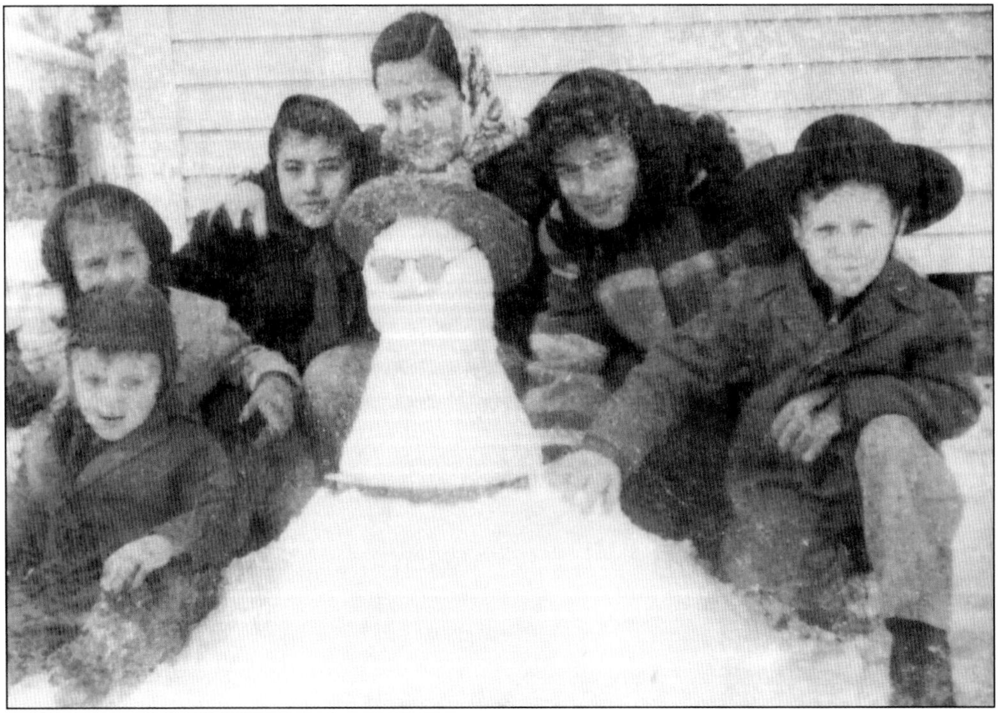

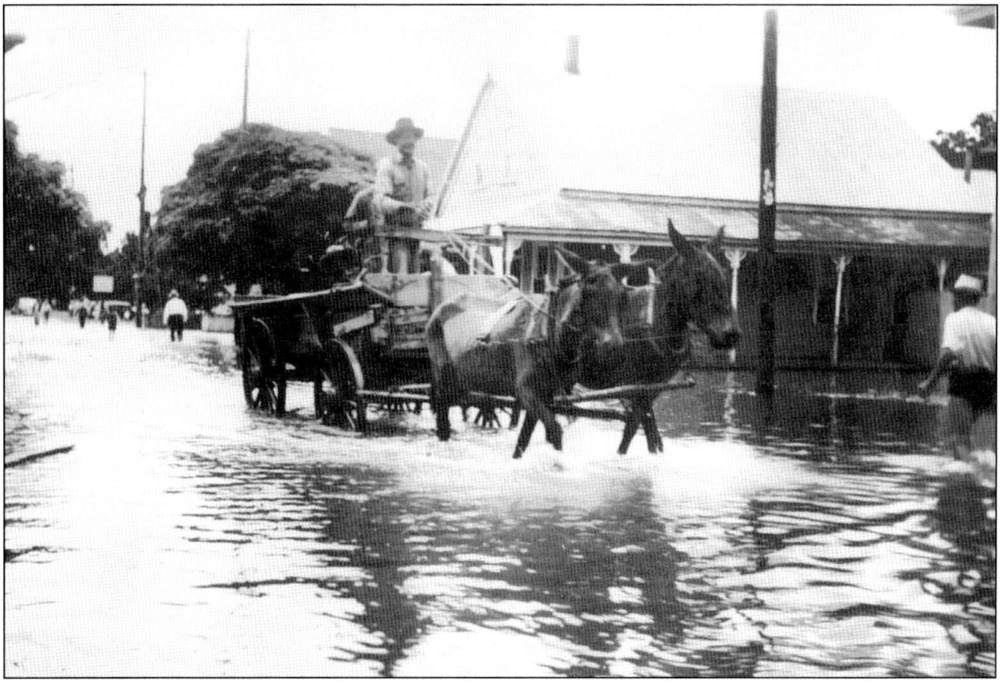

Scott was affected by the floods of 1927 and 1940. In both events, citizens needed to find alternative modes of travel. In this photograph, men walk with pant legs rolled up or ride in mule-drawn wagons that kept riders above the rising water. (Courtesy of Claudette Prejean LeBlanc.)

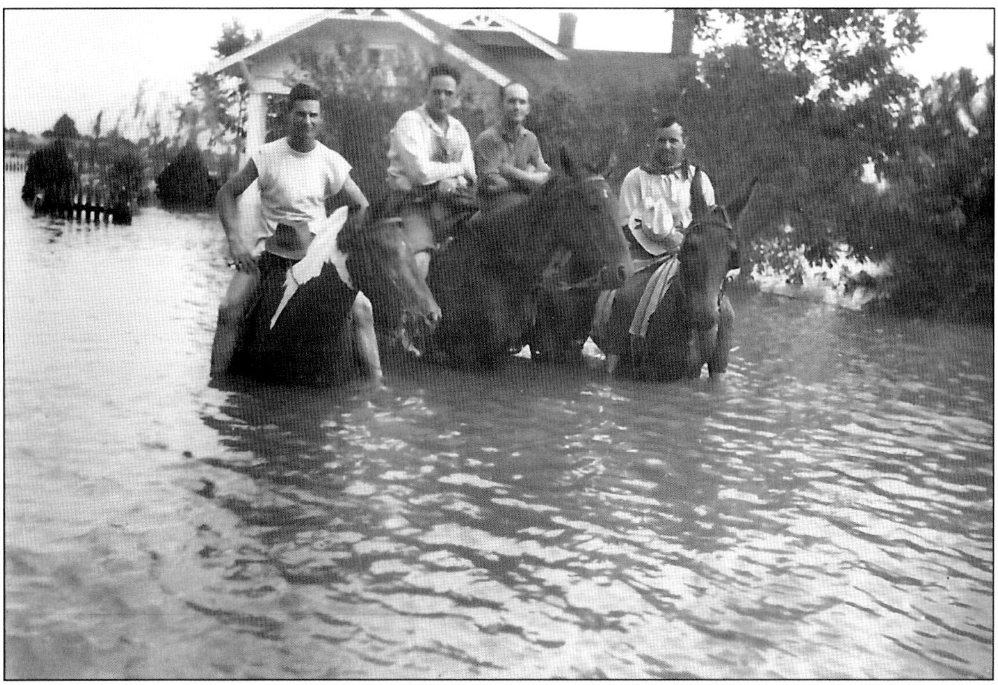

In 1940, severe rainstorms flooded the streets of Scott and surrounding communities of Acadiana. Riding their horses and mules to visit neighbors are, from left to right, Curtis Broussard, Paul Raggio, Dudley Raggio, and Pierre Raggio. (Courtesy of Polly Boudreaux Richard.)

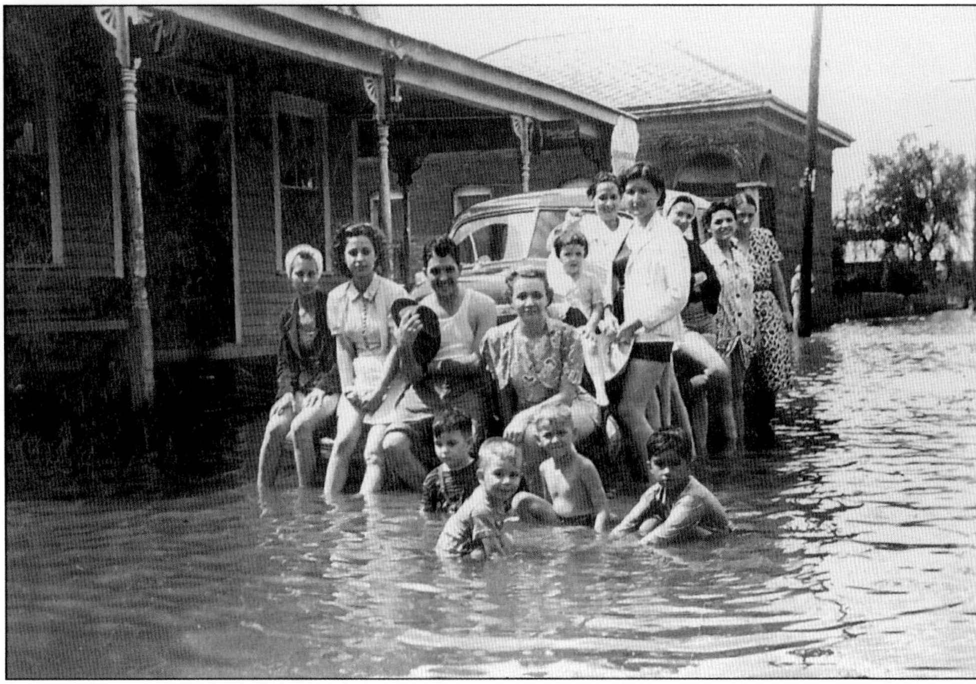

The 1940 flood made it impossible for automobile travel. Neighbors have gathered around a stuck vehicle in the center of town. From left to right are (first row, in the water) David "Boo" Prejean, Charles Oran "Poochie" Abdella, Robert Sonnier, and Gerald Ancelet; (second row) Lucille Prejean, Jeanette Prejean, Clabe "Snook" Begnaud, Rhena Begnaud, Claudette "Titter" Prejean LeBlanc, Lena Bernard Delana, Jeanne Begnaud Prejean, Marie Therese Begnaud, Effie Begnaud, and Nola Sonnier. (Courtesy of Claudette Prejean LeBlanc.)

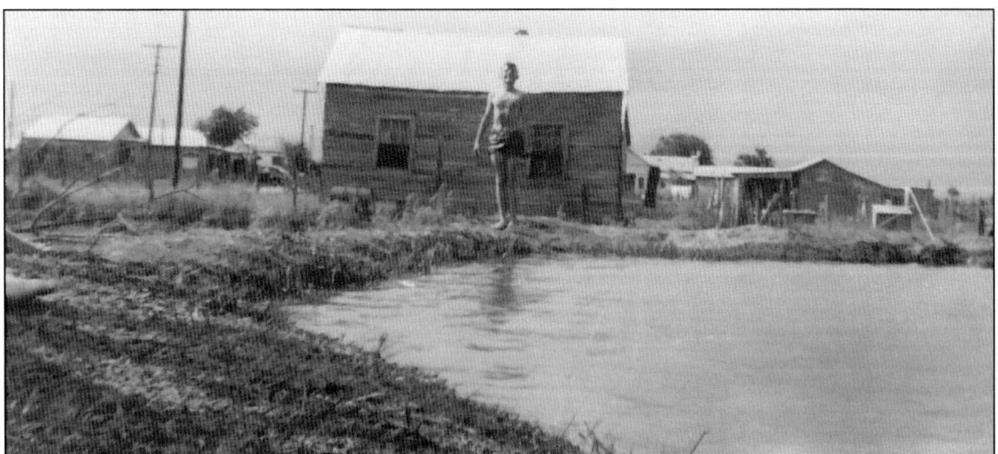

Industrial pumps were used to flood the rice fields; the runoff would flood some of the smaller holding areas. The Pump, a swimming hole located on St. Mary Street, was a popular place in the summer for neighborhood children. (Courtesy of Claudette Prejean LeBlanc.)

Lloyd Stutes's daughter Mary rides her bike on Cameron Street in front of the Scott Hardware and Furniture Store owned by her uncle Turney Stutes. (Courtesy of Mary Stutes.)

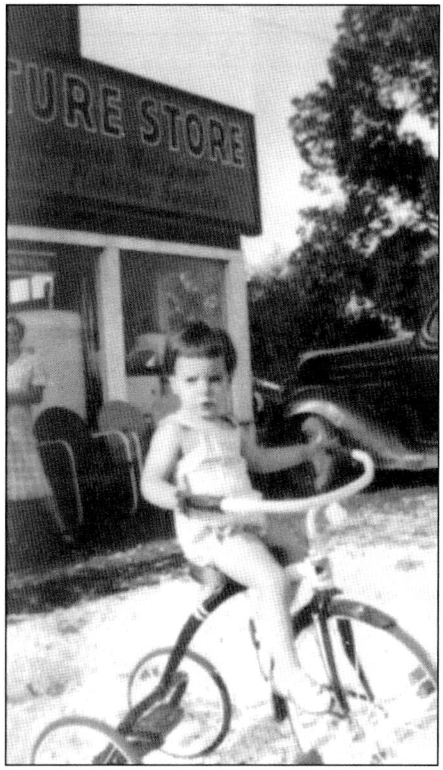


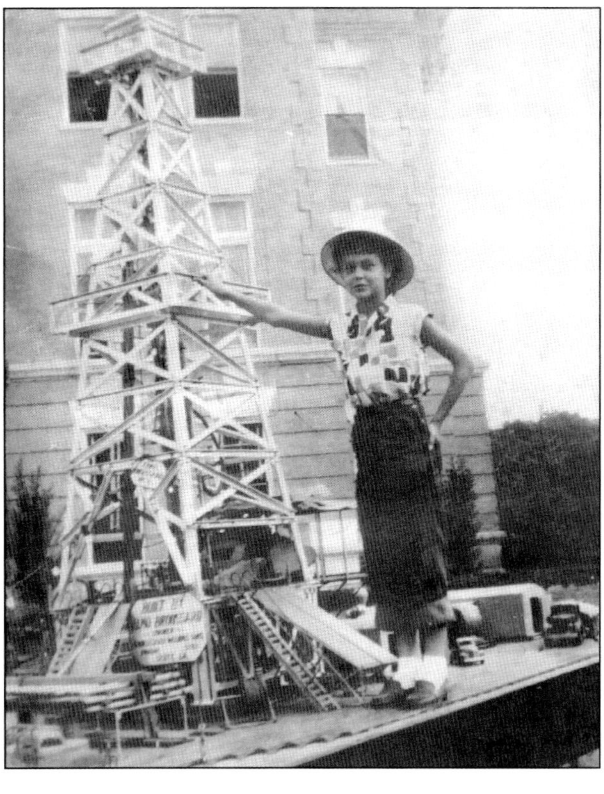

Judith Ann Broussard Leger stands near a working model of a drilling rig at the oil parade in Franklin, Louisiana. The rig was built by her father, Elmo Broussard Sr., and her brother Elmo Jr., who was 14 years old at the time. The drilling rig took three years to build and drilled a 70-foot-deep test well at the Louisiana Gulf Coast Exposition in Lafayette, Louisiana. (Courtesy of Judith Ann Broussard Leger.)

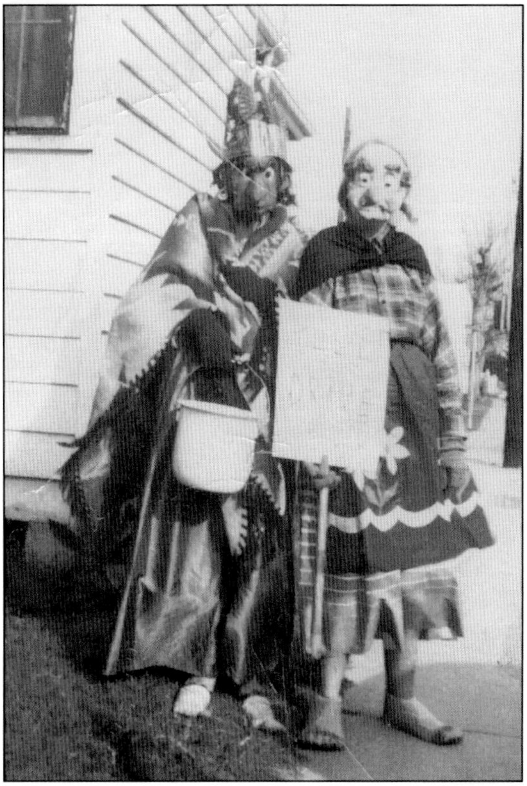

Mardi Gras is a time for dressing up, wearing masks, and having fun before the beginning of Lent. According to their sign, Pearl Guidroz Pellessier and Gertie ? held a relief drive and used a chamber pot for their collections. (Courtesy of Becca Begnaud.)

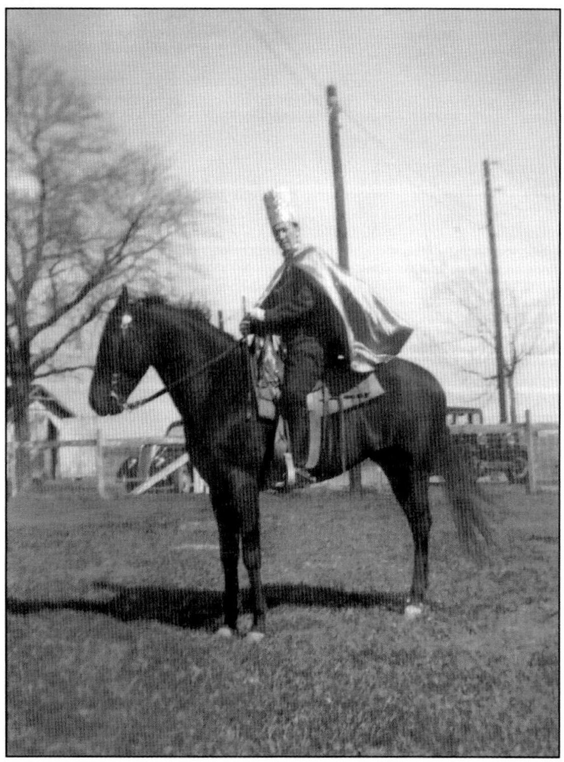

Letha Martin Begnaud is dressed to lead the Scott Mardi Gras parade in the 1930s. An avid and accomplished horsewoman, Letha never owned a horse; however, many of her friends were always willing to loan her their horses for exercise or riding in a parade. (Courtesy of Cassie Richard Blair.)

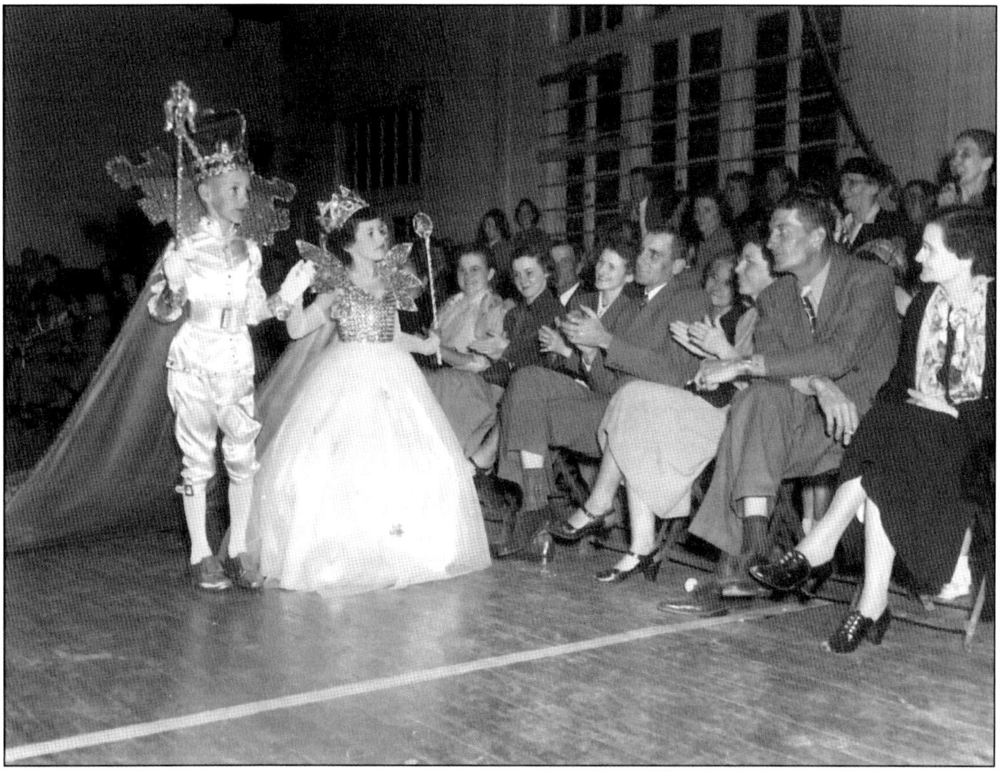

Pageantry is displayed during this 1950s Scott Children's Krewe Mardi Gras celebration. King James "J.J." Sonnier (left) and Queen Anna Marie Boudreaux greet their "loyal subjects" gathered for the revelry. (Courtesy of Deanna and J.J. Sonnier.)

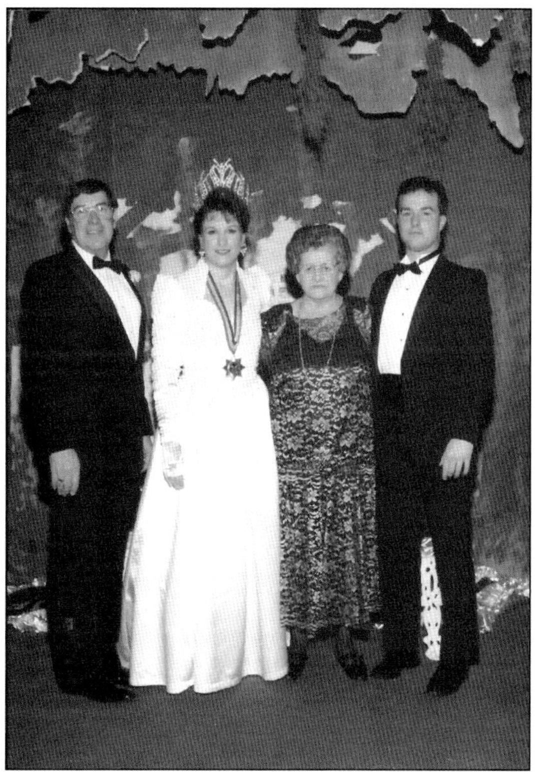

Montez Boudreaux, the second queen of the Krewe of Olympus, poses with her family. From left to right are her father Murphy Boudreaux, Montez, her grandmother Bertha LeBlanc Domingue, and her brother Doyle Boudreaux. (Courtesy of Murphy Boudreaux.)

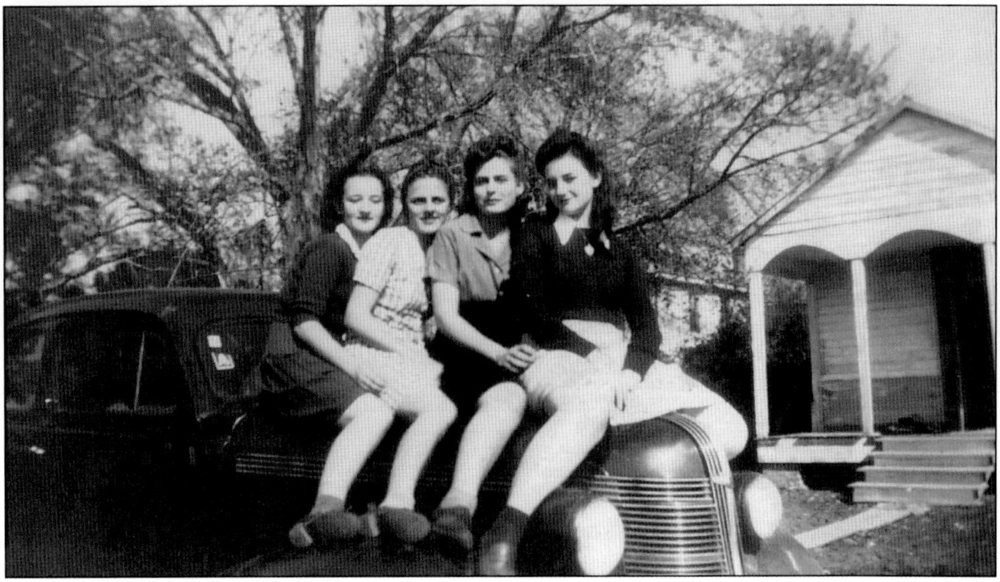

Posing for the camera in the 1940s are, from left to right, Polly Mouton Prejean Lacy, Fannie Martin Morvant, Rita Boudreaux, and Ellen Cecile Campbell Resweber. (Courtesy of Arlene Breaux.)

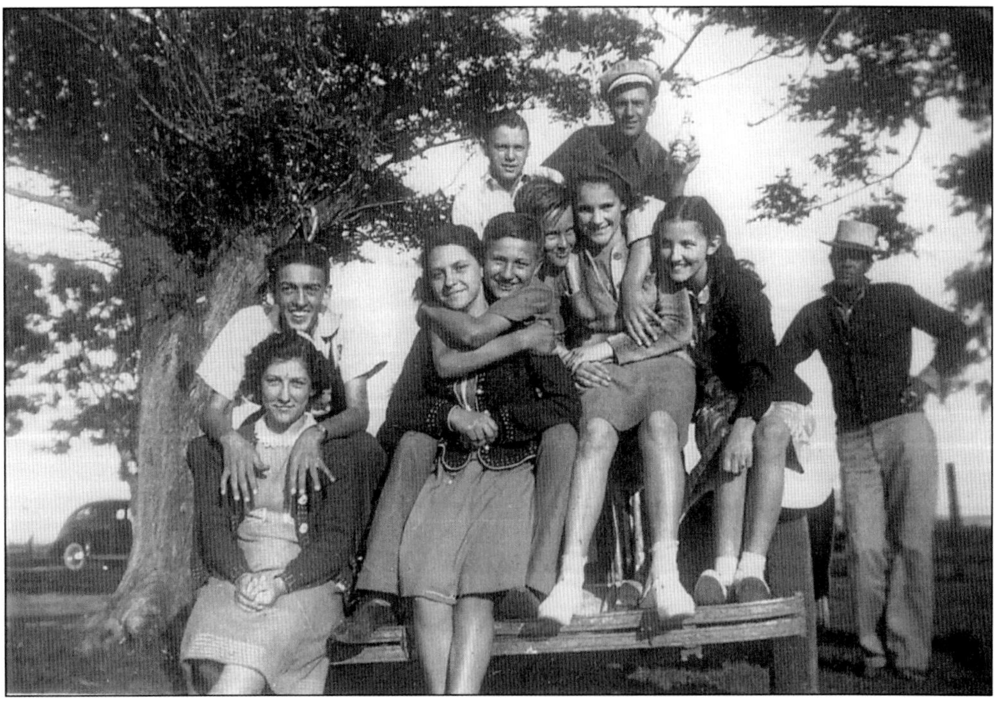

Scott youths sitting atop Martin Begnaud's Ford are, from left to right, (first row) Mollie K. LaLonde, Audrey K. Broussard, Polly Domingue Hebert, and Georgette Knight; (second row) Paul H. Begnaud, Roy Broussard, Frances Sonnier; (third row) Kirby Knight and Aaron Domingue. The man standing on the far right is unidentified. (Courtesy of Pearl Marie Guidry.)

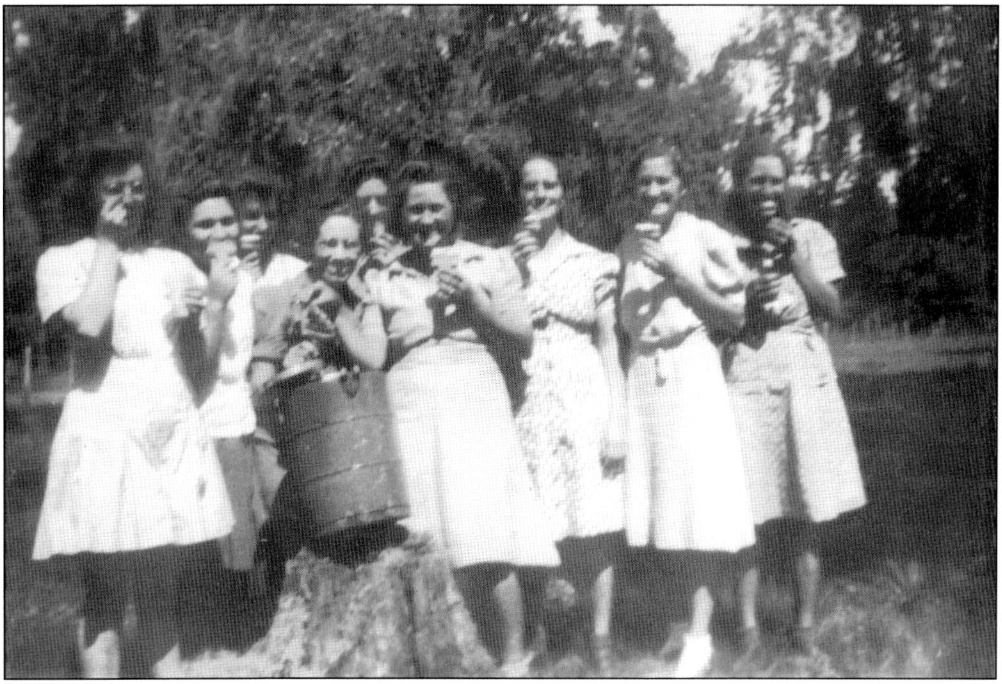

Tasting the first homemade ice cream of the summer are, from left to right, (first row) Nellie Broussard, Luce Cormier, Eva Sonnier, Bertha Sonnier, Iris Sonnier, Agnes Sonnier, and Clothilde Sonnier; (second row) Dorothy Tillman and Loretta Guillot. (Courtesy of Louise Sonnier.)

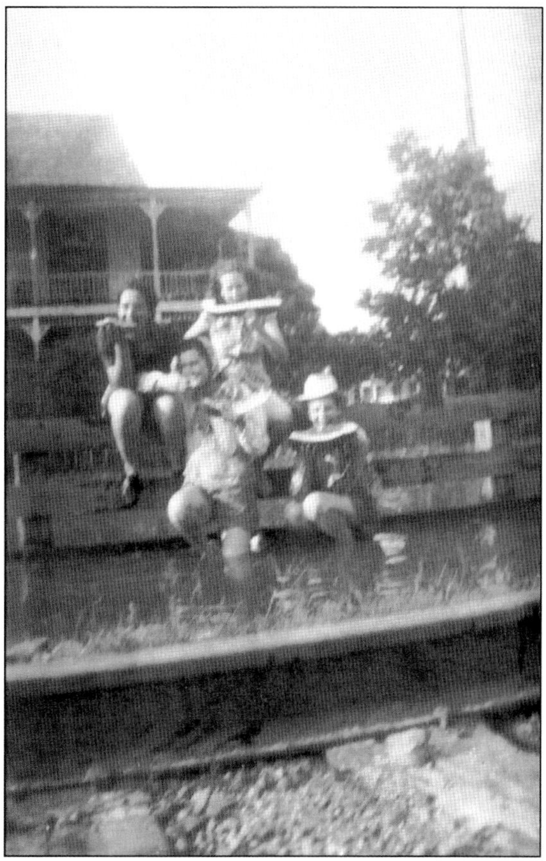

Eating watermelons by the railroad tracks was a great way to cool off on a hot summer day. On the fence by Leon Bernard's house are, from left to right, (first row) Saffer Arceneaux and unidentified; (second row) unidentified and Ruth Begnaud. (Courtesy of Cassie Richard Blair.)

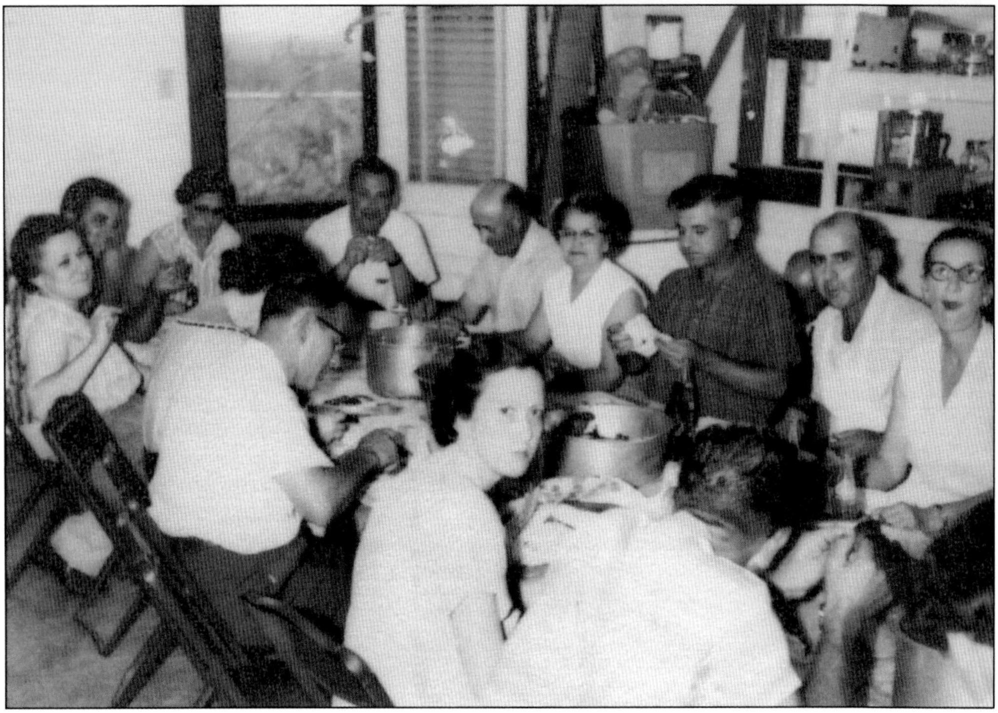

During the early spring months, Scott residents would spread newspapers on the table, open cold beers, and spend an evening peeling and eating boiled crawfish. Around the table are, from left to right, (first row, in foreground) Laura Begnaud, Regina Arceneaux, Henry Begnaud, Marie Therese Begnaud, and Mayo Begnaud; (second row) Floyd Begnaud, Gene Provost, John Gueno, Martin Begnaud, Monique Begnaud, Murphy Broussard, Toby Begnaud, and Letha Begnaud, who stop to pose for the camera while engaging in this Scott tradition. (Courtesy of Becca Begnaud.)

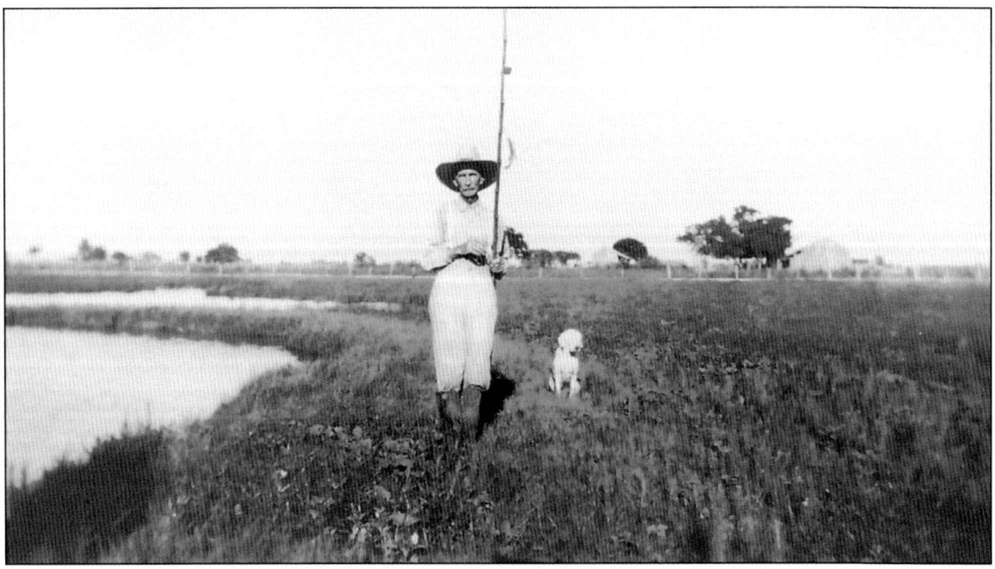

To help feed his 14 children, John B. Sonnier would take his pole and find a place to fish. When neighbors asked about his favorite fishing spot, he would point off in the distance and reply, "*Las bas*," meaning "over there" in French. (Courtesy of Anne Bourgeois.)

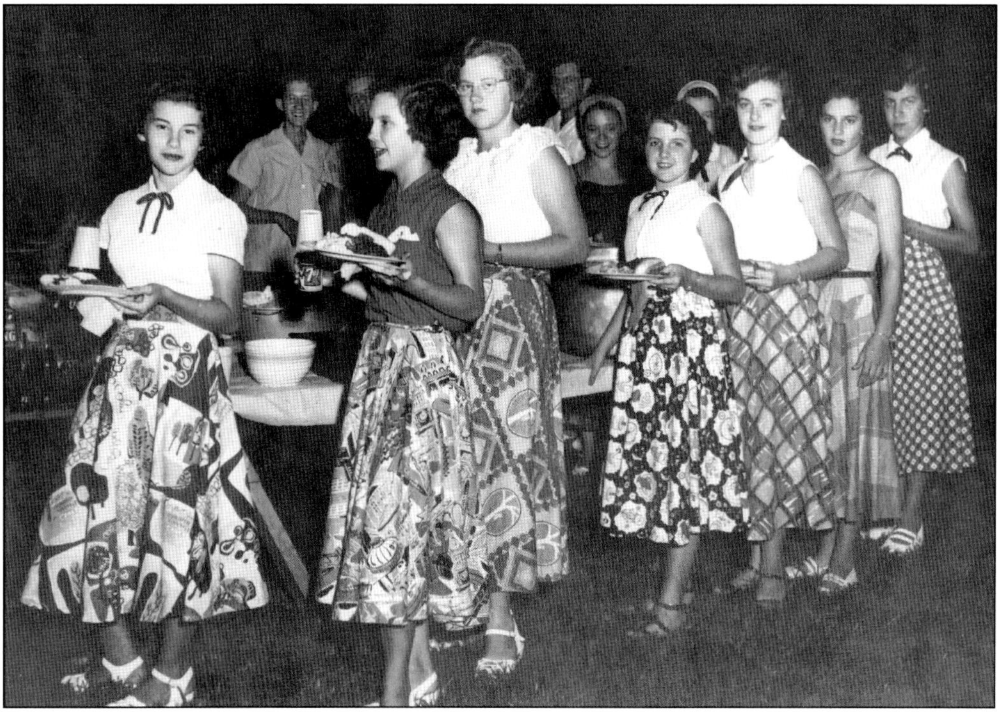

This birthday party was the occasion to dress up in colorful summer skirts and eat barbecue and potato salad. The young women in front include, from left to right, Betty Labauve, Etta Pearl Domingue, Marie Annette Sonnier, Claudette Prejean, Mona Mire, Elaine Bollich, and Marie Falcon. (Courtesy of Claudette Prejean LeBlanc.)

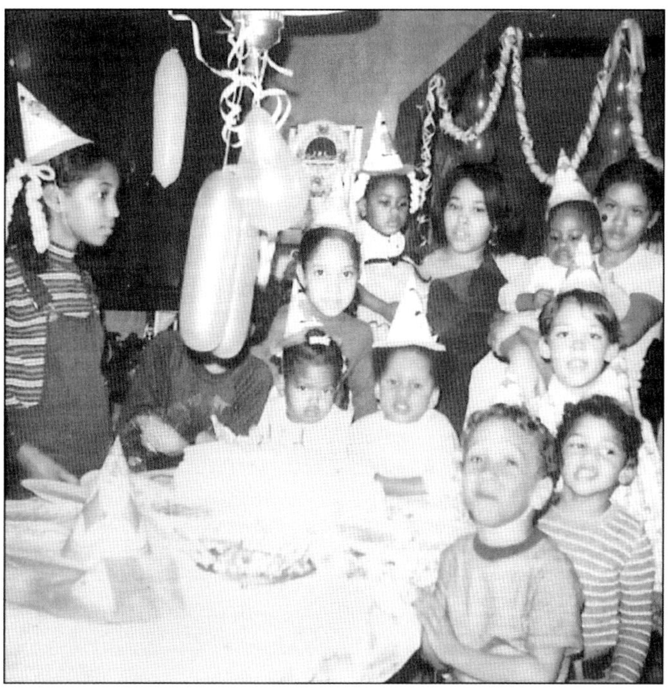

Paper hats, balloons, streamers, and a cake were part of this birthday celebration for the boy hidden by balloons. Among the participants are, on the far right from front to back, Patrick Magee, Harlem Shay, Greg Hammer, and Leana Mire holding an unidentified baby. (Courtesy of Leana Miller.)

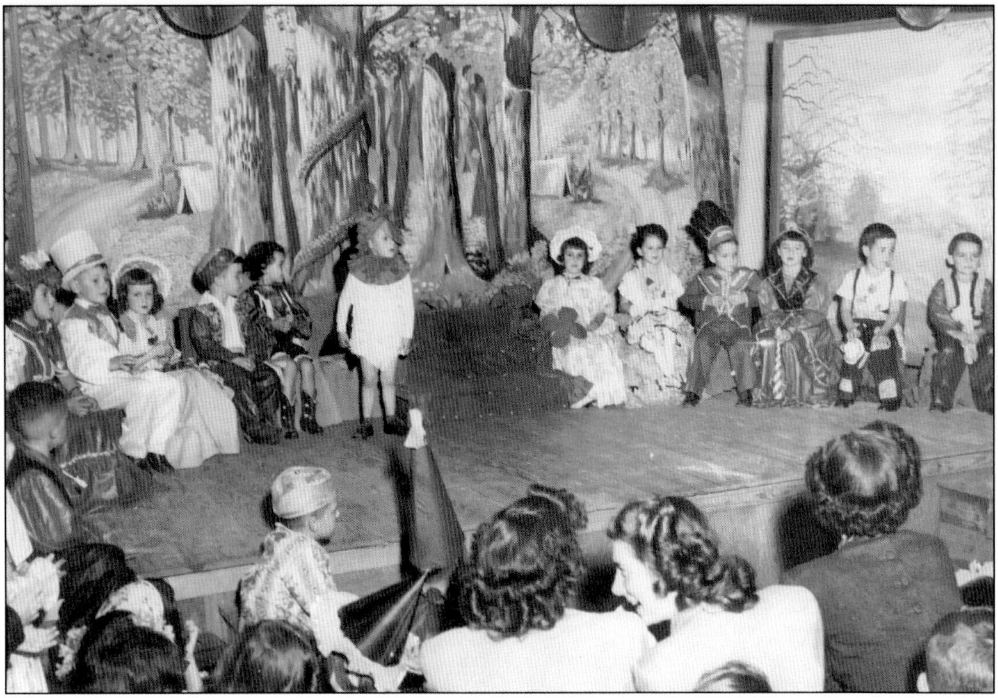

School plays were an important activity in Scott. This Scott Elementary play in the early 1950s features students reciting nursery rhymes or stories. On stage wearing costumes to represent their characters are, from left to right, Judy Broussard, George Broussard, Paula Lagneaux, Johnny Perrin, Patsy Sonnier, Jude Arceneaux, Lucille Sonnier, Carol Martinez, Reggie Bollich, Cathy Begnaud, Sammy Ardoin, and Jessie Domingue. (Courtesy of Becca Begnaud.)

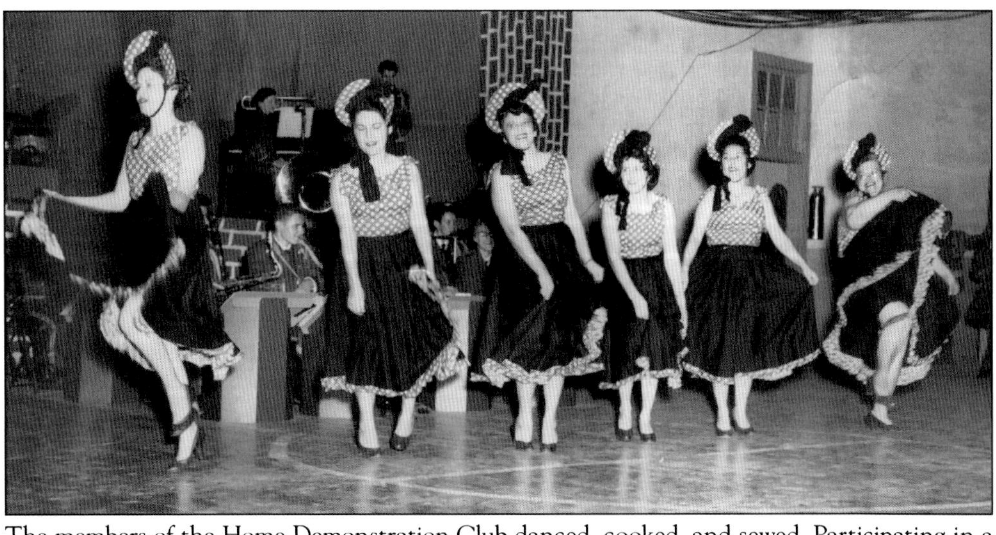

The members of the Home Demonstration Club danced, cooked, and sewed. Participating in a rousing can-can in 1953 are, from left to right, Juanita Braquet Richard, Audrey Knight Broussard, Polly Boudreaux Richard, Mathilde "Mattie" Sonnier Broussard, Verna Mae Knight Domingue, and Lena Doucet Lenstrum. (Courtesy of Marguerite Fontenot.)

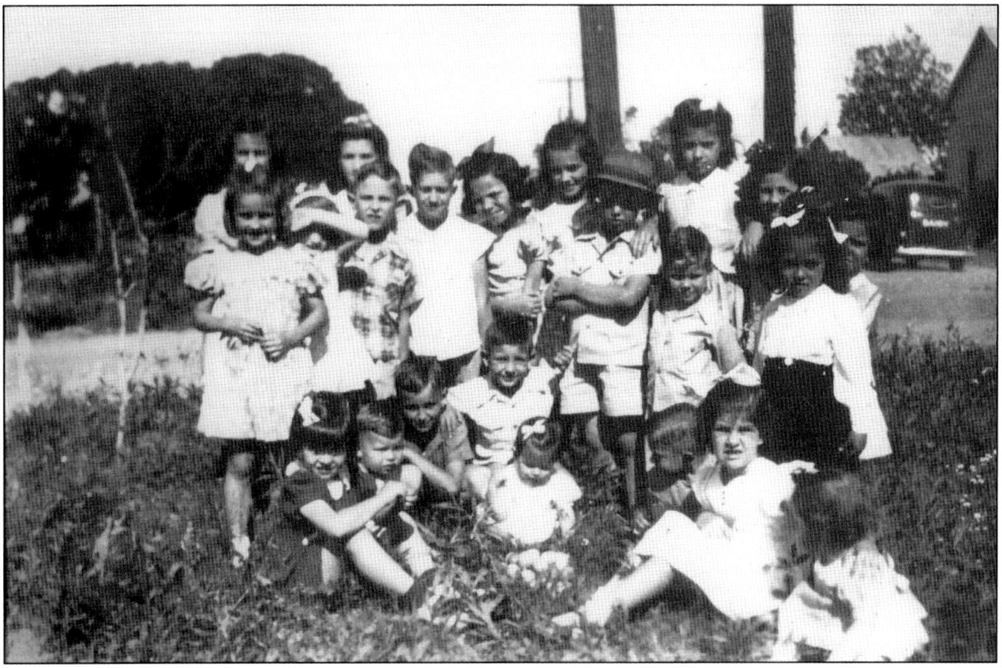

Among those celebrating at this birthday party in the early 1940s are Charles Oran Abdella, Rose Marie Prejean, Ned Boudreaux, and Pearl Marie Provost. Several neighborhood children gathered for the group photograph. (Courtesy of Pearl Provost Guidry.)

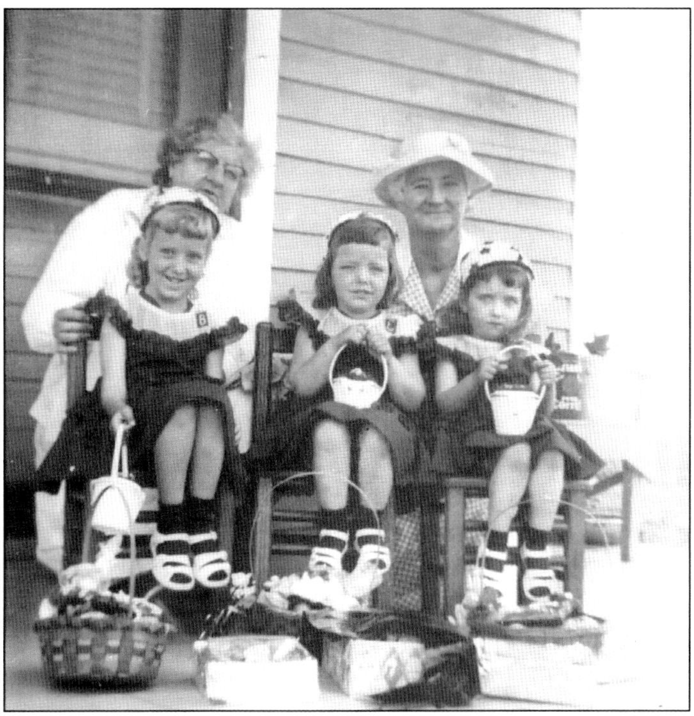

Easter Sunday is a time to get together with family. In this 1956 photograph, three little girls pose with their grandmothers. The dresses were made by the girls' mother, Lorris Carriere, who said she had to put initials on all of their clothes to be able to tell them apart because they were so close in size. From left to right are (first row) Barbara Carriere, Earlene Carriere, and Judy Carriere; (second row) Celemaan Janice Carriere and Marie Sarah Guidry. (Courtesy of Earlene Carriere.)

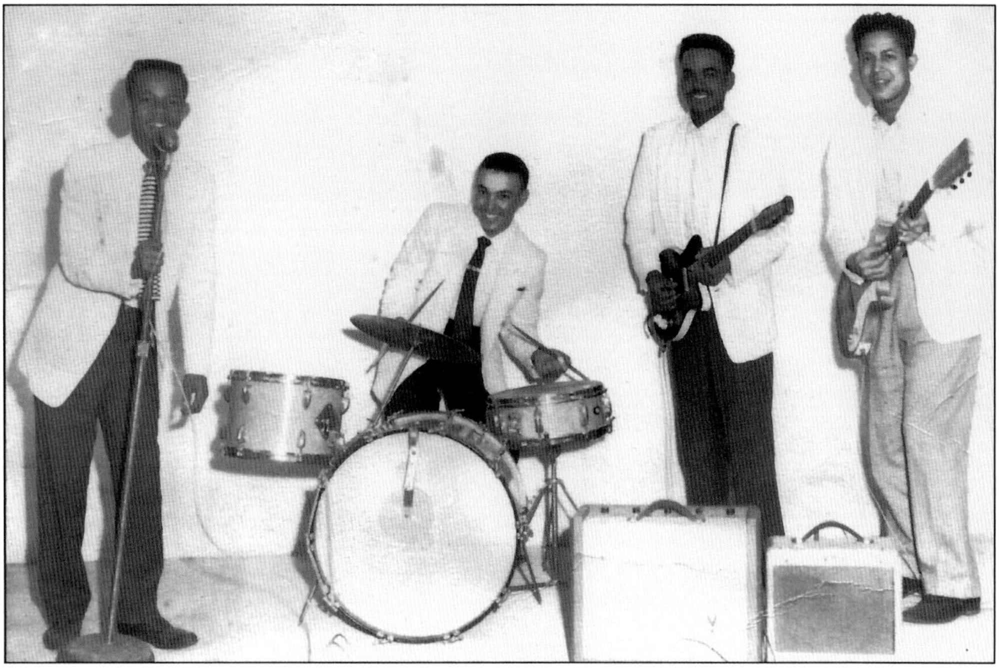

From left to right, emcee and singer Norris Randall, drummer Dennis Bernard, and guitarists Ferris Dugas and Richard Morrison entertained crowds in the late 1950s and early 1960s with jazz and rock and roll. Miss Loom's dance hall on Delhomme Avenue was one of the spots they frequented. (Courtesy of Purvis Morrison.)

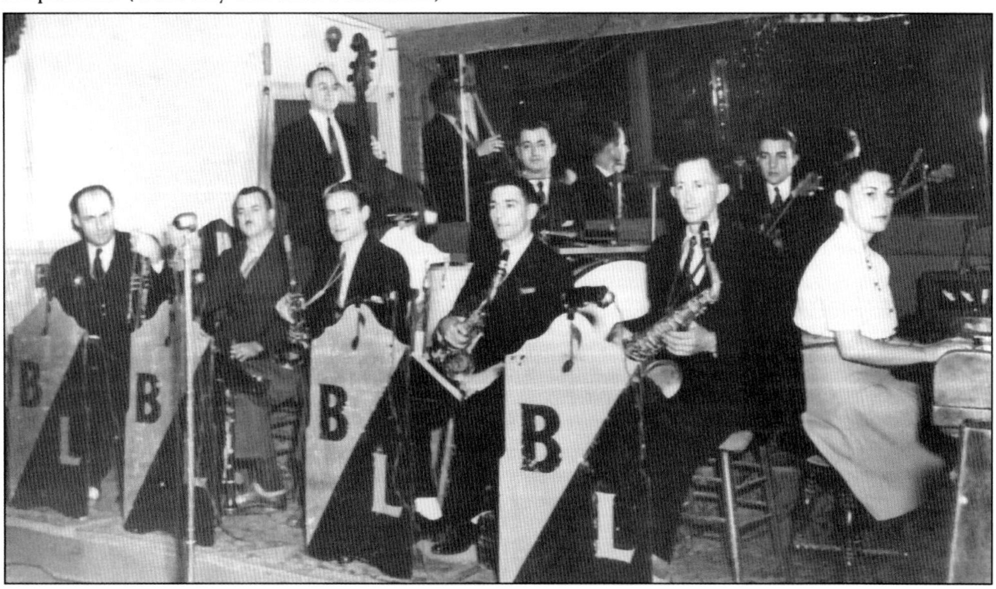


The Bill Landry Orchestra performed at Toby's Oak Grove, a nightclub at "Four Corners" between Scott and Lafayette where Cameron Street and University Avenue now meet. In this 1936 photograph are, from left to right, (first row) Leon "Bill" Landry, Ernest "Bruce" Broussard, Johnnie Minor, Aaron Domingue, and Frank Mier; (second row) Noah Hebert, Lucien Landry, and Hayward "Dub" Domingue. Verna Mae Knight Domingue accompanies the orchestra on the piano. (Courtesy of Lafayette Parish Clerk of Court.)

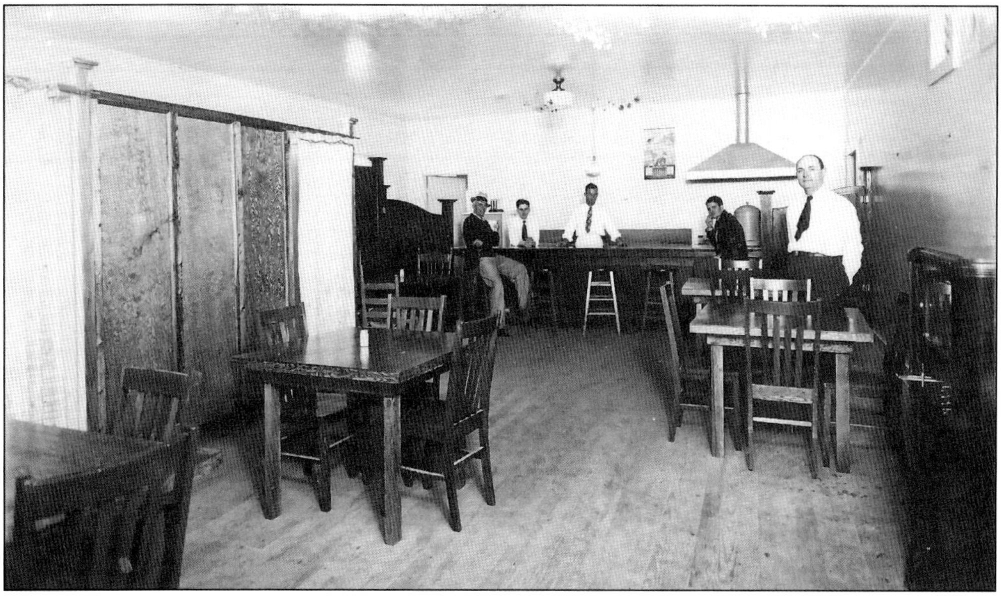

From left to right, two unidentified men, Louis Provost, Clebe "Snook" Begnaud, and J. Orrin Brandt gather at Brandt's Bar before business begins. On this "family side" of the bar, hot dogs and hamburgers were cooked, served, or picked up to go; the family side was separate from the bar serving alcohol. A sign above a swinging door reminded patrons that no minors were allowed on the "bar side." (Courtesy of Caroline Adams.)

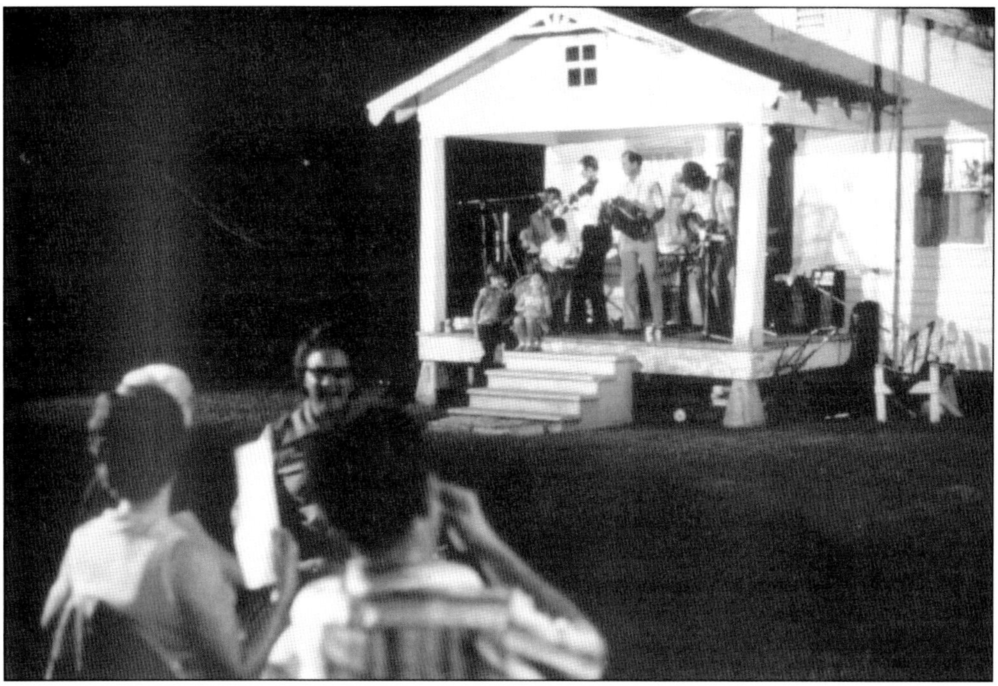

Music was a way of life at many family gatherings in southern Louisiana. Families would get together for a visit or a meal and eventually musical instruments appeared, lawn chairs were taken out, and a jam session would begin. This scene on the Montoucet family porch was typical in Scott. (Courtesy of Terry Montoucet.)

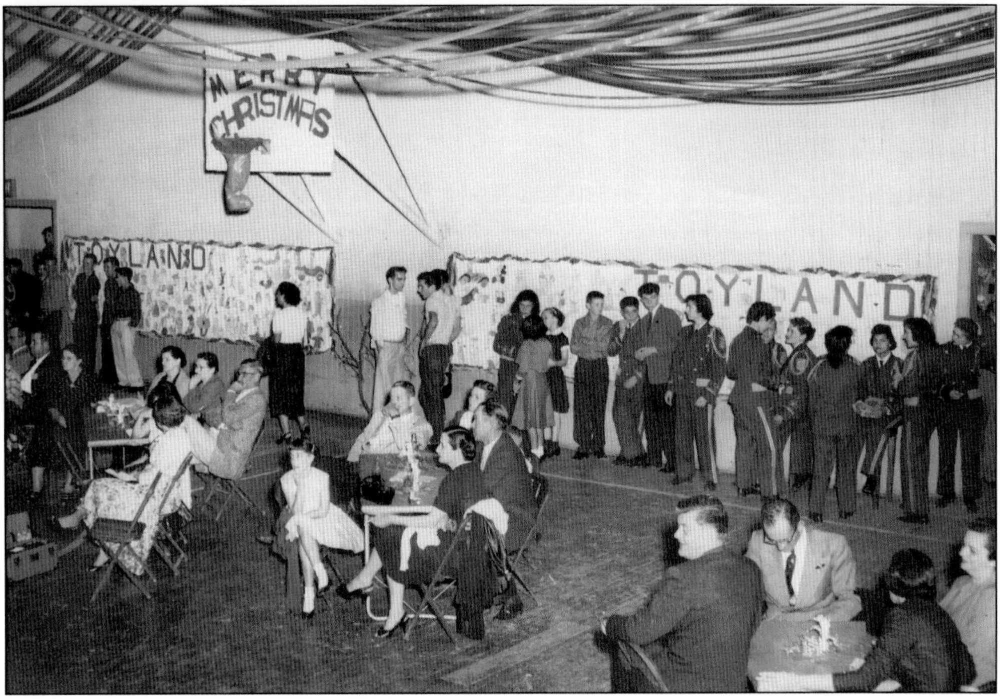


This Scott High School Christmas party in 1956 was a family affair. Young and old have gathered to celebrate the Christmas spirit and listen to the Scott band perform. In the middle of the far left table are Anna Mae Breaux and Roy Broussard, facing left. At the table in the lower right with their backs to the camera are Charles Delana and his wife, Leana. (Courtesy Audrey Breaux Young.)

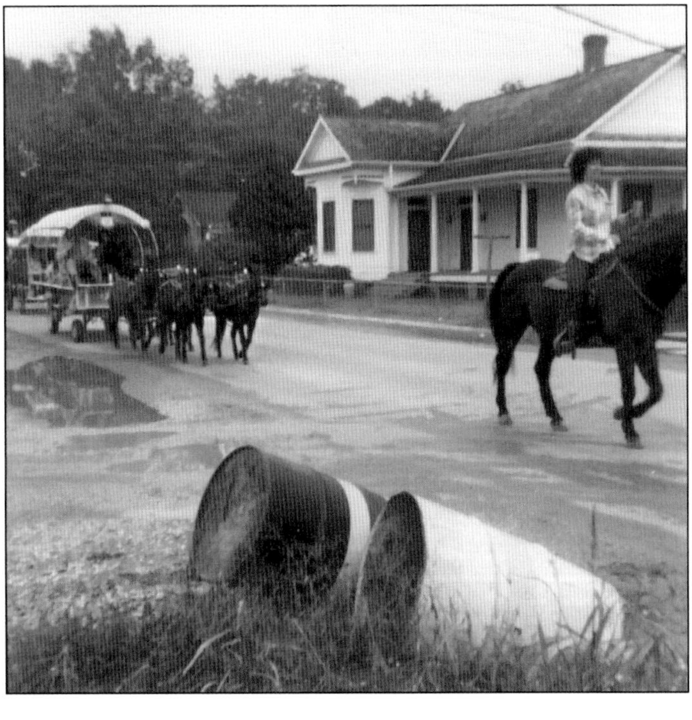

Horseback riders and horse-drawn carriages were part of autumn trail rides through Scott. Music, food, and drink were part of the event. This ride is passing in front of Floyd Sonnier's studio and gallery. (Courtesy of Earline Carriere.)

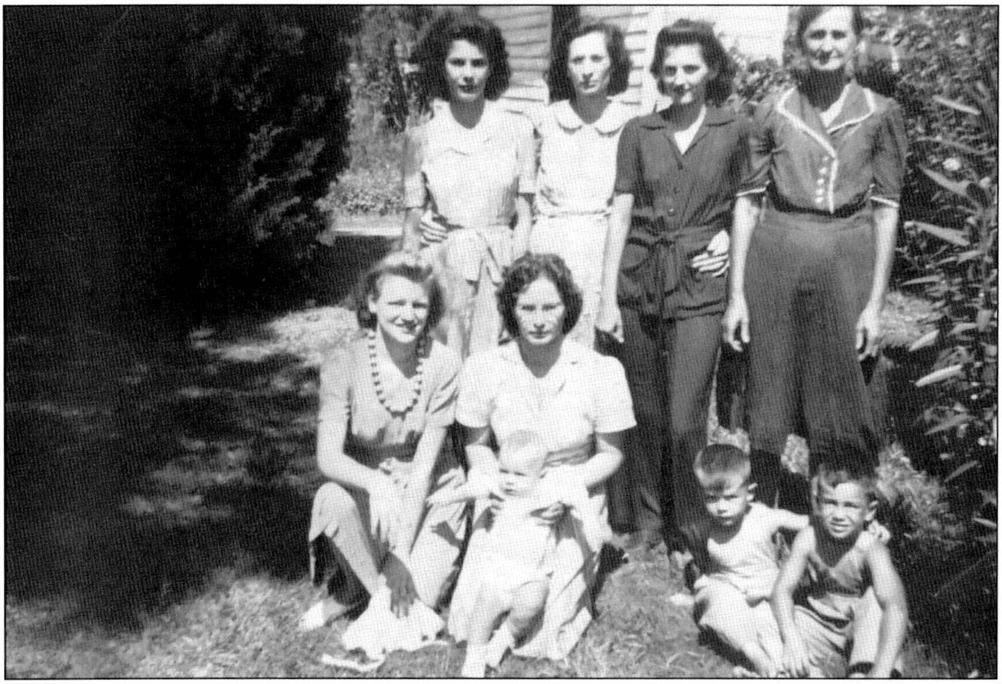

Before air-conditioning, neighbors would visit on front porches and backyards. Pictured here are, from left to right, (first row, children sitting on the ground) Marlene Credeur, Lee Breaux, and Ronald Breaux; (second row) Juanita Braquet Richard and Corita Cormier Credeur; (third row) Lucille Cormier, Marie Hebert Cormier, Pearl Blanchard Lormand, and Monya Blanchard. (Courtesy of Audrey Breaux Young.)

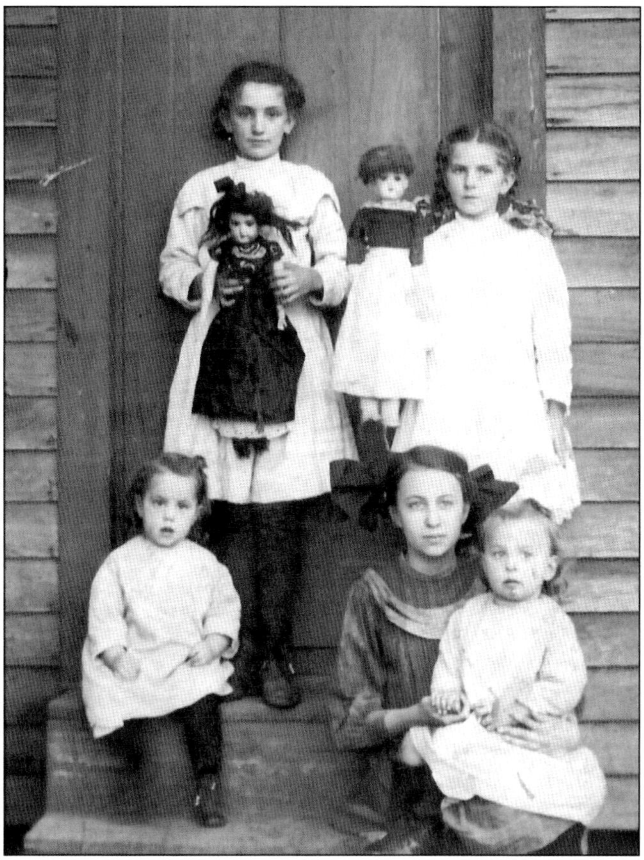

Girls played with dolls and often watched over younger brothers and sisters in the early 20th century. Here, seated on the right, Editha Bourque poses with her sister Milta (left) and brother Milton; standing are two unidentified girls with their china dolls in this c. 1911 photograph. (Courtesy of Macqueline Thibeaux.)

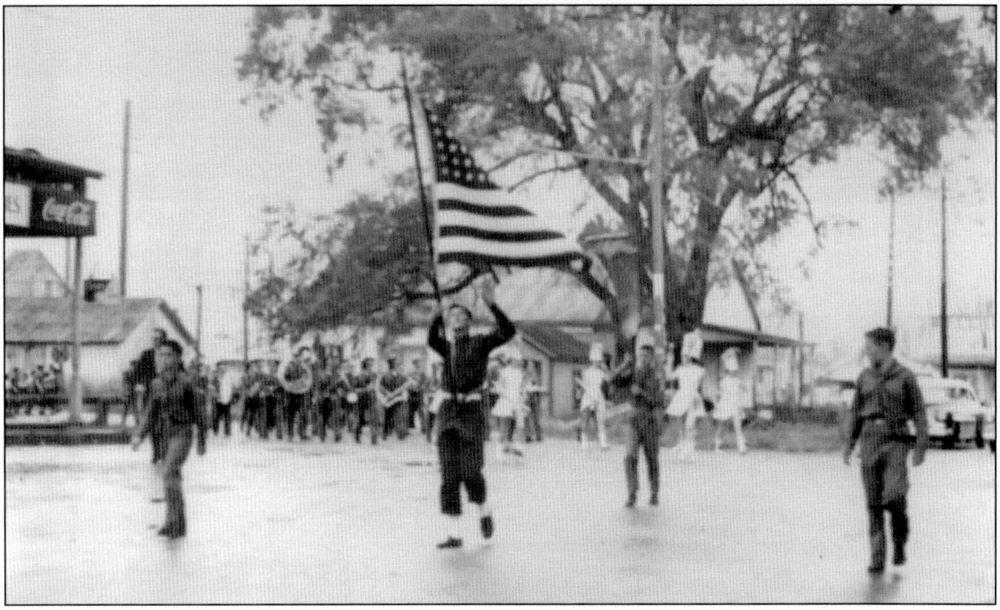

At the corner of Alfred and St. Mary Streets, Boy Scouts and the band lead the 1956 parade in celebration of the first fire truck purchased by the Scott Volunteer Fire Department. Visible in the background are the Scott Depot (left) and the porch of the Judice store. The feed store under the tree was converted into the Coffee Depot in 2011. The tree was registered in the Live Oak Society as the Laughlin Oak in 2012. (Courtesy of Louise Sonnier.)

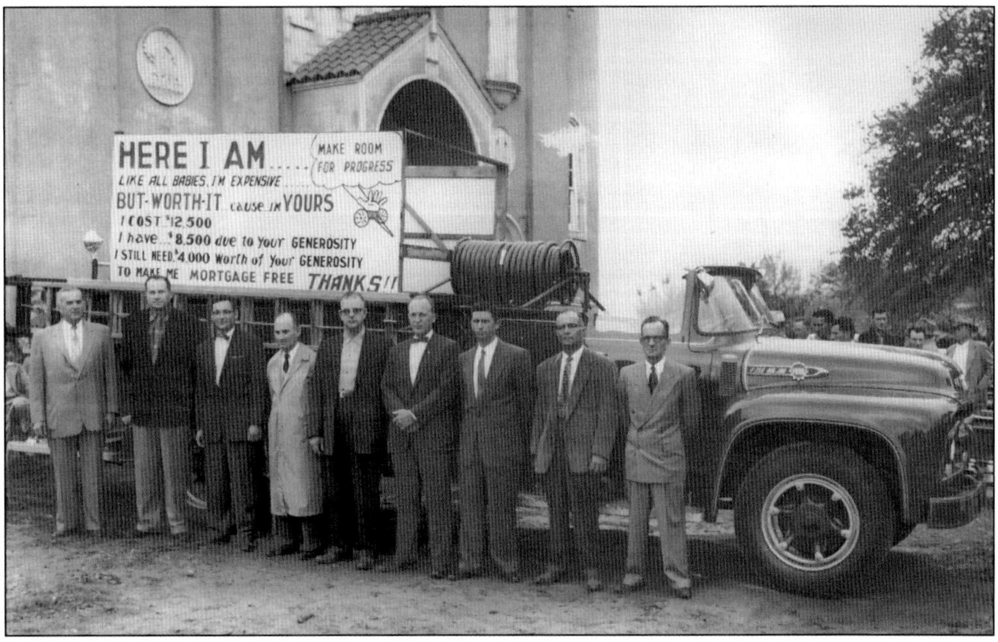


From left to right, Howard Dugas, Andrus Martinez, Johnny Comeaux, Nathan Mouton, Louis Prejean, Warren "Buddy" Landry, J.B. Richard, Voorhies Raggio, and Mayo Begnaud present the goals for Scott's latest fire truck, a $12,500 investment. The photograph was taken to commemorate the community's $8,500 donation toward the total cost. Dugas and Martinez organized the volunteer fire department in the 1950s. (Courtesy of Cassie Richard Blair.)

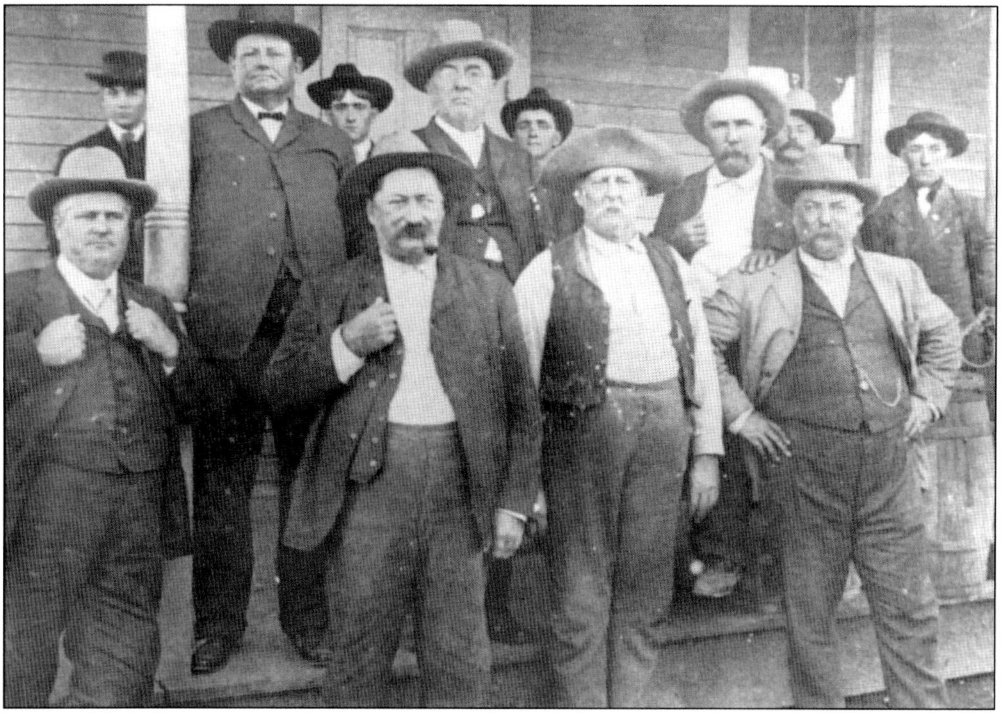

Albert Bourque's Saloon, a "gentlemen's only establishment," was called a general merchandise store during Prohibition. In this 1900s photograph are, from left to right, Adam Bourgeois, G. Chaisson, Cleopha Chaisson, Henry Pellessier, ? Dugas, John "Bebe" Begnaud, unidentified, Oliver A Boudreaux, Alexandre Hernandez, Antoine Hernandez, ? Dugas, and Ancebay Ancelet. Years later, artist Floyd Sonnier celebrated such men in his pictures and used the bar as his gallery. (Courtesy of Polly Boudreaux Richard.)

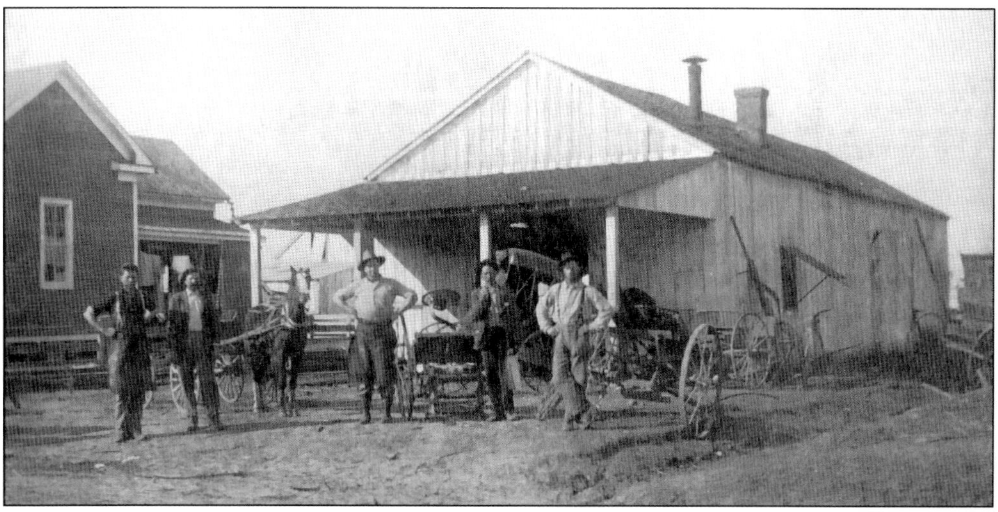

Pictured here among this group are O.Z. Boudreaux (far left) and his brother George Boudreaux (center) at the blacksmith shop on Delhomme Avenue and Scott Street. They purchased the shop after apprenticing with Charles May. The brothers built coffins, repaired buggies, and serviced cars. O.Z., a master of many trades, modified a tool used for oil wells by J.P. Getty to drill water wells for area farmers with filtered water. (Courtesy of Mona Stutes Caldwell.)

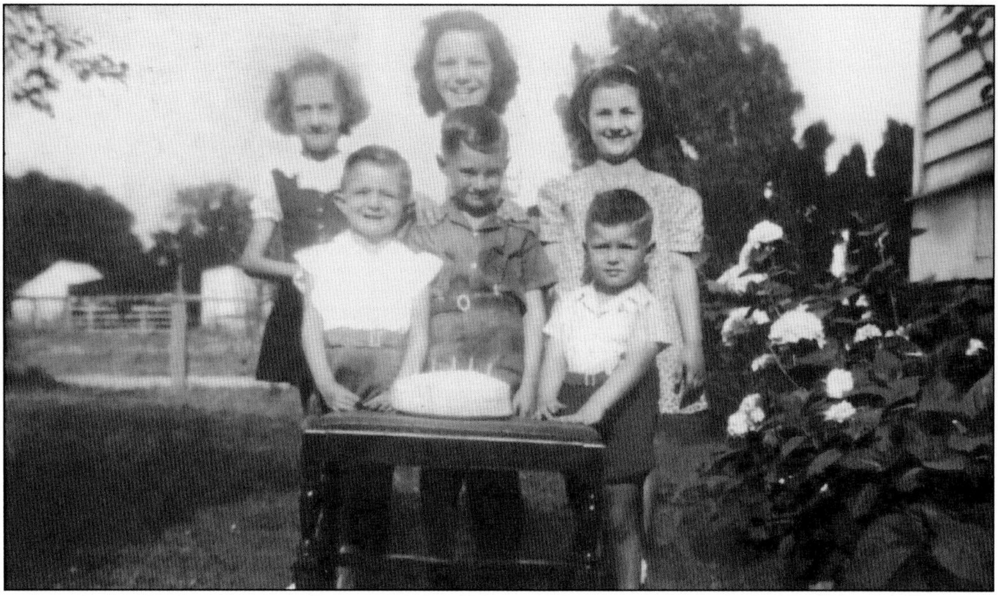

Francis J. Boudreaux celebrated his fourth birthday on May 12, 1943, in the yard of his grandparents Andre and Julie Martin Boudreaux. Ready to sing Happy Birthday and eat cake are, from left to right, (first row) Francis Boudreaux, Kenneth Simon, Bill Arceneaux; (second row) Cecile Jane Broussard, Pearl Marie Provost, and Elia Louise Doucet. (Courtesy of Jeff Laughlin.)

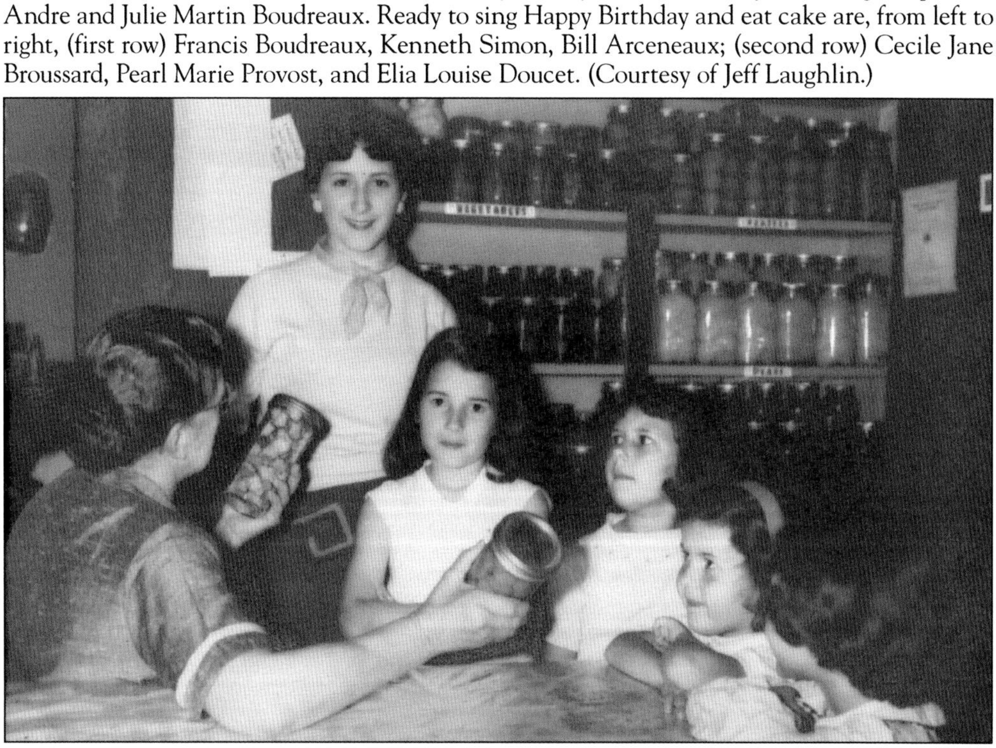

Norinne Pellessier, with her back to the camera, gives her granddaughters pointers on canning. Paying attention to the demonstration are, from left to right, Joyce Arceneaux, Cathy Pellessier, Beth Pellessier, Marty Pellessier, and Becca Begnaud. Crops grown on the Pellessier farm were preserved for the table until the next year's harvest. Canning, a means of preserving food, was very important before refrigeration was available. Some people still can foods today. (Courtesy of Becca Begnaud.)

## *Six*

# PEOPLE ALONG THE WAY

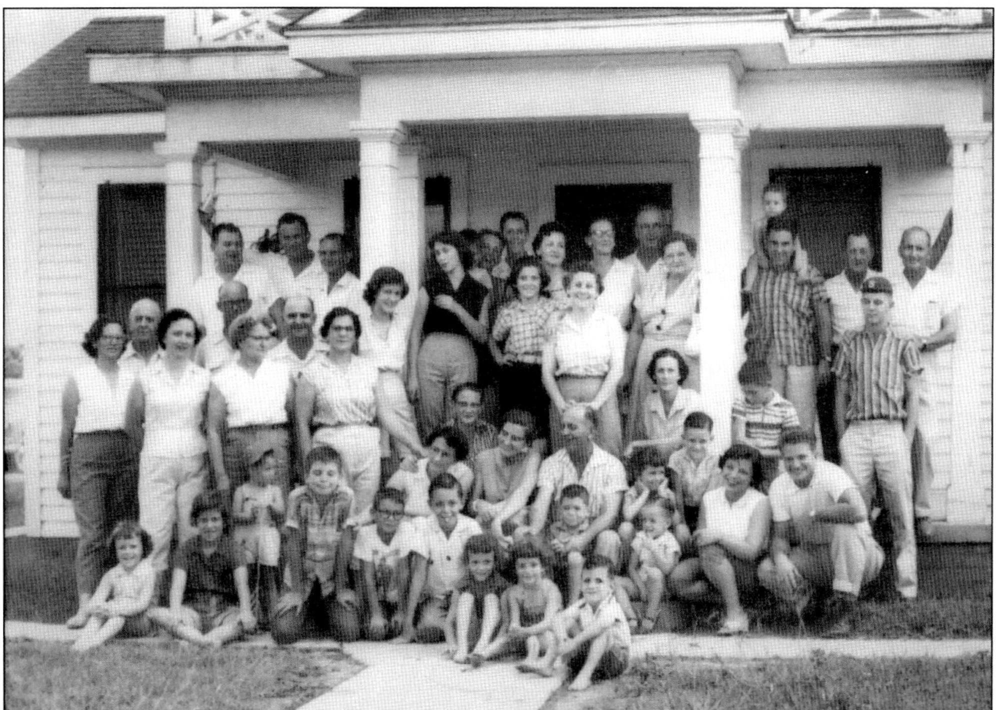

Descendants of Theophile "Sonce" Begnaud, the husband of Pearl Mouton, gather for a reunion at the home of Louis and Georgine B. Provost in the mid-1950s. The photograph includes three generations. The children of Sonce and Pearl include Martin, Mayo, Toby, Raoul, Henry, John, George, Regina, Georgine, Rita, and Carmalite. The image also includes their spouses and children. (Courtesy of Becca Begnaud.)

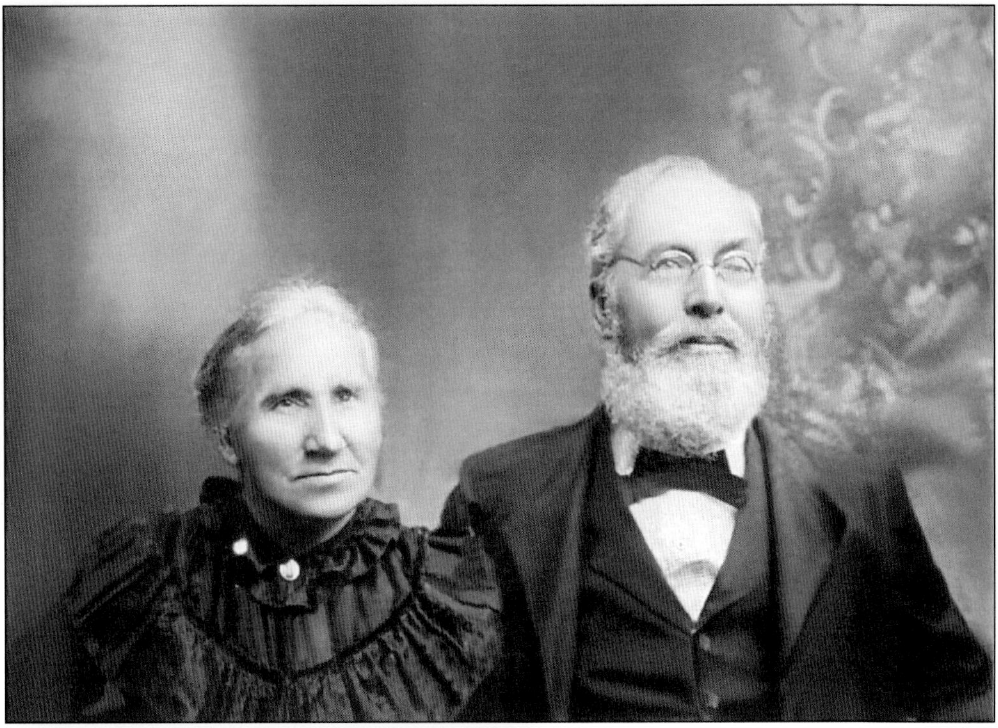

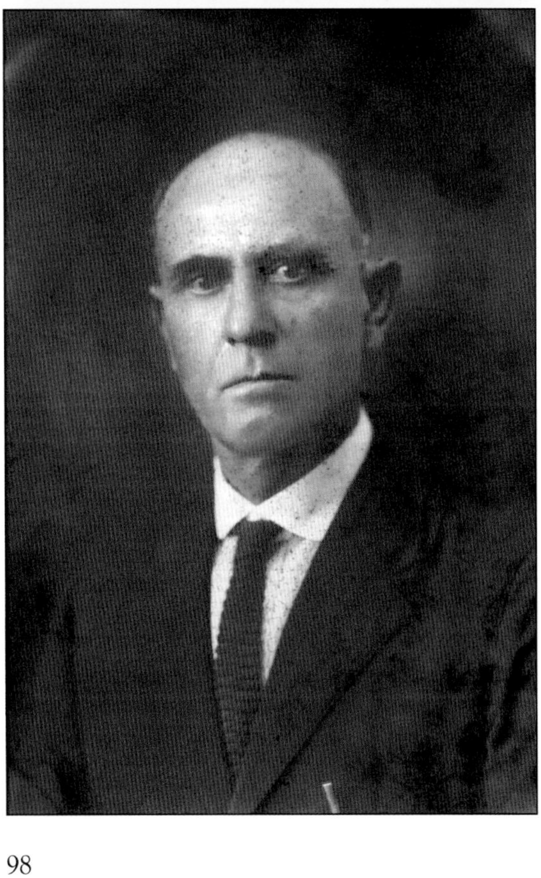

Col. Aurelien Drouzin Boudreaux married Azema Martin on June 8, 1842. They made their home on a plantation encompassing over 500 acres in Lafayette Parish, near Scott, and raised eight children. (Courtesy of Mona Stutes Caldwell.)

Luke LeBlanc was born on November 19, 1869. He married Amelia Martin, and they had three children: one son, George, and two daughters, Marie Louise and Lucille. Luke had a lumber company and is credited with assisting with the development of the sweet potato industry in the Scott area. (Courtesy of Camille Martinez.)

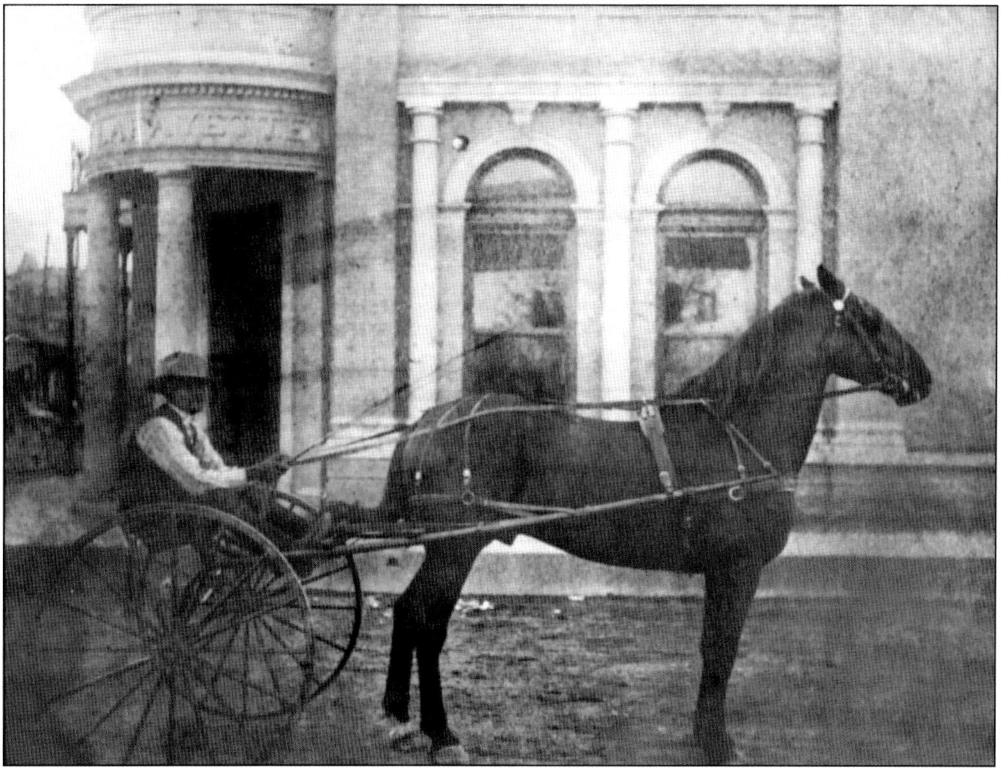

Louis "Deh Deh" Anderson was a very wealthy landowner. He owned approximately one square mile of land along with a store and other businesses. He built a school for African American children of the area. (Courtesy of Viola Mallet.)

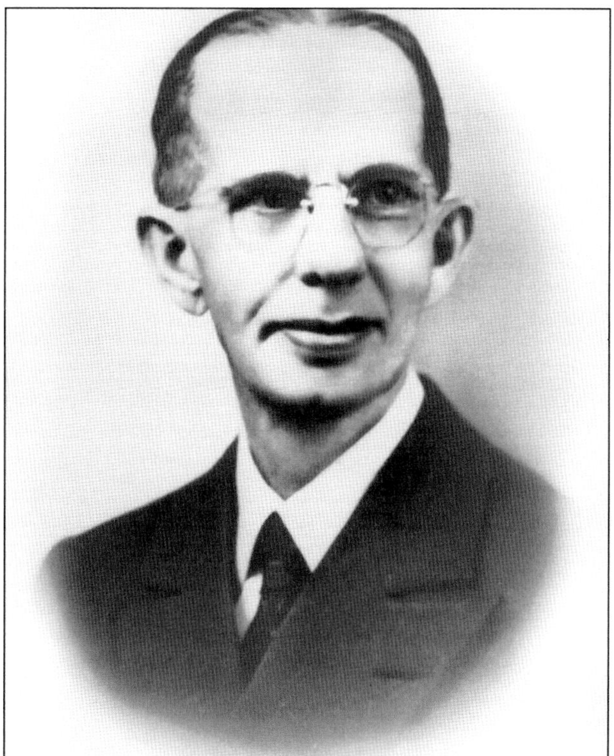

Dr. Louis A. Prejean, the first mayor of Scott, was one of the most successful physicians and surgeons of Lafayette Parish. He answered calls anytime, day or night, with no regard for monetary compensation. The building, which was his office, remains on St. Mary Street. He married Maude Gatz of Baton Rouge on April 22, 1907; she was a schoolteacher. They raised three children: Louis, Oran, and Lucille. (Courtesy of Scott City Hall.)

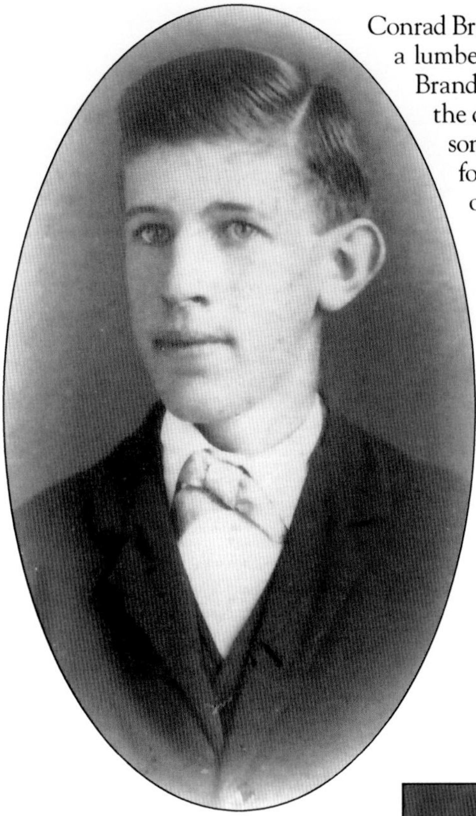

Conrad Brandt married Lelia Bernard. He owned a home and a lumberyard on Delhomme Street. His father, William Brandt, came to Louisiana from Germany and became the clerk of court for the Vermillionville area. Conrad's son Orrin owned Brandt's Bar on Cayret Street, a place for frequent gatherings of local residents. (Courtesy of Carolyn Boudreaux Adams.)

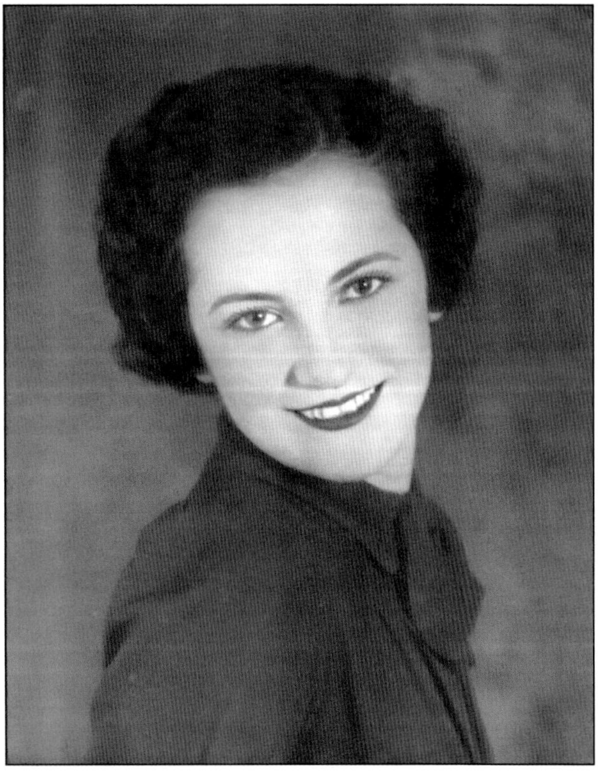

Noelie Martin Provost was a woman whose love of Scott, family, and church could not be contained. She shared her encyclopedic knowledge of Scott as teacher, historian, and genealogist and joined in community parades and plays. She cared for three generations of her family, and as a loyal Cajun Catholic participated in church functions. She was named Catholic Daughter of the Year and served in the Ladies Altar Society. (Courtesy of Annadine Credeur.)

Dr. Lastie John Broussard (1920–2011) was born in Maurice, Louisiana, and resided in Scott. He was a schoolteacher, and in World War II he served as a French and German interpreter. He finished his premed studies after the war and practiced medicine in Scott from 1953 to 1984. He married Rita Royas from Eunice. She was a nurse, and together they had a family of eight children. (Courtesy of Madelyn B. Maragos.)

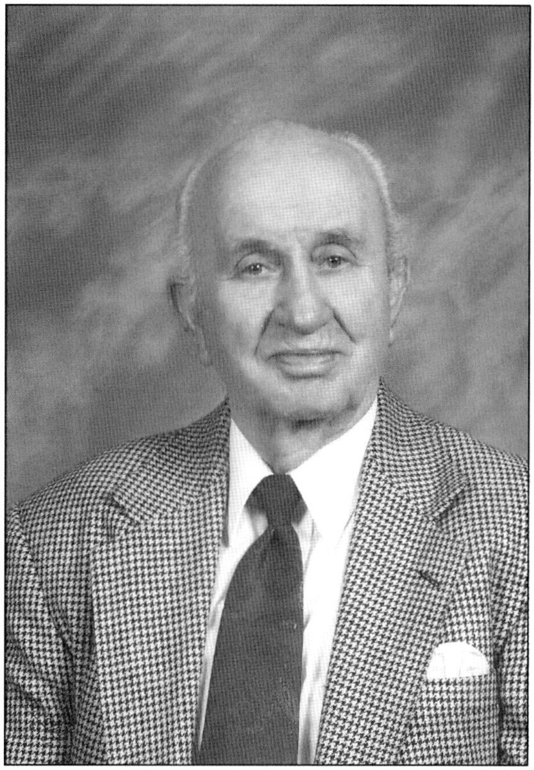

As a child, Floyd Sonnier dreamed of becoming a professional artist. He used bits of charcoal and drew on any available surface. Dedicated to promoting the Acadian culture and heritage and portraying the Cajun lifestyle he loved, he exhibited his art throughout the United States, France, and Canada. The Floyd Sonnier Beau Cajun Gallery is located in the area of old Scott. (Courtesy of the estate of Floyd Sonnier.)

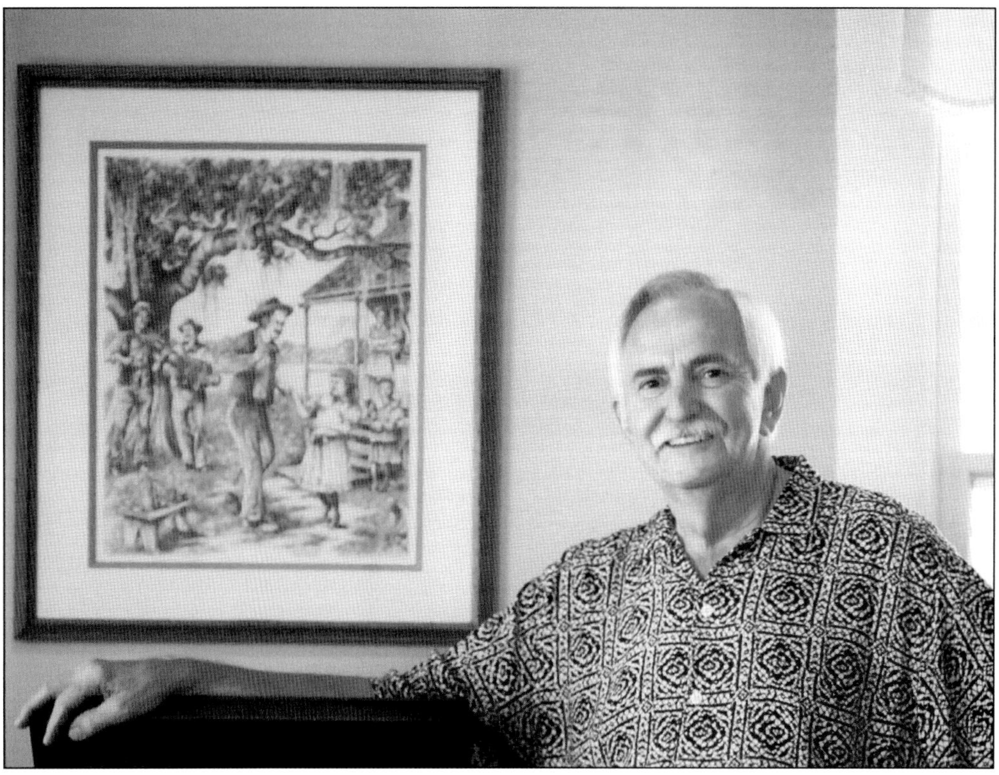

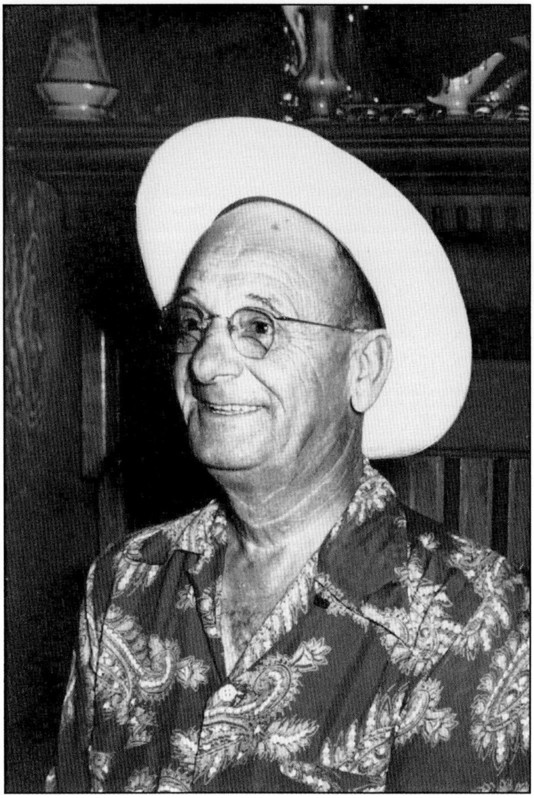

George LeBlanc was married to Celemine Boudreaux. He started the first insurance company in Scott. His father, Luke LeBlanc, owned a lumberyard and a sweet potato kiln. (Courtesy of Claudette Prejean LeBlanc.)

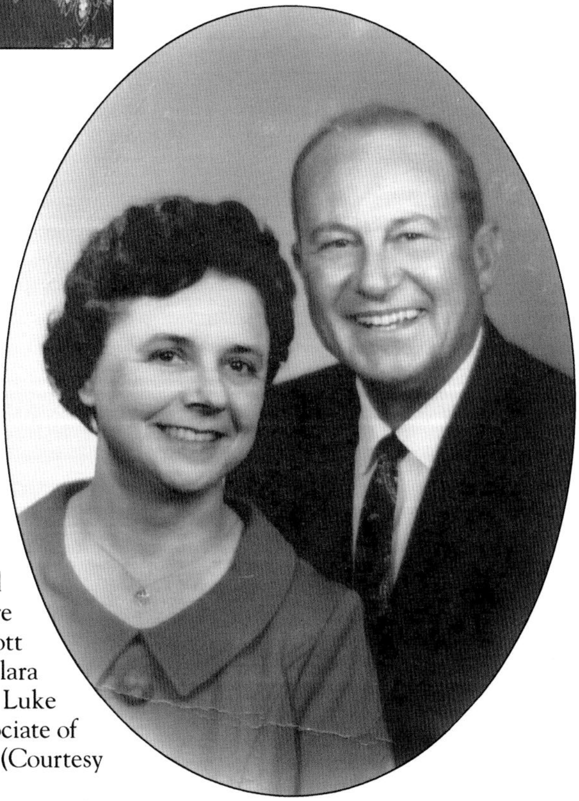

Andrus Martinez worked in a furniture store with Roy Broussard, where Martinez started also an insurance business; he sold insurance for 25 years. He and Howard Dugas began the first Scott Volunteer Fire Department. He also organized the Scott Lions Club with friends. Andrus's wife, Clara Belle, was the office manager for the Luke LeBlanc Lumberyard and a lifetime associate of the Sisters of the Eucharist Covenant. (Courtesy of Camille Martinez.)

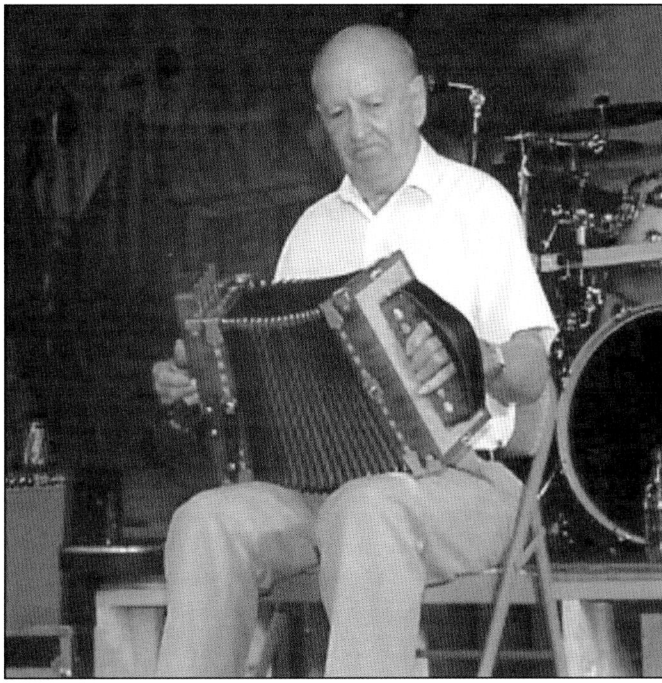

Donald "Mr. Don" Montoucet, an accomplished accordion player, has played around the world, most notably in Russia and at the 1984 World's Fair in Louisiana. He made triangles, called *tit-fers*, a trade learned from his grandfather, a blacksmith from France. He has been featured in the *New York Times* and *Reader's Digest*. His triangles have been sold around the world; there is one in the Smithsonian. (Courtesy of Donald Montoucet.)

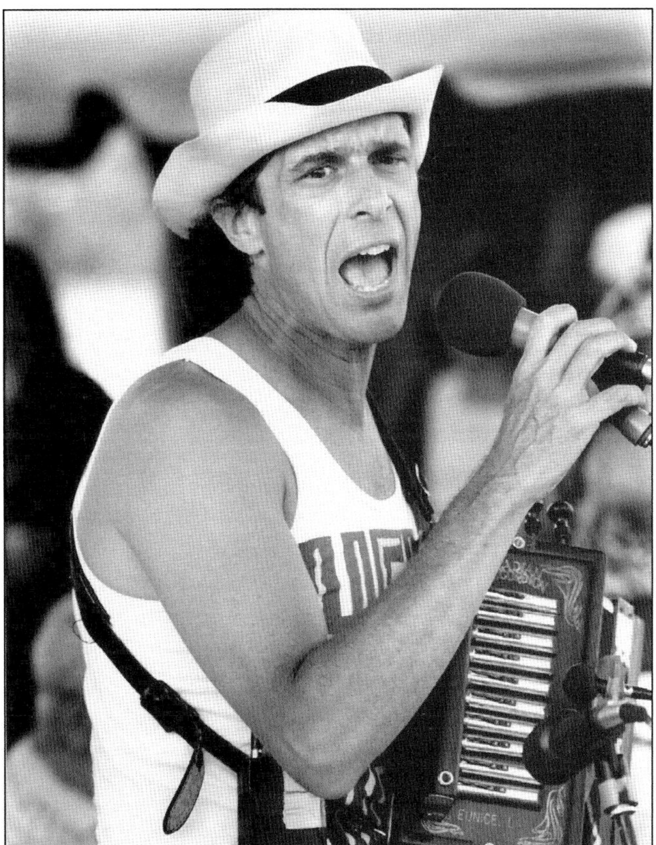

Zachary Richard is a world-renowned musician with 16 albums, including one double platinum and five gold albums. He learned to play the accordion from his neighbor, the late Felix Richard (no relation). He is an environmentalist, cultural activist, poet, and singer-songwriter and has collaborated on several documentaries. Zachary founded Action Cadienne, a volunteer organization to promote the French language and Cadien/Cajun culture. (Courtesy of Stuart Brinin.)

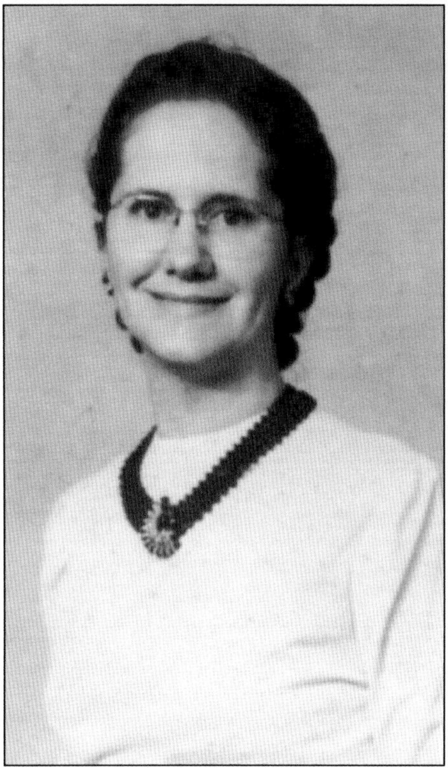

Iris Sonnier Boudreaux was Scott's second librarian, replacing Lucille Arceneaux. The library was located at the old church hall. It later moved into a small room in the home of Andre and Julie Boudreaux. The necklace Iris is wearing was given to her by actress Dorothy L'Amour during a visit with Iris's sister Clothilde Sonnier in New Orleans. (Courtesy of Louise Sonnier.)

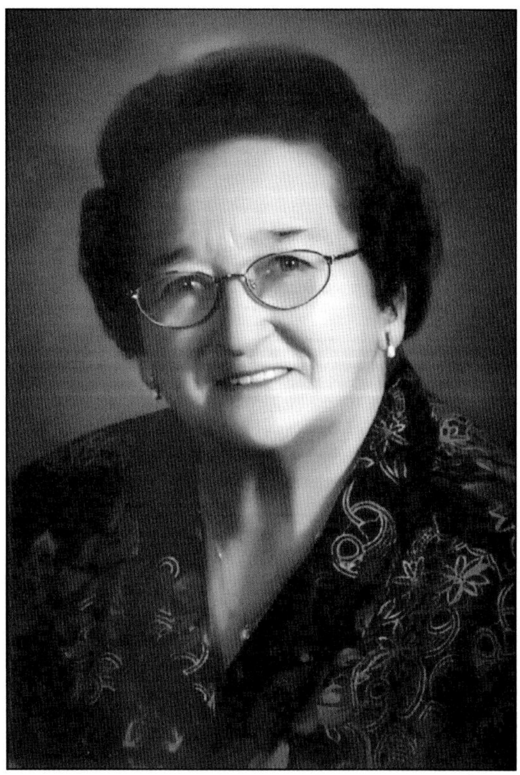

Rita Prejean served as the librarian for the Scott branch of the Lafayette Public Library from 1977 to 2002. She started out as a part-time employee and took over after Iris Sonnier Boudreaux retired. During her 25 years of service, the library moved from a camper that was gutted and fitted with shelves to a room in a house and finally to a library building on Cameron Street. Her service to the community grew during her days as librarian. (Courtesy of Anna Bernard.)

Louis Charles Prejean, the 10th mayor of Scott, worked for the Scott cotton gin, the Bank of Scott, and managed the Lafayette School of Aeronautics during World War II. He opened Lafayette Frozen Foods for public storage of frozen foods. During his term as mayor, the first municipal building was constructed, a proposal for a sewage system was initiated, and a new 50,000-gallon, elevated water tank was constructed. (Courtesy of Claudette Prejean LeBlanc.)

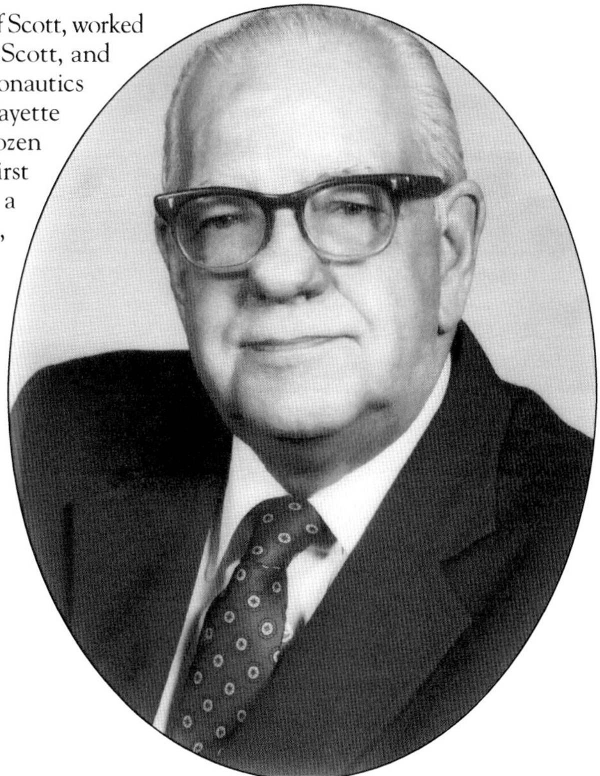

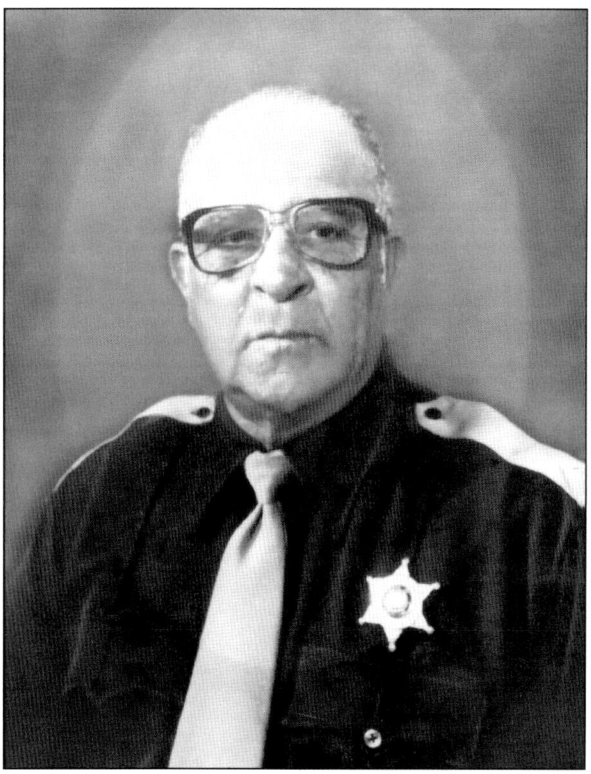

Frank Glaude, the great-grandfather of Scott's current mayor Purvis Morrison, was the first African American from Scott to work for the sheriff's department in Lafayette Parish. (Courtesy of Purvis Morrison.)

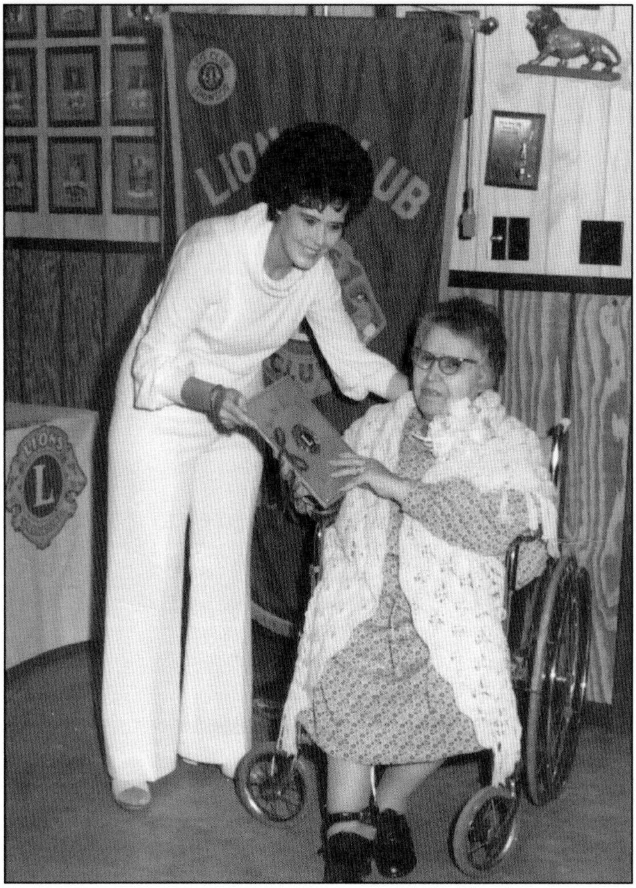

Disability did not deter Orta Patin. Orta was a schoolteacher and a professional seamstress who cared for her father after her mother's death. She answered calls for the Scott Volunteer Fire Department from her home and sounded the alarm every day at noon and for every fire. Here, Delta Leger presents Orta with an award from the Scott Lion's Club for her years of service. (Courtesy of Joshua Patin.)

Claude and Emerite Hebert, known as Mr. and Mrs. Santa Clause, were notable citizens of Scott. They were honored at Founders Day events, Mardi Gras Balls, and Lafayette Council on Aging events. Claude, a horticulturist, taught agriculture at Scott High School. Their yard was filled with fruit trees and vegetables plants, which they harvested and gave to local charities and soup kitchens. (Courtesy of Charles and Joyce Faulk.)

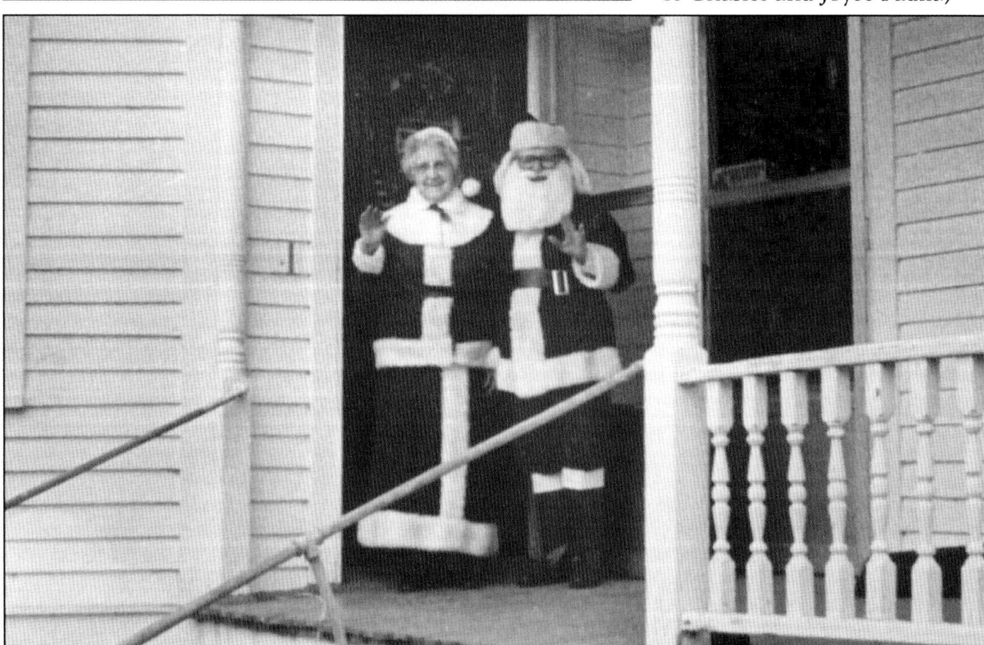

Julie Martin Boudreaux and her husband, André, lived on the corner of Cayret Street and Old Spanish Trail. They had a small hamburger stand near the local school where many students would gather to visit and eat lunch and after-school snacks. The front room of their home was once used as the Scott library. (Courtesy of Polly Boudreaux Richard.)

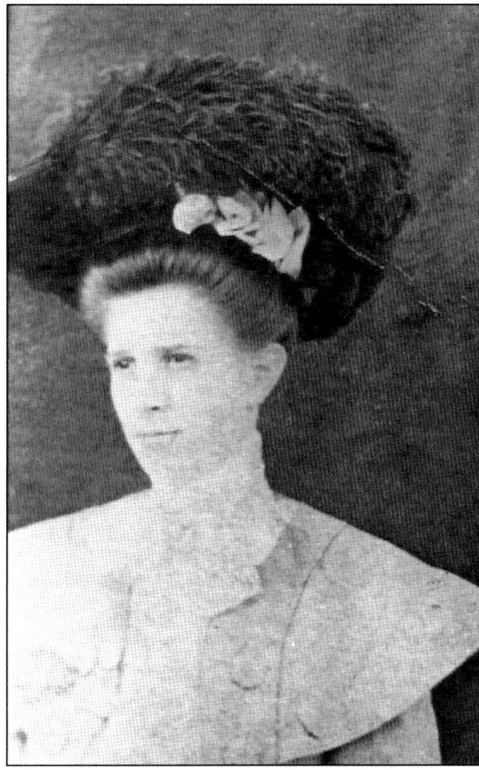

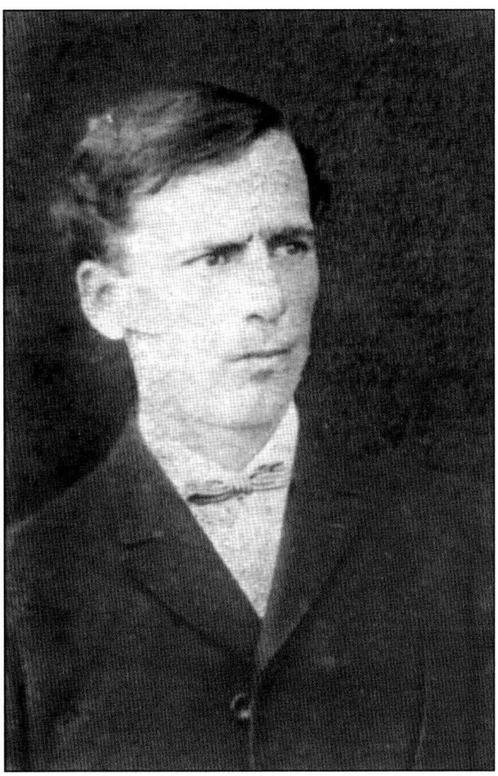

André Boudreaux, a horse jockey at the local bush tracks in the 1880s, rode against Gabriel "Gobb" Strauss in many races that drew the attention of the Cajun country. Much has been written about the rivalry between the two men. Boudreaux and his wife, Julie, were the parents of Emick, Edward, Edvar, Charlie, Cinquieme, and Pauline. (Courtesy of Polly Boudreaux Richard.)

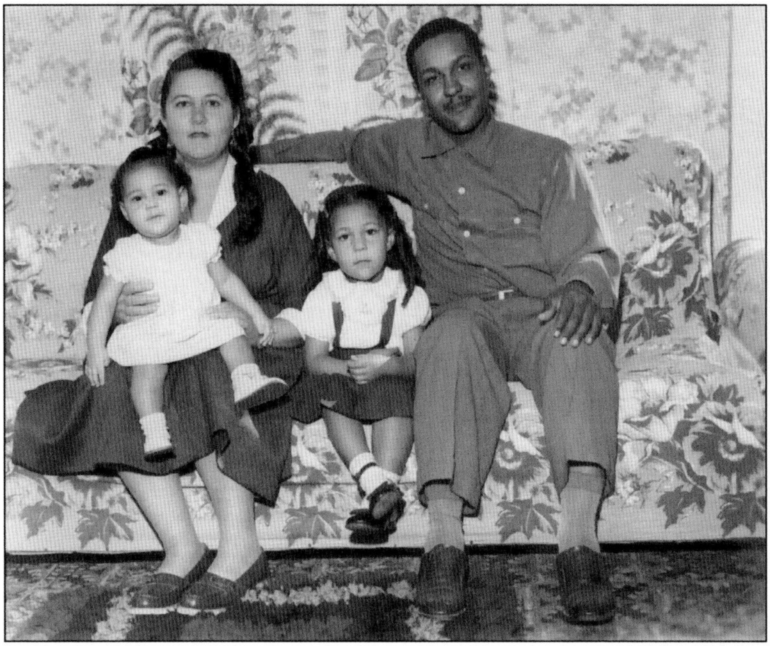

Gumbleton and Viola Mallet with their two daughters, three-year-old Donella and seven-month-old Camella, pose on a typical Sunday afternoon. This photograph was taken at their home by a visiting parish priest in 1954. (Courtesy of Viola Mallet.)

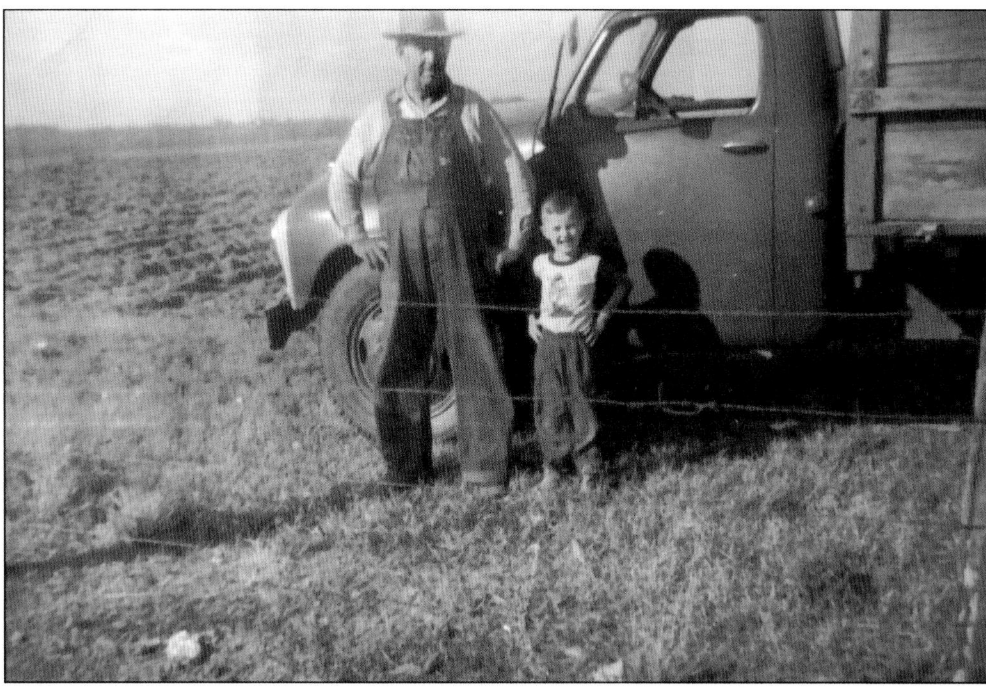

Cyprien Guilbeau, a Scott farmer shown with his first grandchild, Ronald James Noel, was well known in the area for hauling fence posts and boards. He purchased the truck for his hauling business. Cyprien's wife, the former Beulah Hebert, worked side by side with her husband in the fields, as was common in those days. (Courtesy of Clara Baudoin.)

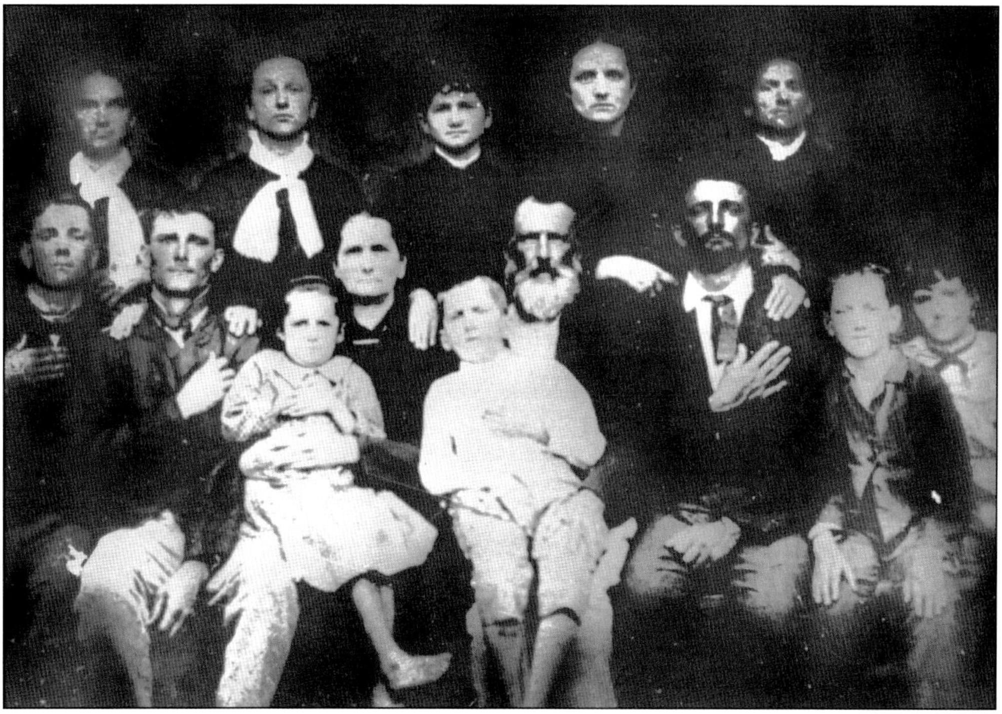

Members of the Basile Sonnier Sr. family posing for the camera in 1885 are, from left to right, (first row) Theophile Sonnier, Basile Sonnier Jr., Philomene Gilbert Sonnier with Sophie Sonnier in her lap, Basile Sonnier Sr. with Jean Sonnier in his lap, Honore Sonnier, Joseph Sonnier, and Bernadette Sonnier; (second row) Selma Sonnier, Alzina Sonnier, Marie Sonnier, Odiedes Arceneaux Landry, and Cecilia Sonnier. The couple had 15 children and 116 grandchildren. (Courtesy of Lafayette Parish Clerk of Court.)

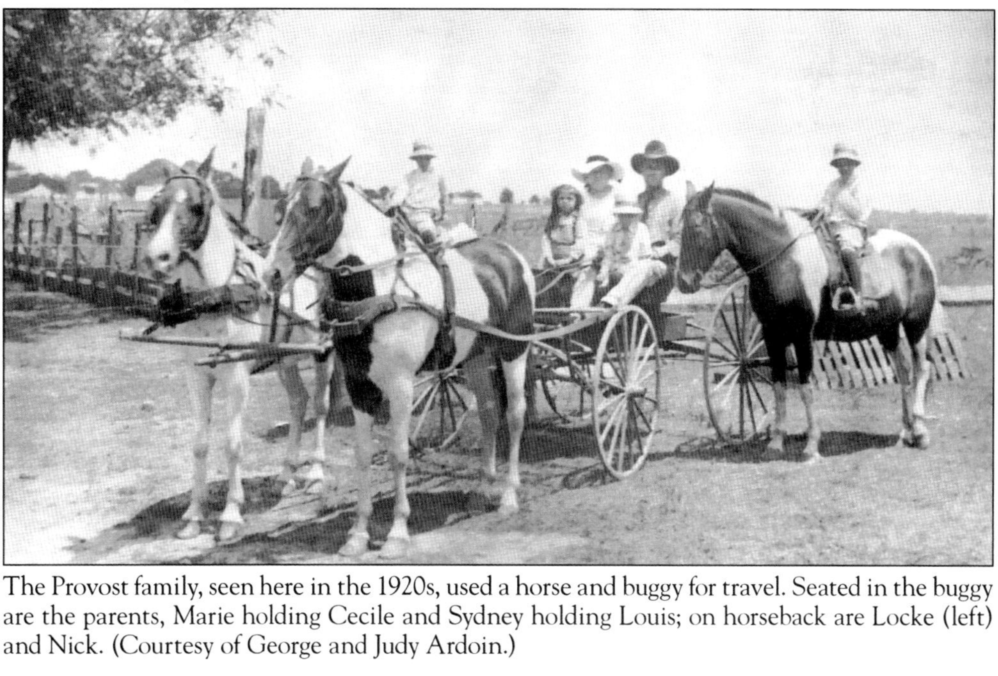

The Provost family, seen here in the 1920s, used a horse and buggy for travel. Seated in the buggy are the parents, Marie holding Cecile and Sydney holding Louis; on horseback are Locke (left) and Nick. (Courtesy of George and Judy Ardoin.)

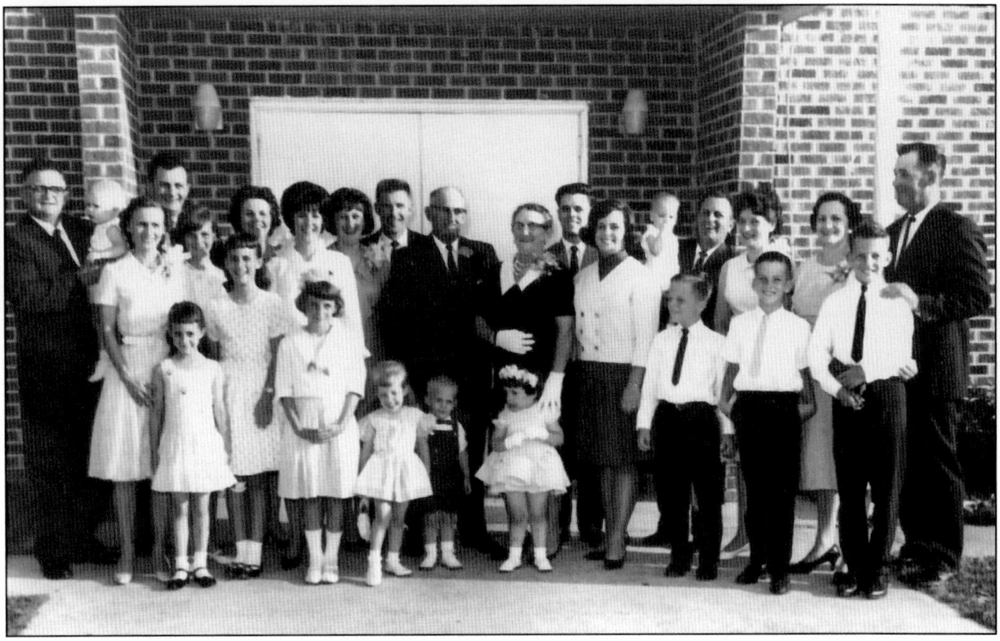

John Martin Sr. and Carmen Hebert Martin are seen in the 1960s celebrating their 50th wedding anniversary with three generations of the Martin family. John was the son of Alex Martin and Azema Begnaud. Carmen was the daughter of Theophile Hebert and Marie Sonnier. (Courtesy of Annadine Credeur.)

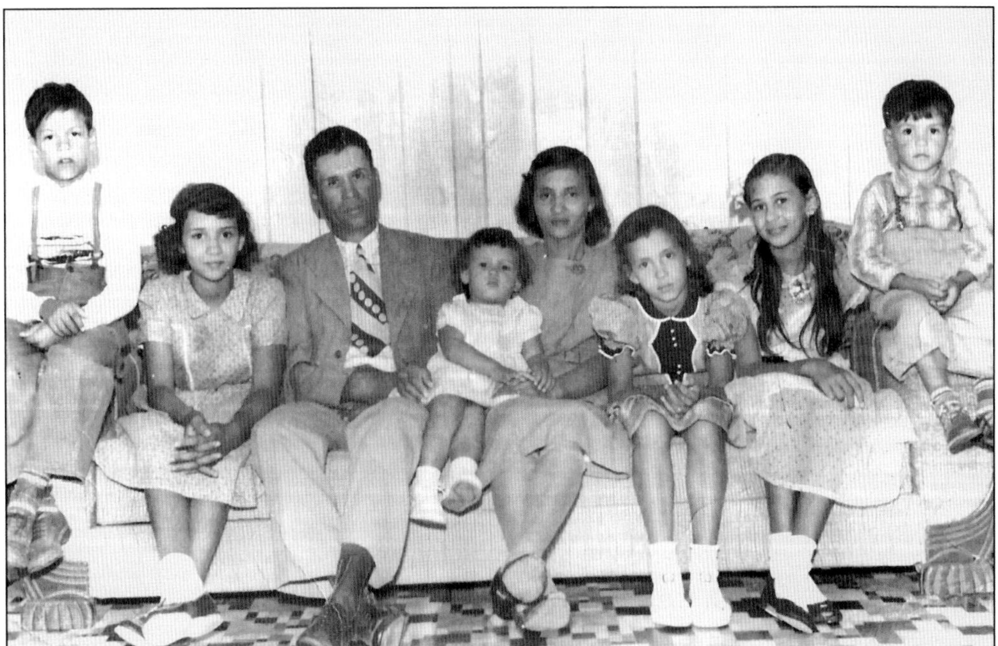

This 1950s photograph of the Mire family was taken prior to their move to California. It was taken by Father Rousselle, SVD, who photographed many area families in those days. From left to right are Weldon, Alicetine, Davis, Linda, Arlean, Dorothy, Helen Joyce, and Wilbert. (Courtesy of Leana Miller.)

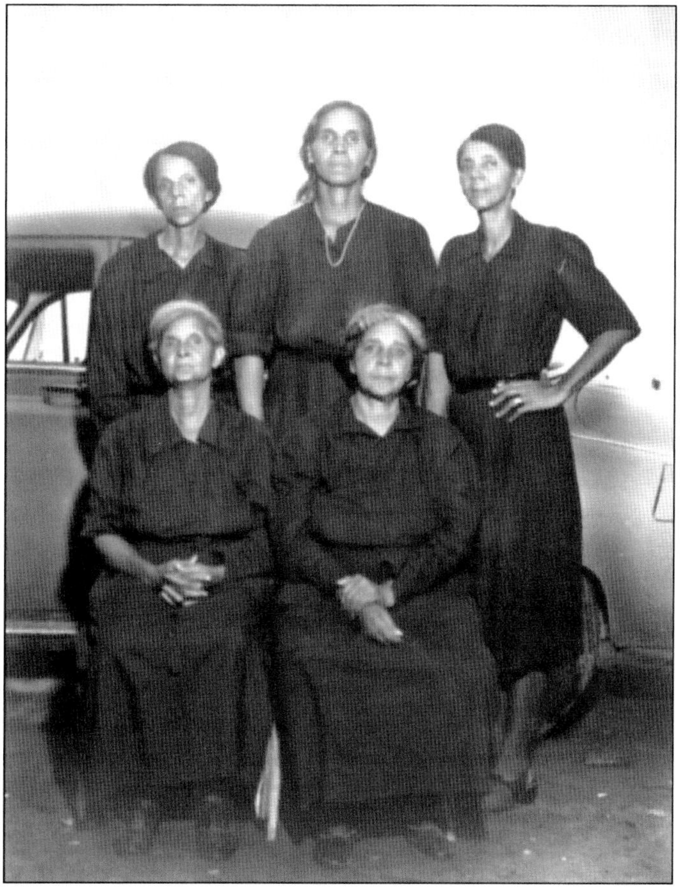

These five Morrison sisters were part of a family of 17 children who lived on the outskirts of Scott, part of a large farming community. When in mourning, the women wore black dresses, and the men wore a small black ribbon attached to their hats. Their nephew remembers the women did everything from smoking pipes to cooking and cleaning. From left to right are (first row) Louise and Dophina; (second row) Celeste, Alicia, and Helen. (Courtesy of Purvis Morrison.)

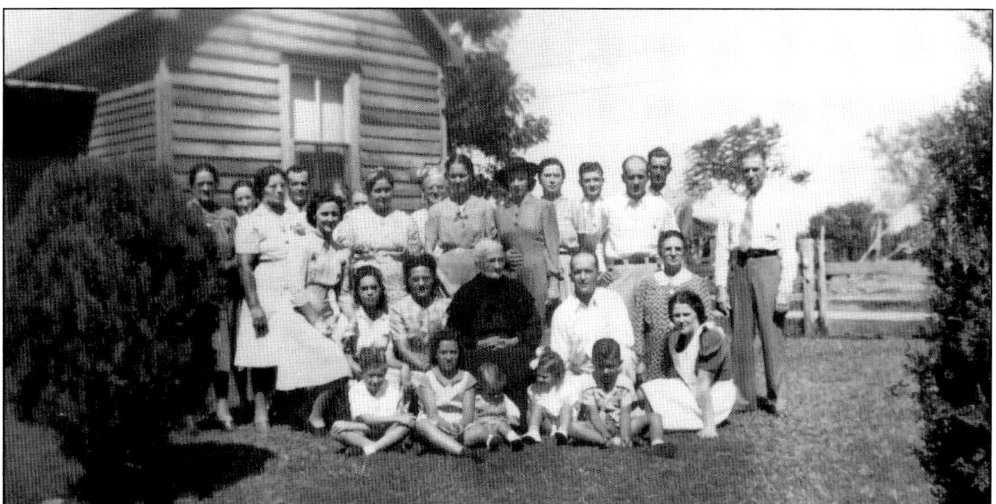

A surprise party for the 82nd birthday of Philomene (Begnaud) Boudreaux was attended by family and friends. She and her husband, O.A. Boudreaux, raised 12 children. During her lifetime, she saw the introduction of radio, television, cars, and moving pictures. (Courtesy of Mona Stutes Caldwell.)

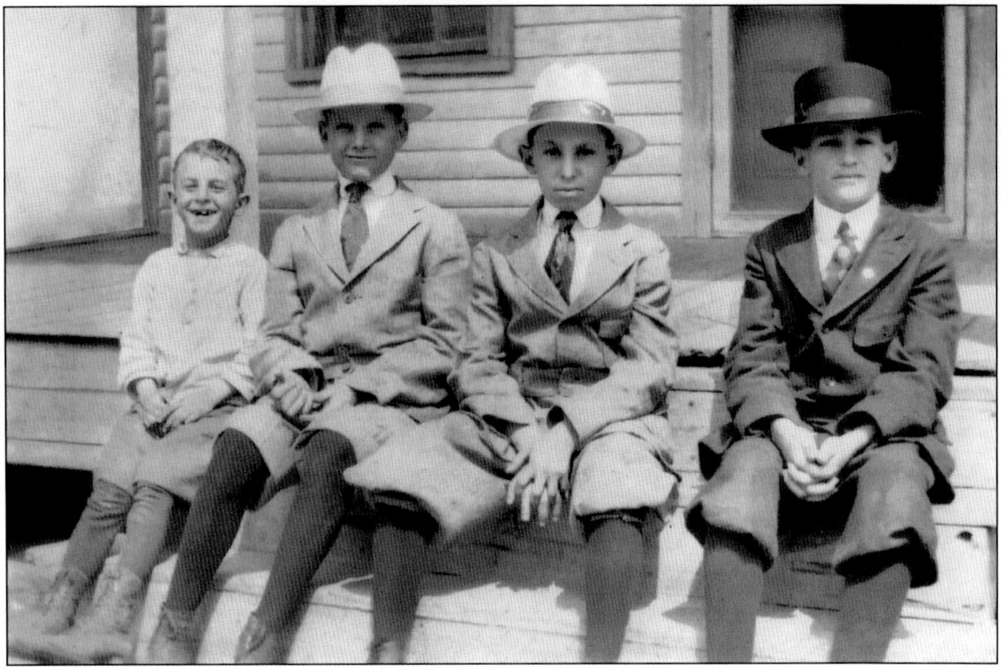

The Bourque boys pose for a group photograph taken by a visiting photographer. From left to right, Milton "Tan," George, Clovis "Pete," and Lester "Lep" are dressed in their Sunday best. Tan decided at the last minute that he wanted to be in the photograph, too, and managed to get in just before it was taken. (Courtesy of Macqueline Thibeaux.)

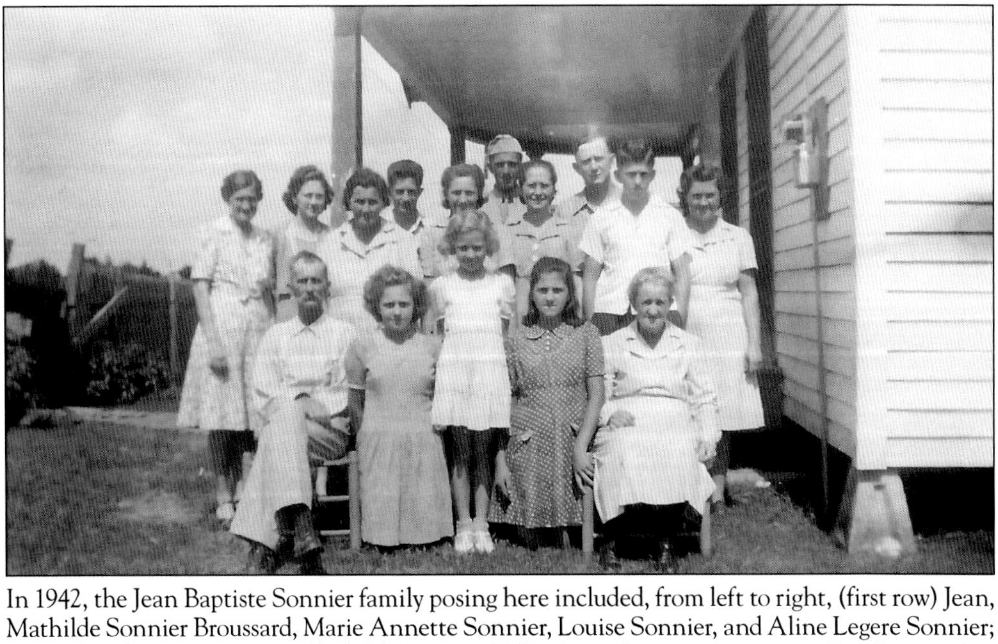

In 1942, the Jean Baptiste Sonnier family posing here included, from left to right, (first row) Jean, Mathilde Sonnier Broussard, Marie Annette Sonnier, Louise Sonnier, and Aline Legere Sonnier; (second row) Agnes Sonnier, Clothilde Sonnier Hills, Anna Sonnier Arceneaux, Eva Sonnier, Iris Sonnier Boudreaux, Johnny Sonnier, and Bertha Sonnier; (third row) Ulysses Sonnier, Claude Sonnier, and Leon "Doc" Sonnier. (Courtesy of Louise Sonnier.)

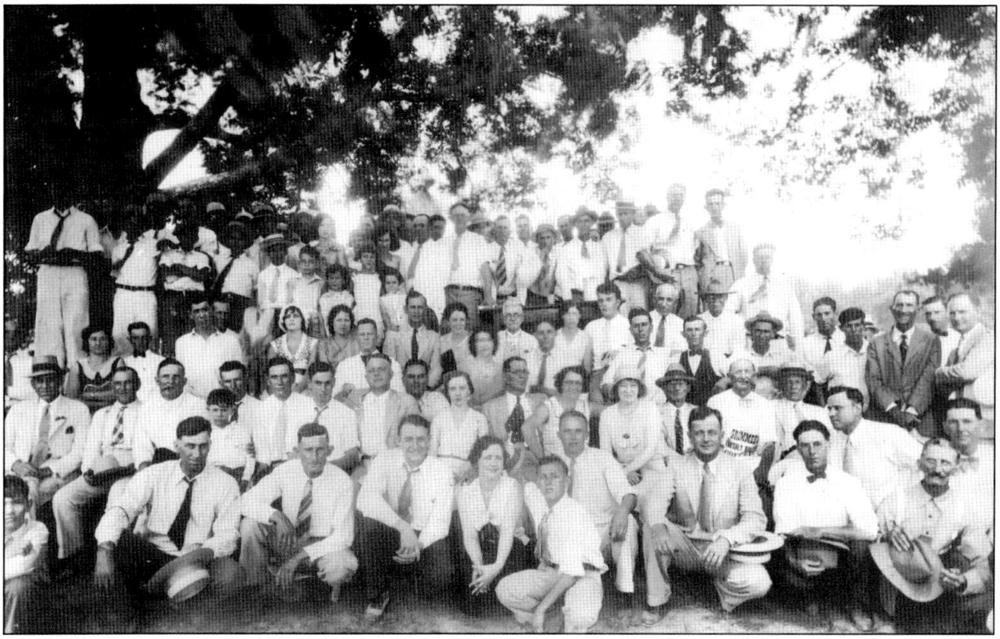

In the 1920s, horse racing was a favorite pastime. There were several dirt tracks throughout the area where residents could go to every weekend. This group of regular attendees included, in the first row on the far right, Alus Leger and Lucian Leger. (Courtesy of Earlene Carriere.)

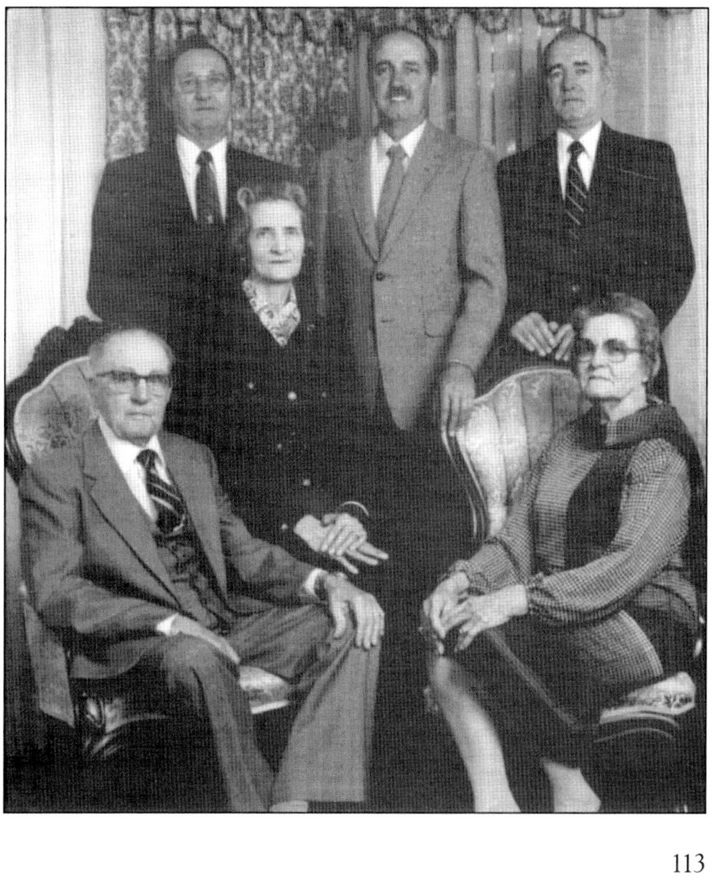

Freddie Sonnier, a mechanic, and his brother Alcee owned Scott Service Garage. When electricity arrived in Scott, Freddie climbed the electric pole near his garage at dusk and dawn to flip the switch. He and his brother Saul owned the Sonnier Brothers sweet potato packing and shipping company. Pictured here with his family are, from left to right, (first row) Freddie, Mildred, and Alida; (second row) Carrol, James, and Hubert. (Courtesy of Fran Bihm.)

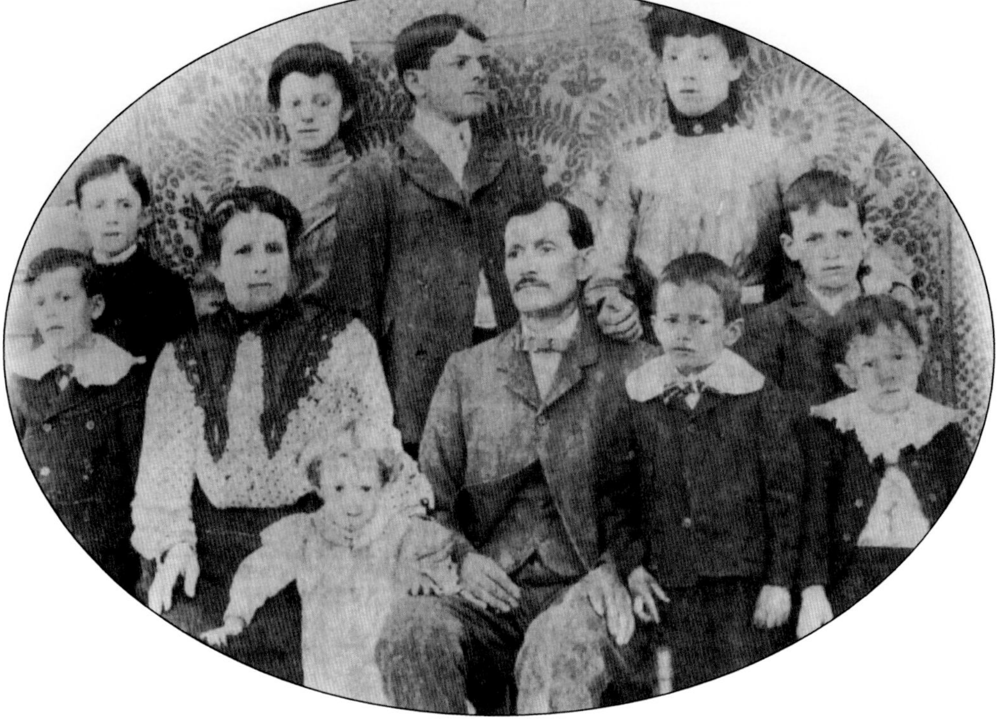

Alex Martin Sr. and his wife had a farm northwest of Scott. Alex often set broken bones for area residents who could not reach a doctor. Martin used old sheets donated by neighbors to wrap the limb tightly, keeping the broken bones in place. Pictured are, from left to right, (first row) Alfred, Azema B. Martin, Leah, Alex Martin Sr., John, Alex Martin Jr., and Elie; (second row) Gabriel, Noelie, Leo, and Honorine. (Courtesy of Annadine Credeur.)

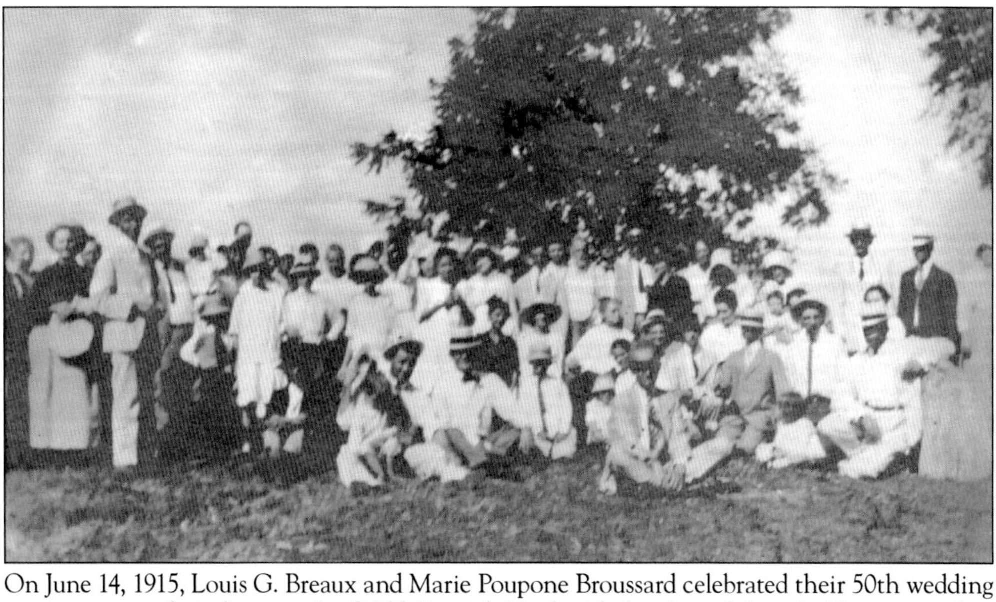

On June 14, 1915, Louis G. Breaux and Marie Poupone Broussard celebrated their 50th wedding anniversary at their farm south of Old Spanish Trail with family and friends. He was a police juror and a deputy sheriff. (Courtesy of George and Judy Ardoin.)

*Seven*

# Honoring Those Who Served

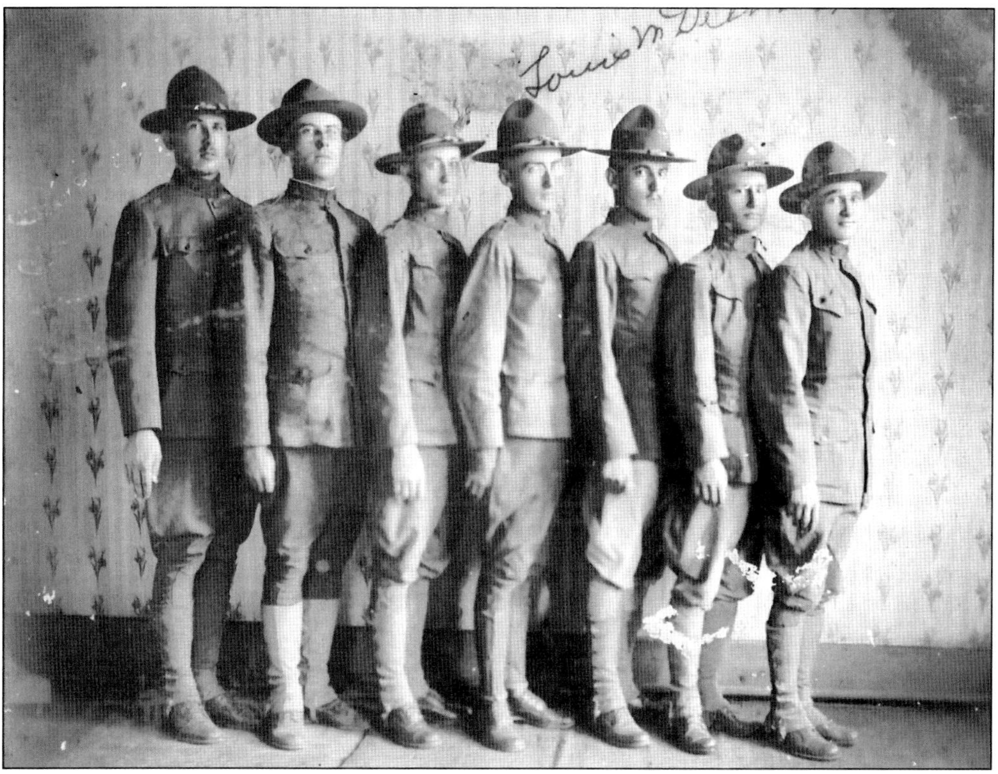

French interpreters were needed among the American soldiers during World War I. Louis M. Delhomme (fourth from left) was assigned to the 113th Signal Battalion as a French interpreter. His battalion was deployed to assist in the liberation of Cour Cheverny, France, in 1919. He was later awarded honorary French citizenship by the citizens of Cour Cheverny. (Courtesy of David Delhomme.)

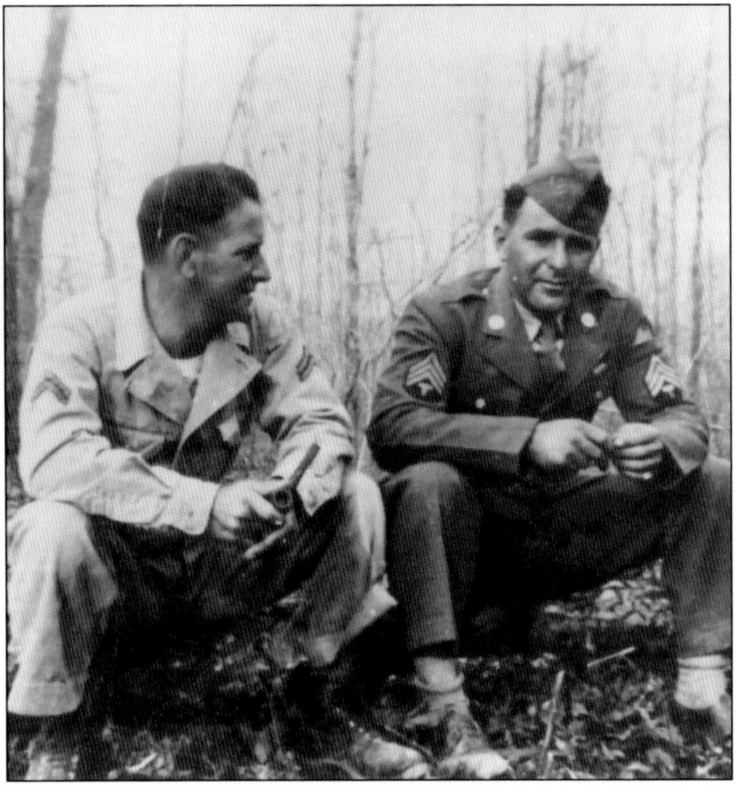

Brothers Henry (left) and Toby Begnaud met by chance while on Army training maneuvers in Tennessee during World War II. This meeting was captured by a Tennessee newspaper photographer and was later published in a local area newspaper. (Courtesy of Cassie Richard Blair.)

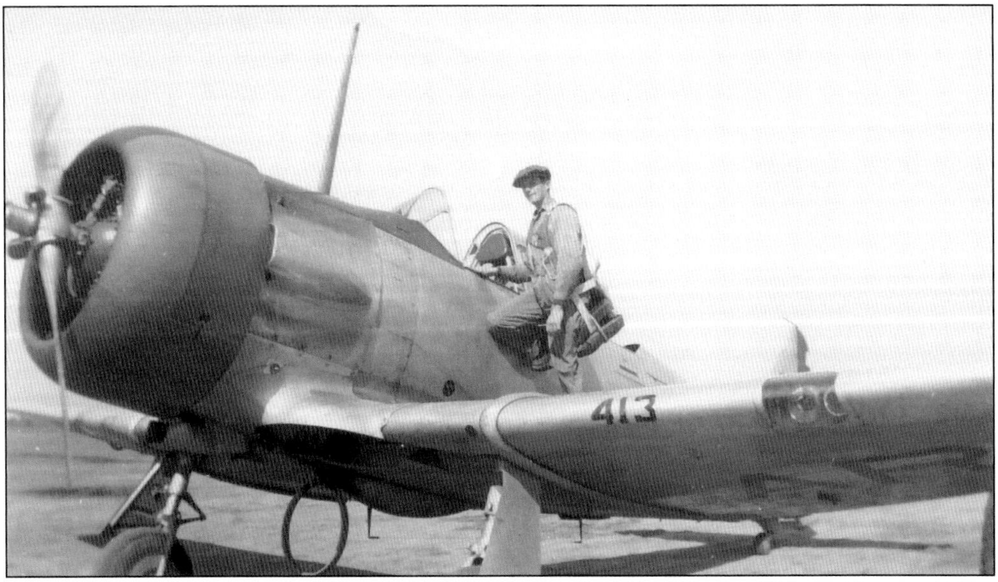


John Baptiste Richard, son of Feregus and Sara Richard, enlisted in the US Air Force in 1940, where he attained the rank of master sergeant. He was deployed to the Philippines during World War II and discharged in 1946. He is pictured here with an AT-6 Texan advanced trainer. (Courtesy of Cassie Richard Blair.)

Gumbleton Mallet served in the US Army during World War II. He attained the rank of staff sergeant and was deployed from 1942 to 1945. During a presentation by Pres. Harry S. Truman, he received the Good Conduct Medal for his time in service. (Courtesy of Viola Mallet.)

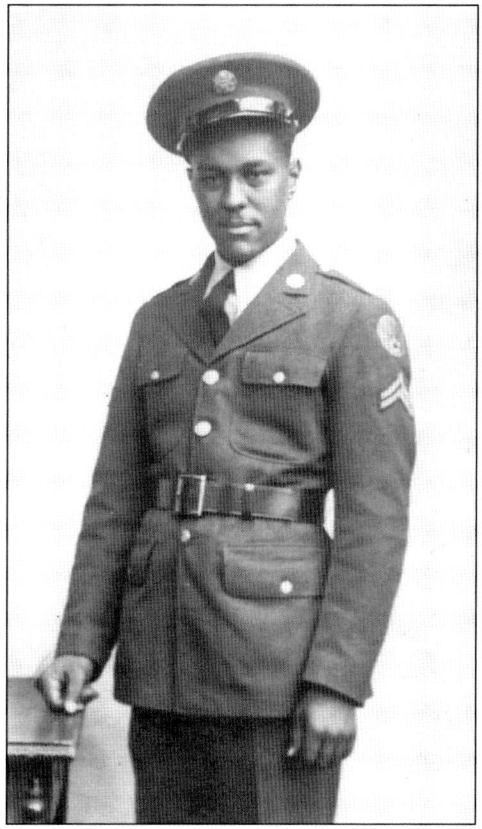

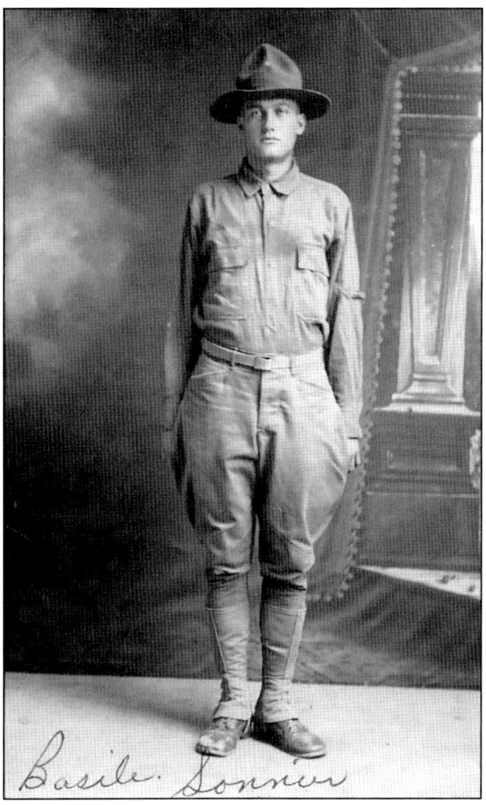


Basile Sonnier entered the Army in 1917 and served in various locations during World War I. He was discharged and returned to the Scott area at the end of the war. (Courtesy of Mary Ann Raggio Bourgeois.)

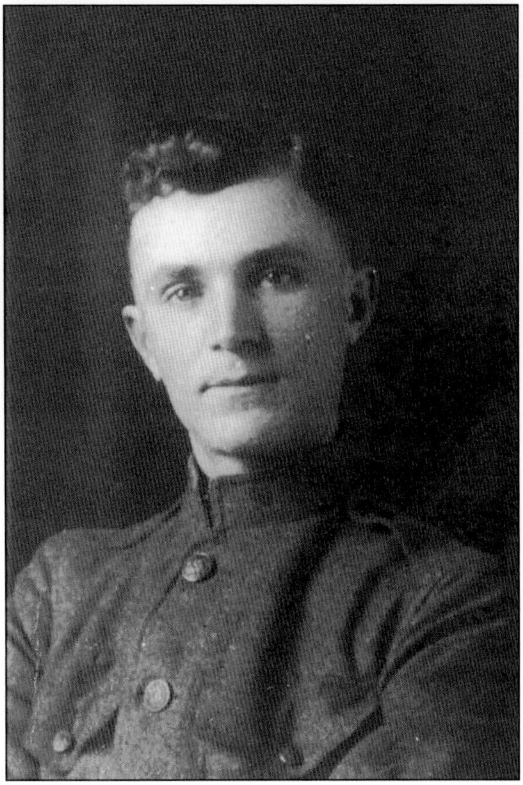

Sosthene O'Neal Guidry enlisted in the Army in 1917 and was stationed at Fort Pike, Arkansas. His unit was undergoing training for a deployment to Europe; however, the war ended prior to it being deployed. (Courtesy of Pearl and Aubrey Guidry.)

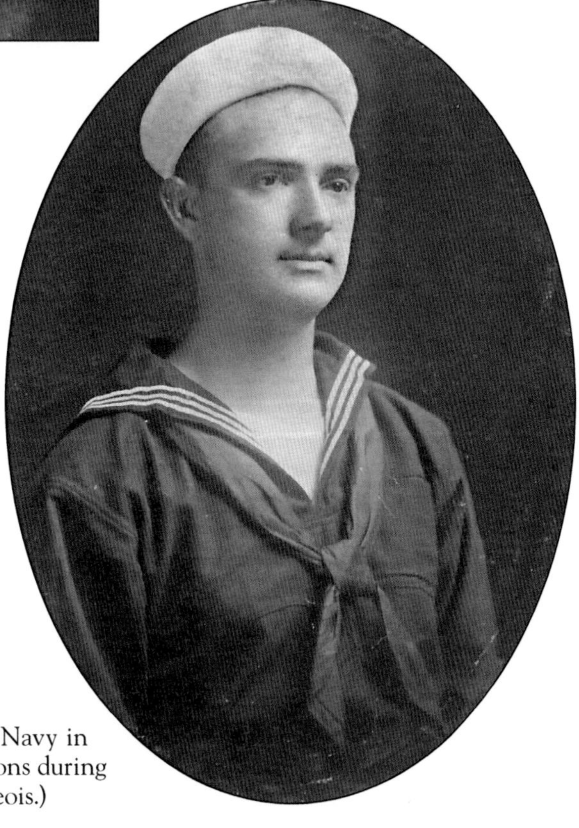

John Orrin Brandt enlisted in the US Navy in 1917. He was deployed to various locations during World War I. (Courtesy of Anne Bourgeois.)

O'Donnell M. "Chief" Pellisier was a ship fitter with the Navy Seabees during World War II. He served in the Navy from 1942 to 1945 and trained in Virginia, Rhode Island, and Florida. He served in New Hebrides, Tonga, Fiji, and Admiralty Islands. (Courtesy of Annadine Credeur.)

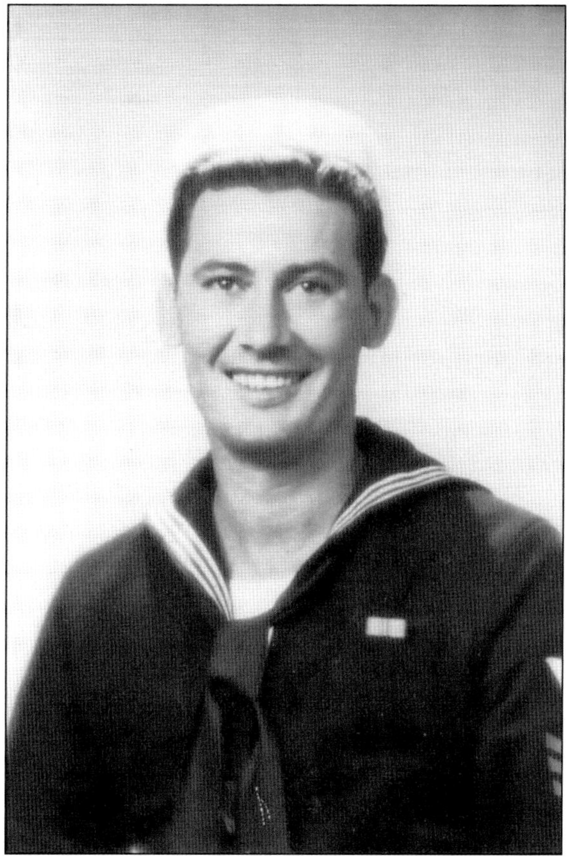

Louis Delhomme Jr. served in the Navy from July 12, 1941, until October 15, 1945. He was trained at Norfolk Naval Station, Virginia. He was assigned to several different ships during his time in the service, including the USS *Block Island*, a CVE-21; *Kasann Bay*, a CVE-69; and *Mission Bay*, a CVE-59. (Courtesy of David Delhomme.)

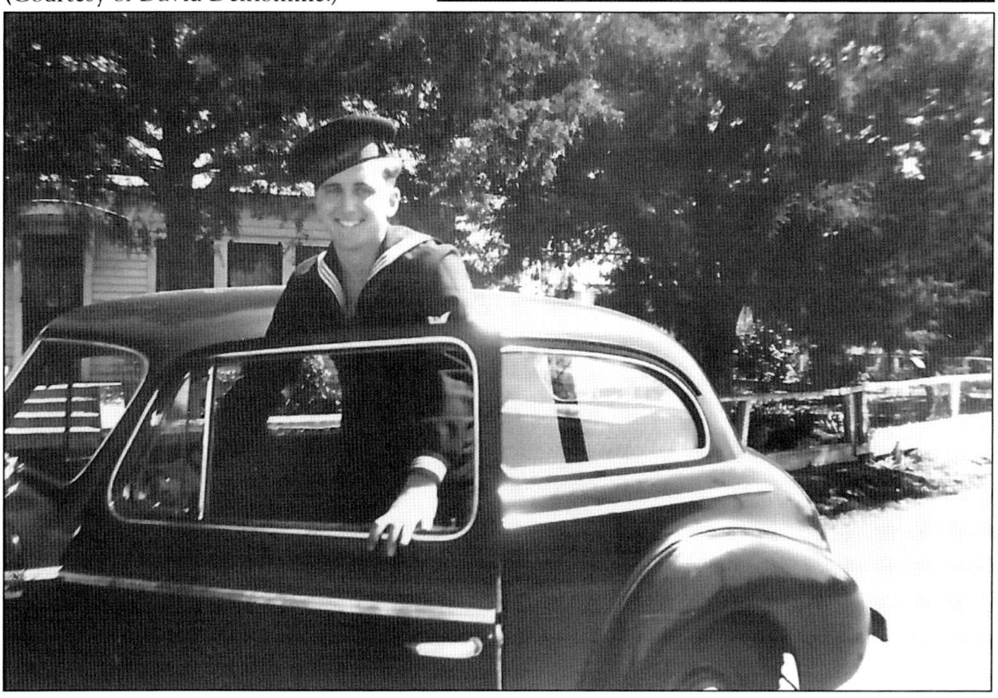

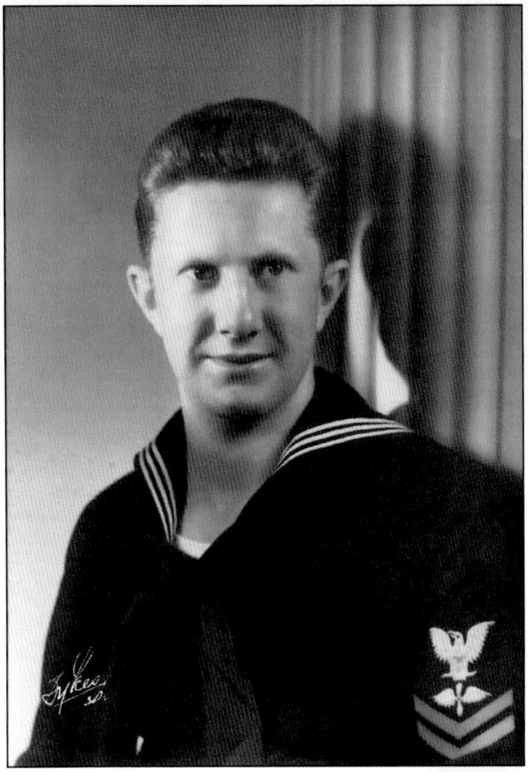

Ulysses Sonnier enlisted in the Navy in 1942 at the age of 19 and served as an aviation machinists mate, 2nd Class, in World War II on the USS *St. Lo*, a CVE-63. His was the first ship sunk by a Kamikaze plane, and Ulysses was one of the 128 men killed instantly in the attack. Nathan Mouton was working at the depot and delivered the telegram to notify the family of Sonnier's "missing in action" status. Sonnier was posthumously awarded the Purple Heart. (Courtesy of Macqueline Thibeaux.)

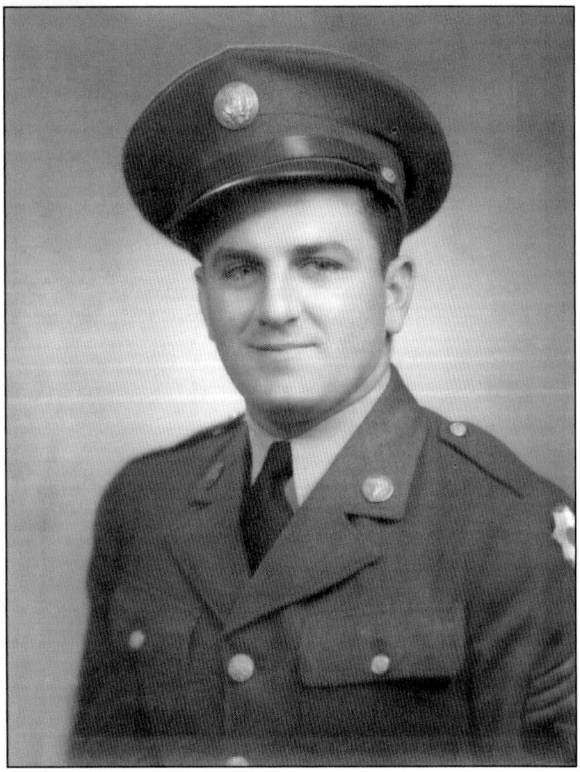

John Martin Jr., son of John and Carmen H. Martin Sr., served in World War II. He was trained to work as an assistant in the military pharmacy. (Courtesy of Debbie M. de Gravelle.)

Odus Ardoin was a tank mechanic with the 3rd Armored Division in World War II. His tour of duty included time in Belgium and Germany. (Courtesy of Sam Ardoin.)

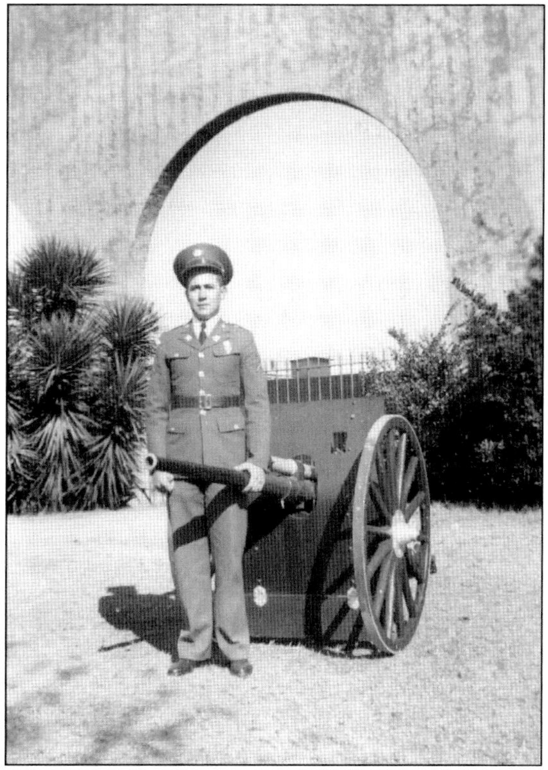

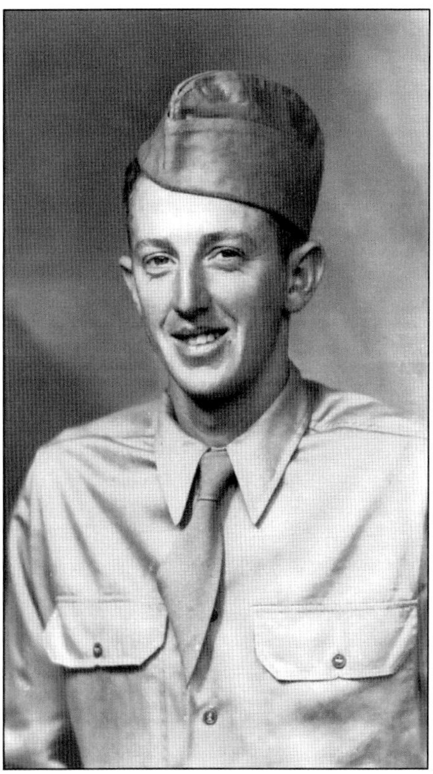

Numa Richard Jr. served with the 179th Thunderbird Infantry Division in the European Theatre. He participated in the liberation of France after D-Day. His wife, Juanita, also contributed to the war effort by volunteering to watch for suspicious airplanes in the Scott area. The women would take turns sitting in the cupola on the top of the Hotel St. Paul. (Courtesy of Louise Sonnier.)

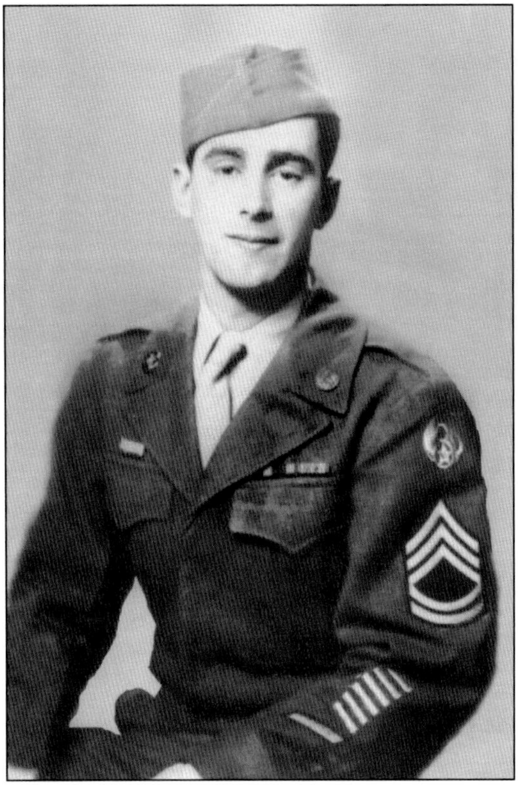

Lloyd Domingue entered the service on February 16, 1942, at Camp Beauregard, Louisiana. He trained at Keesler Field, Mississippi, with the 97th Bombardment Group and the 92nd Bombardment Group at MacDill Field. He was a clerk for the Group Headquarters officers before being transferred to the 327th Bombardment Group, where he was the assistant to the first sergeant. He was stationed in England and French Morocco. (Courtesy of Wayne Domingue.)

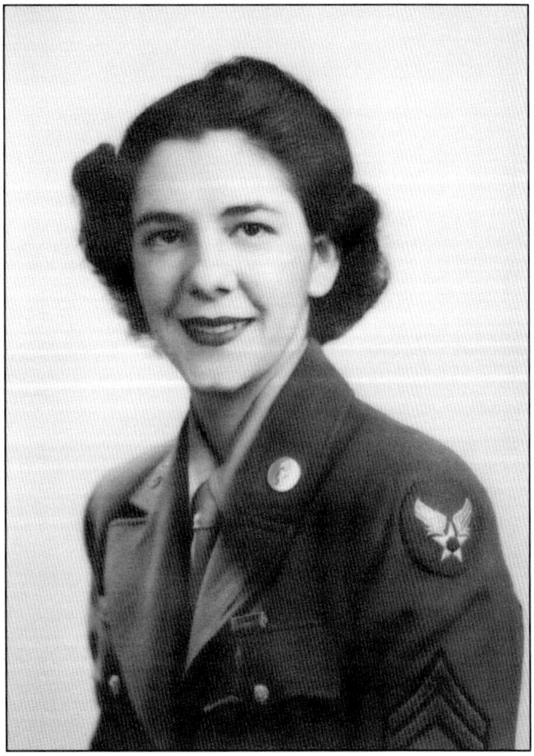

Pauline Broussard entered the Army in 1943 and was trained in Iowa, Florida, and Virginia. She attained the rank of corporal and served in the European Theatre. (Courtesy of Mary "Bruci" Gauthier.)

Lee Martin Sr. and Leanac "Nick" Provost were brothers-in-law. They served in World War II and were both deployed to the Philippines. Lee was assigned to General McArthur's headquarters, and Nick served as a radio operator and airplane mechanic. Nick served a total of seven years, and Lee served in both World War II and the Korean War. (Courtesy of Annadine Credeur.)

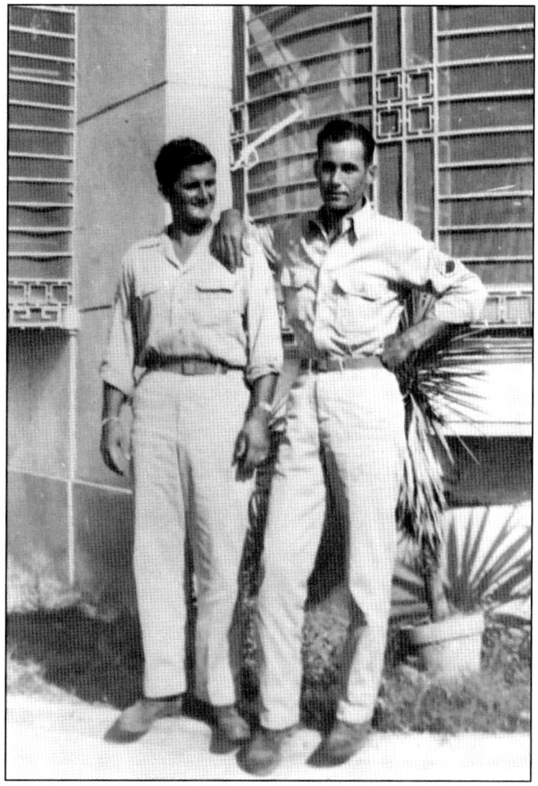

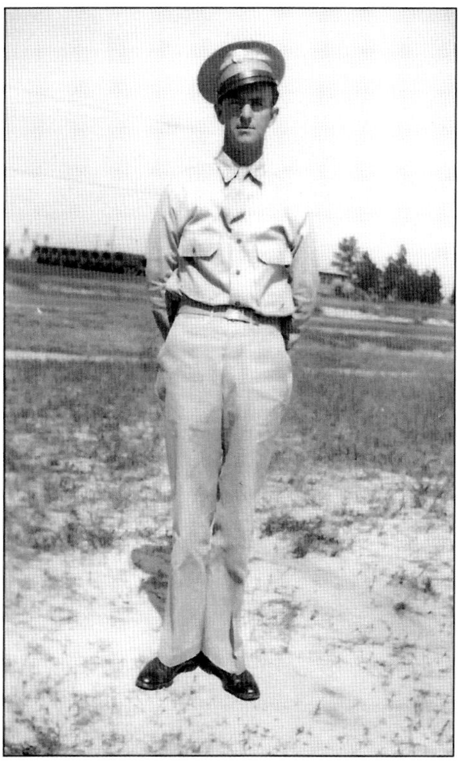

Milton "Tan" Bourque enlisted in the Army on June 5, 1942. He attained the rank of warrant officer and was discharged on April 8, 1943. (Courtesy of Macqueline Thibeaux.)

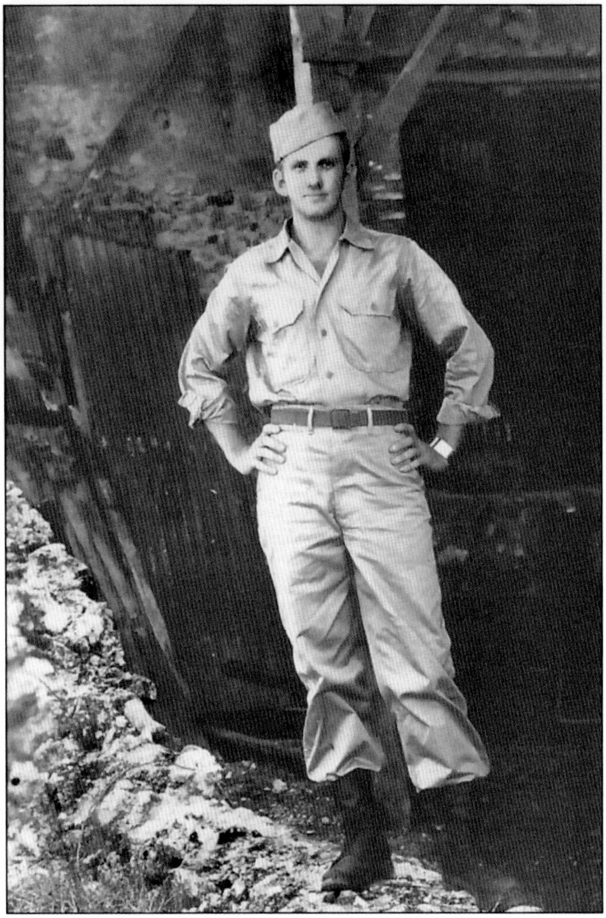

Johnny Sonnier enlisted in the Army on December 14, 1944. He served in various locations during World War II and was discharged on October 4, 1946. (Courtesy of Louise Sonnier.)

Wilson Sonnier (second from the left in the front row) served his country during World War II. He enlisted in the Army and was deployed to the European Theatre, spending most of his tour in Germany. (Courtesy of Mary Ann Jolivette.)

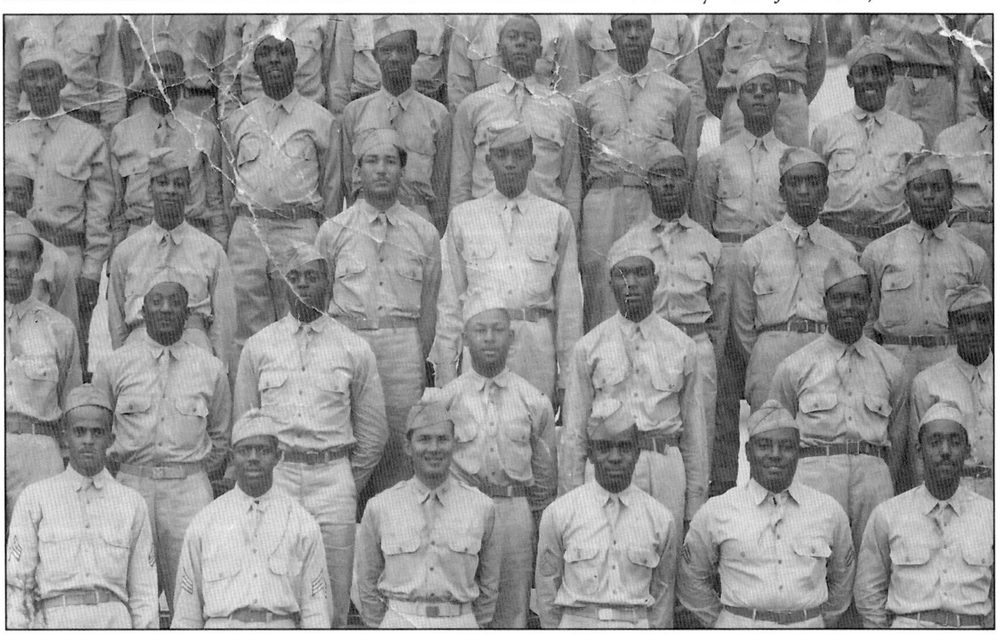

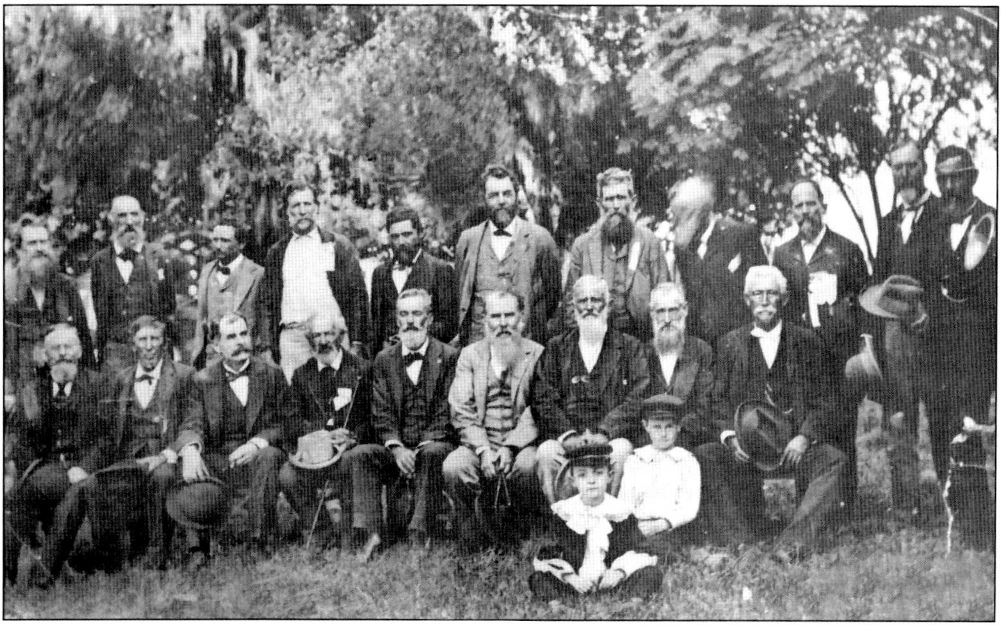

Pictured in 1890 at the Confederate veterans reunion picnic near Lafayette are, from left to right, (first row) children Frank Meyer and Dave Church; (second row) Judge Allen, Chris Steiner, William Clegg, Aurelien Broussard, two unidentified, Sosthene Mouton, ? Greig, and William Torian; (third row) Samuel Montgomery, Arthur Greig, Alexander Comeaux, Tibus Dugas, Lucien St. Julien, Louis Breaux, Leonidas Creighton, Auguste Lisbony, J.C. Buchanan, Douglas Cochrane, and Cinquieme Mouton. (Courtesy of Lafayette Parish Clerk of Court.)

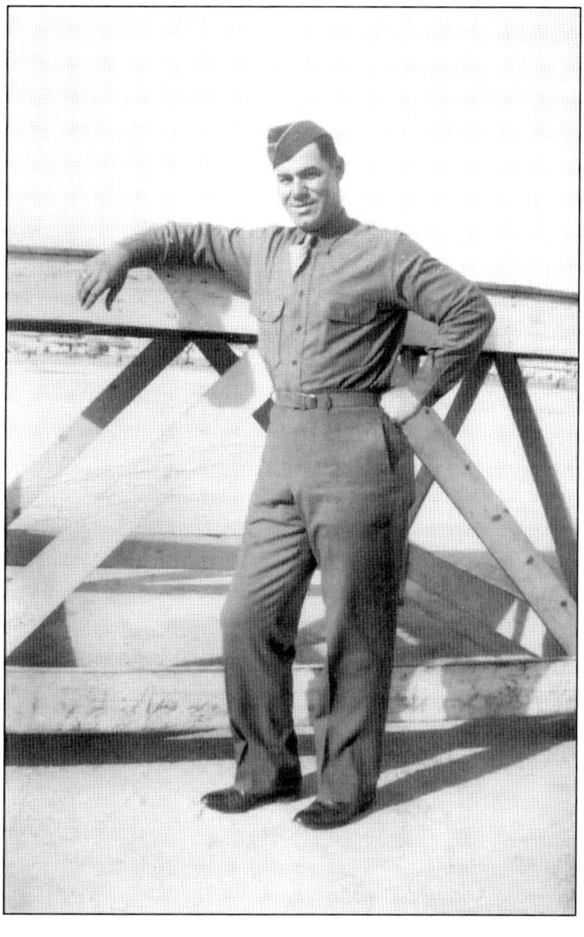

Locke Provost served in the Army during World War II and was stationed in the Aleutian Islands for the Asiatic-Pacific Campaign. He received the American Theater Campaign Ribbon, Victory Ribbon, and the Overseas Service Bar. (Courtesy of Stephen L. Provost.)

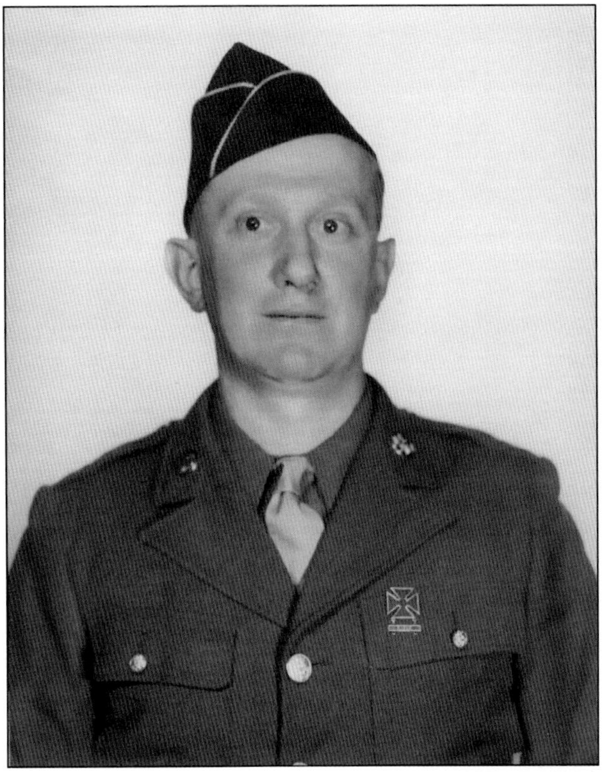

Leon "Doc" Sonnier was an installation repairman for the military during World War II. He installed, repaired, and maintained telephone communications. Deployed to the Battle of Normandy, he served in northern France, Ardennes, Rhineland, and central Europe. He attained the rank of private T/4 with the 3892nd Quartermaster Truck Company. He was awarded the Honorable Service Lapel Button, Victory Medal, Good Conduct Medal, five battle stars, and the European Theatre Ribbon. (Courtesy of Louise Sonnier.)

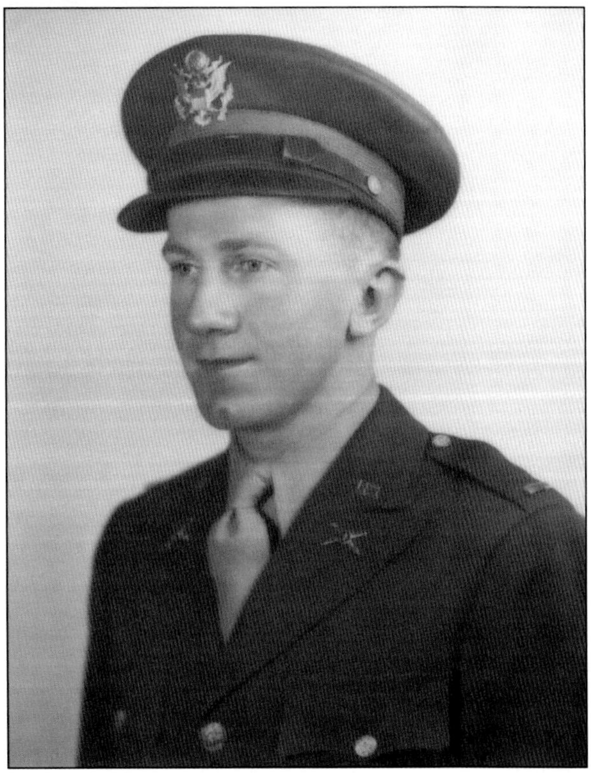

Claude Sonnier was commissioned as a captain in the US Army in 1941. He trained in Texas, New York, California, and North Carolina. He was assigned to the Aberdeen Proving Grounds, Maryland, where he was responsible for ballistics research and the testing of new weapons. (Courtesy of Louise Sonnier.)

Ulysses "MeGee" Arceneaux, son of Israel and Arcade Arceneaux, served in World War I. Born on February 8, 1896, he died in 1982. (Courtesy of Louise Sonnier.)

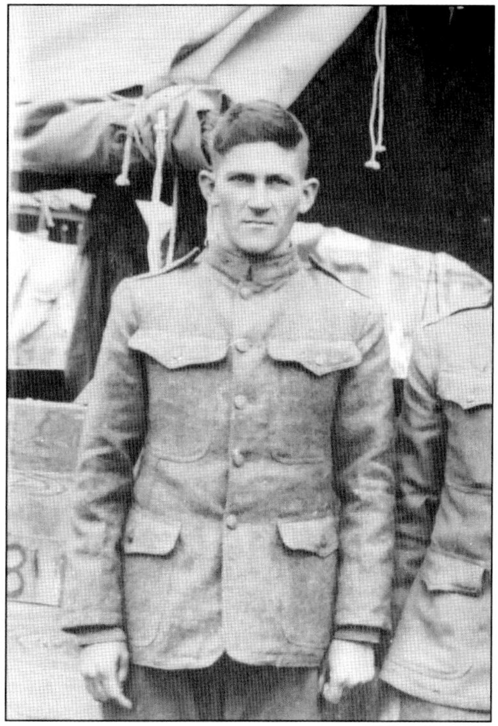

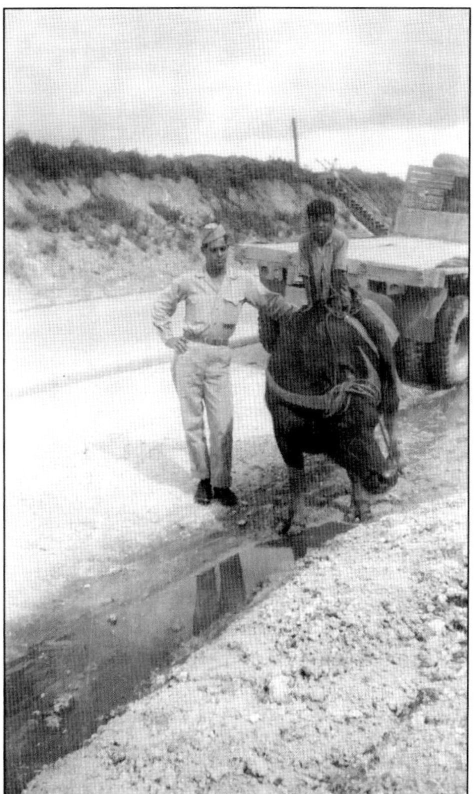

Paul Albert Broussard enlisted in the Army in 1943. He trained at Camp Adair, Oregon, and was assigned to the 70th Field Artillery Division. He was later deployed to the Philippines. He was discharged in 1946. Broussard is pictured in the Philippines with a local boy and a water buffalo. (Courtesy of Bruce A. Broussard.)